Issues in Contemporary Documentary

Issues in Contemporary Documentary

JANE CHAPMAN

With additional research by Kate Allison

polity

First published in 2009 by Polity Press

Polity Press
65 Bridge Street
Cambridge CB2 1UR, UK.

Polity Press
350 Main Street
Malden, MA 02148, USA

ISBN-13: 978-0-7456-4009-9
ISBN-13: 978-0-7456-4010-5 (pb)

A catalogue record for this book is available from the British Library.

Typeset in 9.5 on 12pt Utopia
by Servis Filmsetting Ltd, Stockport, Cheshire
Printed and bound by MPG Books Group, UK

For further information on Polity, visit our website: www.politybooks.com

To Miles and Toby

Contents

Acknowledgements

It is difficult to describe adequately or ever do justice to the team effort that goes into projects like this one that have taken years to reach fruition. Without the instinctively sound judgement of Andrea Drugan and John Thompson, it would never have happened, and I am eternally grateful to them for their continuing confidence.

At the very early stages, Paul Stainthorp at Lincoln University library did tremendously wide literature searches for me and this work has been invaluable. Kate Allison's contribution to the ideas, research, writing, checking and correcting has been equally essential – a really important and enthusiastic contribution. The comments of Brian Winston, Sylvia Harvey, Ann Gray and other colleagues at Lincoln have provided further insights, as have those of friends and colleagues at the BEA in the United States, especially Lisa Mills.

I am grateful for the efficiency and dedication of Neil and Jonathan at Polity, and of Tim Clark, who has ensured the highest standards, and Susan Beer. Finally, my thanks to John Simons as Faculty Dean, and to John Tulloch, head of Lincoln School of Journalism, for giving me the space and time for this writing and research, and to Miles and Toby for tolerating my passion when it comes to turning out books!

The publisher would like to thank the following for permission to reproduce copyright material:

Page 61, © WELLSPRING MEDIA / THE KOBAL COLLECTION; Page 66, © DOG EAT DOG FILMS/ WEINSTEIN COMPANY / THE KOBAL COLLECTION; Page 99, © LAWRENCE BENDER PRODS. / THE KOBAL COLLECTION / LEE, ERIC; Page 109, © JIGSAW PRODUCTIONS / THE KOBAL COLLECTION; Page 129, © WARP X/FILM 4 / THE KOBAL COLLECTION; Page 147, © CH4 FILMS / THE KOBAL COLLECTION / SPARHAM, LAURIE.

Introduction

The question: continuity and change

Documentary is now so popular and diverse that it needs to be understood as complex, multi-faceted and influenced by a range of different contexts. The genre simultaneously shapes and is shaped by the public communicative space, also fast changing as the range of information and the range of outlets for reception continue to increase. The effect of diversified distribution offered by the Internet and sites such as YouTube has been to offer a range of opportunities relating to how a screen can be used for viewing and associated activities.

Yet, clearly, documentary's history cannot be ignored. Indeed, the genre is so well established that a 'documentary tradition' is frequently referred to (Jacobs 1979). Assessing the balance and relative importance of continuity versus change is the challenge of this study. What are the issues for documentary studies now? Are the traditional themes of study still valid or are they changing, and if so, how?

The task of the documentary studies interpretative community has always been to work with and through a number of frequently irreconcilable critical positions and aspects of analysis. In this book I identify ongoing elements – or themes – as chapter headings, then pose the question 'are they still relevant?'

The digital revolution and the enormous increase in Internet usage have prompted much discussion about change and this has inevitably influenced the field of documentary. As technology becomes more sophisticated, cheaper and more readily available, so concerns over the genre's evolution and authenticity also escalate, although continuities are sometimes overlooked. Definitions of the genre, resonant with film's early days, are becoming more fluid; in fact it is precisely documentary's fluidity that provides a continuity of argument. In this study continuity has a number of different manifestations. One is the continuity of themes taken as chapter headings; another concerns the tension between the creative role of the documentary maker and the actuality of the real world, a tension that still generates arguments about whether documentary is reportage or art. Other continuities will emerge from individual chapter discussions.

Contextual issues

Issues of continuity and change require that we respond both to the micro-level of social phenomena and to the broader contextual picture. A number of media analysts, such as Dahlgren (1995) and Thompson (1990), stress the importance of context, pointing out that media representations are only one method amongst others by which knowledge is socially produced. Marxist analysis of culture and the arts has highlighted the role of political and ideological factors, arguing that aesthetics should have a morally and ideologically acceptable basis.

In his seminal 1936 essay 'The Work of Art in the Age of Mechanical Reproduction', Walter Benjamin defends the integrity of an art work, stating that no critical theory will have a lasting claim on the work that it interprets, for it is never a substitute for the original artistic product. He argues that we must return constantly to the work itself (Benjamin 2008: 3–9, 195–205, 315–20). In this evolving process of artistic criticism, history will find its way in, but the aim is not to present cultural history. Any consideration of what values and debates might be valid worldwide is impossible without addressing contextual issues that need to be understood historically and within a variety of social conditions and contexts. But this book is not a history of documentary;[1] rather, I have used documentary history selectively to explain context rather than attempt to present an all-embracing chronological evolution.

Any enquiry will be influenced by wider changes in emphasis and approaches within other areas of media research such as television, film studies, media history, cultural theory and the sociology of the media. The question for documentary in a broadcasting context centres on how television documentary's textual system has come to develop a more 'popular' approach. TV documentary has moved from an earlier period of scarcity, when it was used to archive social consensus, to the present period of plenty, in which it reflects the uncertainties and tensions of the modern world. According to Ellis (2002), TV management participate in this process, and their approach to scheduling and increased use of digital graphics have become central. This has been in competition with other realist formats such as docu-soap, docu-drama and presenter-led 'location challenge' series that cherry pick elements of the documentary style. The context is changing, the experience of TV viewing has changed, and this has rubbed off on documentary making more generally. For independent television producers, this overcrowded market is a buyer's market, not a seller's. This scenario has changed the form of documentary itself (Chapman 2007: 25–8, 50), and has impinged on levels of self-censorship (see Chapter 4).

Documentary gives us situated knowledge, but the specifics of cultural representation are linked to larger historical and social forces, such as the pressure on television executives to deliver critical success at a time when audiences are fragmenting across a range of delivery and exhibition platforms and channels of distribution. The Internet has made access and audience participation easier, but it has not greatly influenced the criteria normally used for analysis, interpretation and criticism. One aspect of the influence of the Internet often overlooked in discussion about contemporary documentary is the potential for marketing. The success of *An Inconvenient Truth* (2006) and *Super Size Me* (2004),[2] for example, both of which enjoyed strong marketing support and a prolonged afterlife, also illustrates how our perception of the public sphere has changed. Advertisers and distributors have recognized the shift from 'nationally defined audiences to individualised interactivity on a potentially global scale' (Gillespie 2005: 4).

The main difference that has interested academics is the potential of the Web for extending democracy and communication: the general public can more readily participate in a variety of forms of response using the Internet. Participatory and interactive attributes allow people to have a different sort of relationship with the public sphere than hitherto existed, in that it is now much easier to become a creator of documentary. 'Amateurs' can then upload their films onto YouTube and wait for the response, which in Britain may include interest from television commissioning editors who if they spot potential may fund a longer documentary version to fit their scheduling requirements.

Of course, YouTube has a wider application than simply posting documentaries. The video-sharing site, rivalling the BBC as the most visited in Britain, is used for election campaigns, and for a host of other didactic as well as entertainment purposes, some of which implicate documentary. For instance, the Church of Scientology used YouTube to counter a BBC current affairs documentary exposé, by posting footage of the reporter John Sweeney 'losing it' by screaming at a Scientology spokesperson during the filming of a *Panorama* programme. Sweeney claims that 'For an hour and a half they showed me these appalling images. I felt as though I was being brainwashed and that if I didn't fight it they would have taken over my mind' (Swinford 2007). In addition to the YouTube footage, the Scientologists also distributed 100,000 DVDs as part of their campaign to combat the 'negative' messages of the *Panorama* film. The virulence of this particular organization's campaigns to influence hearts and minds may well be extraordinary, but their distribution methods are open to everyone to emulate, and this all forms part of the phenomenon referred to as the 'democratization of documentary' – itself another element of continuity in this study.

Methodology and how to use this book

The evidence may well suggest that the balance of power between filmmaker and audience is changing, and addressing how this shift affects the issues raised in the main chapter themes will be one of the tasks of this book. Are these themes still relevant for the analysis of contemporary films? That question constitutes our underlying, discursive, research question. I do not examine how documentary elements are used in other media categories, nor engage in a general study of the impact of the Internet and the digital revolution on documentary. This is, rather, a study of how far these aspects of change, important and dramatic as they are, impact upon the issues that are traditionally addressed in documentary studies.

The criteria for selecting case studies has been to propose contemporary films, made since 2002, that are accessible either on DVD or on the Internet, and are in some way provocative. The only exception to this rule is *Titicut Follies* (1967), presented as a case study in Chapter 8 exclusively in terms of the concept of 'informed consent', since it remains the most striking example of ethical practice in this area, and its presence here also enables comparisons with other recent films.[3] The case studies can be looked at discretely before a screening of the film in question, or as part of the whole chapter as general background, but they are only indicative, intended as an introductory road map towards greater insight and further research. The choice of case studies is eclectic and non-exclusive – there are many others that could equally have found their way into the pages that follow, had space permitted. Some films provoke a feel-good factor, others provoke anger or discomfort on the part of the audience. Others yet again are important for a particular issue that emerges from a close reading relevant to a given chapter's theme.

Chapter summary

Chapter 1 discusses how documentary deals with the world we live in, or the world as it was in the past, exploring how the genre consists of reality-driven representations, based on the premise that there is some form of bond or connection between what is filmed and the end product. These factors create an imperative to retain a legitimate, referential importance for the documentary image. Nevertheless, any non-fiction film will remain a depiction that reflects the intentions of the filmmaker as much as it does the available real. The authority of documentary as a genre has traditionally been supported by the fact that it is different from fiction, yet there have always been questions about a genre that requires acceptance of a multi-dimensional role for the filmmaker – as discoverer, observer, inventor of approach and form, composer of style. Epistemological considerations may have been the lifeblood of documentary studies in the past, but will they continue to be in the future? Sub-genres of documentary, such as 'mockumentary', influence documentary's self-definition, but does this have a more limited value in the twenty-first century as the level of fluidity and pace of change both escalate?

The realist tradition has encouraged the viewer to assume that unproblematic access to the truth can be achieved in a documentary. This assumption will be challenged here on a number of fronts that are examined in various case studies. Truth is connected to claims for reality, and both of these concepts are problematic for the documentary as a genre. The achievement of absolute truth within the documentary genre represents a mission impossible, yet it still appears to act as a central motivation for the form. 'The documentary genre depends on a series of assertions of the truthfulness of its material, and the criteria of truthfulness differ between cultures and historic periods' (Ellis 2002: 206). A documentary will never be wholly true to reality; but neither will it eliminate reality altogether simply because it is representational.

Chapter 2 examines forms of representation, and problems associated with them, underlining the obvious point that the way real people are represented can be controversial. Even when the aim of a factual film is to examine a particular issue, or when the filmmaker wants to emphasize the extent to which the portrayal is close to reality, what and who is filmed will continue to pose a problem. For this reason, analysis of the dialectical relationship between events and their representation tends to be central to any discussion about documentary. The reaction has sometimes been to suppress this issue in favour of some kind of 'naturalism', or else to take up the challenge by introducing aspects of the impact on the design of films (Rosenthal and Corner 2005: 8). Whatever style of representation is selected, there will be strengths and weaknesses to the combination of sound and images and to the kind of usage envisaged for the film.

Marginalized and minority communities in many countries look to documentary as a communication vehicle that will reveal the 'true picture' of their situation, anticipating that the research process will uncover hitherto hidden evidence. Historically, public service broadcasting (PBS) has often provided a platform for such communities. The significance here is not simply one of visual technique, but a political one of representational form in the broader sense of the word. When this is examined more closely, issues of subjectivity and/or objectivity will emerge as part of the political equation of representation.

Chapter 3 discusses the feasibility and desirability of objectivity as an aim. In the post-colonial situation, native film and video can play an important role in the rediscovery of the history of indigenous peoples, giving a platform to local perspectives on the past. Documentaries and photographs can supplement or replace oral history as a means of providing continuity and a sense of community. In this context, documentaries with an apparently subjective perspective can serve a dual purpose of providing a platform for a lesser known viewpoint whilst correcting an imbalance that will itself provide a new 'objectivity'. Subjectivity comes in various forms. When a film is viewed, the subjective voice can appear as the subjectivity of the spectator – dealt with in Chapter 7. Subjectivity is also a product of the film-text and a quality that is assigned to that text. Above all, there is the subjectivity of the filmmaker. Here the documentary form acknowledges different levels of personal influence, while also relying on the integrity of the filmmaker not to 'fake it' and to show viewers 'what really happened'.

Chapter 4 considers how, in the future, it is likely that indirect forms of control on expression, such as self-censorship and market influence, will become increasingly important, and it is only pressure from citizens that will help to create the climate for attitudinal change. On the one hand, the effect of deregulation on funding has been to reduce the role of politics, difference and dissent within the nation-state, and this has had an impact on determining which documentaries see the light of day. On the other hand, technological advances and increased audience awareness have combined to make the Internet an accessible alternative platform for the communication of dissent. This binary feature is reminiscent of the Gramscian hegemony versus counter-hegemony media analysis.

Chapter 5 examines the role of the authorial voice. Just as every documentary is individually crafted, so also every analysis of authorial voice will be different. In order to fully appreciate 'voice', both visual and linguistic factors need to be taken into account. The way these are juxtaposed, interact and are synthesized will influence any assessment. The message of a film depends on a triangle of the author's intentions and skills (both aesthetic and technical), the film's subject matter, and the audience interpretation. In fact, manifestations of voice may be found everywhere in a documentary. Reality TV, by contrast, may provide authentic footage, but it cannot be categorized as 'documentary' because there is no editorial content: the voice as message is overshadowed by the entertainment function.

Documentary viewers may become engaged in a film's content and editorial approach as well as its style and structure. Although digital and non-linear formats potentially offer a fresh way of approaching authorial voice, the traditional narrative form still remains a dominant factor in many digital films. Documentaries distributed via the Internet often form part of a wider discursive and/or marketing strategy, an approach examined in relation to *An Inconvenient Truth* in this chapter. 'Agit prop' and advocacy emerge as the main beneficiaries here: through the documentary viewers and makers become engaged in social production by contributing to sub-spheres and counter-spheres within society.

Chapter 6 analyses how reflexivity works to destabilize belief in the verisimilitude of documentary. This leaves us with a dilemma. Realism may appear to be stratified, but if epistemic relativism becomes an end in itself we may then be tempted to reject any attempt to explain reality or to seek the truth behind the appearance. This chapter examines the various categories of reflexivity, among them the self-reflexivity involved in setting out the specific position from which one speaks. Of course, such positions may shift over time as particular issues (political, social, personal) flare up, mature or settle. Similarly, new technologies, cheap software and the Internet have enabled a crossover of roles between viewer, editor, and producer, and reflexivity as a technique for aesthetic expression – introduced by Vertov in the 1920s – must be analysed within this contextual framework.

How does political reflexivity differ from the stance taken in more traditional political films? The latter will tend to invite the viewer to adopt a clearly committed position, whereas reflexive films will challenge the viewer to analyse the complexities of the theme, and also acknowledge some of the intricacies involved making a film about the subject in question. Political reflexivity may also use parody, satire, pastiche or irony to transport the viewer beyond the text to an awareness of a wider social agenda. However, these too can be problematic from the viewer's point of view, and in much of the writing on reflexivity, the needs, potential perceptions and expectations of the audience have often been overlooked.

Chapter 7 discusses the understanding between the parties involved in the communication of documentary's reality. Precisely because the central space documentary occupies is located in 'the gap between life as lived and life as narrativized' (Nichols 1986: 114) one can argue that there is such an understanding, based on a kind of unwritten contract. 'In documentary, the viewer is asked to participate in a series of contracts – between film and its object, between film-maker and audience, between reality and representation' (Rabinowitz 1994: 31–2). That contract is based on a central core value of realism, which is mediated. The documentary-making community may realize that any production will be a construct, but the general public still have certain expectations of the genre.

The problem for scholars is how to measure audience reaction, not least since the data is limited. If there is no accepted standard measure by which to collate and assess audience perception then there will be no quantitative data to analyse. Thomas Austin (2005, 2007) has begun outlining various issues concerning audiences, but as yet the area is still being mapped out in relation to documentary studies. The challenge is all the more formidable due to the fast-changing nature of the field, but this is arguably one of the most important aspects for the future. Older issues still remain: if audiences, either subconsciously or overtly, are still influenced by the claim to authenticity of the genre, then some integrity should be expected and maintained. The only alternative is to give up on the word 'documentary'. The chapter uses case studies (*The Family* [1974; 2008] and *Battle for Haditha* [2007]) to challenge the definition of documentary practice as the conveying of true stories to the audience.

Chapter 8 outlines how discussion about ethics in relation to film falls into two categories: concerning the production procedures and process on the one hand, and the form and effects of the finished product on the other. A documentary maker needs to gain the trust of social actors before filming can start, but needs also to maintain a respectful distance. In this chapter the conflict between creative output and reality is explored in terms of its impact on the shifting boundaries of power, privacy and the public interest. One element of continuity here is fakery: it has been around since the early days of documentary, although its presence hardly puts the existence of all documentaries into question. Greater audience awareness does not mean that the spectator will dismiss *all* documentaries as 'fake'. This issue is just one indication that elements of continuity and change need to be put into perspective in the light of current trends – a point that is applied more generally in this final chapter.

The conclusion to the book argues that documentary amounts to a negotiation between image and reality, subjectivity, interpretation, objectivity and bias. There will always be a tension between documentary understood as a category of factual representation that respects authenticity and the impossibility of aiming for the 'truth' in the presentation of 'reality'. One factor that will weigh heavily on our consideration of the issues is the aspect of scale represented by the World Wide Web: does the existence of virtually limitless numbers of films and allied material mean that we should give up on any attempt to determine the boundaries of the canon and on documentary as a genre? The answer has to be an optimistic 'no'. The need for critical appraisal of documentary is greater than ever before: discourses are likely to be shared increasingly with specialist online communities as viewers become makers, and as both may also become activists. Indeed, the smart money has to be on activist documentary as a category to follow in the future.

1 Definitions
Issues and Influences

Summary

Documentary is a discursive formation, presenting first-hand experience and fact by creating a rhetoric of immediacy and 'truth', using photographic technology. 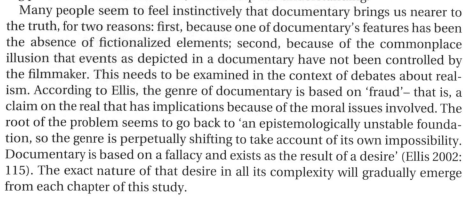 Documentary is also recognized as being a very engaged sort of cinema, which means that there are inevitably pressures and sometimes conflicting claims on verisimilitude, several of which will emerge throughout the pages of this study. Today documentary is so diverse and diffuse that the genre is hard to define. This chapter argues that contextual factors, including historical consciousness, institutional influences such as that of documentary on television, and prevailing politico-economic climates, can all help our understanding.

Many people seem to feel instinctively that documentary brings us nearer to the truth, for two reasons: first, because one of documentary's features has been the absence of fictionalized elements; second, because of the commonplace illusion that events as depicted in a documentary have not been controlled by the filmmaker. This needs to be examined in the context of debates about realism. According to Ellis, the genre of documentary is based on 'fraud'– that is, a claim on the real that has implications because of the moral issues involved. The root of the problem seems to go back to 'an epistemologically unstable foundation, so the genre is perpetually shifting to take account of its own impossibility. Documentary is based on a fallacy and exists as the result of a desire' (Ellis 2002: 115). The exact nature of that desire in all its complexity will gradually emerge from each chapter of this study.

Introduction

Corner has described documentary studies as a 'rather instable category' (Corner 2000: 681) and noted that the term 'documentary' is much more safely applied as an adjective rather than as a noun: 'To ask "is this a documentary project?" is more useful than to ask, "is this film a documentary?" because it suggests firm definitional criteria and an existence as an object rather than a practice' (Corner 2002: 258). It could be that it is more a matter of degree than of kind, with documentary influence dispersed throughout television and advertising, cinema fiction, news and presenter-led TV (cookery, travel, motoring, sport and reality formats, games, challenges, tests, etc.). The crossover in use of techniques between documentaries and other categories, particularly evident in television, has made it more difficult to define and recognize a documentary, and this has contributed to a weakening of the status of the genre.

It may be that this is more of a problem in countries where documentary has traditionally blossomed within a television public service framework, rather than in, say, the United States where the sometimes precarious existence of independent documentary cinema has led to a greater emphasis on the study of form rather than context, function, or the themes and issues treated by documentary. In Europe and elsewhere, documentary struggles for survival within an increasingly commodified television framework where economics, cultural change and scheduling practices have resulted in an enormous growth in accessible actuality-based formats.

Evolution of the genre

From around 1921, early films captured real people in everyday situations and pioneer filmmakers edited such footage to create a structure with either a story or an argument – which became documentary. By 1932, John Grierson had formulated a definition which distinguished between documentary and other factual forms such as cinematic journalism (newsreel), travelogue and scientific or nature films. For Grierson, documentary went beyond arrangement and description because of the way it used 'a creative treatment of actuality': this aesthetic shaping offered a unique capacity for revelation rather than merely mechanistic observation or reflection of the real.

Grierson needed to formulate a definition for his own fundraising purposes (Winston 2000: 20; 2008). This demonstrates that artistic licence – in this case the licence to employ any of fiction's techniques except the use of actors and the invention of a story purely from the imagination – is always influenced by contextual or pragmatic factors and never exercised in a vacuum. The definition has stood the test of time because it allows for all manner of producer intervention along with, or following after, the recording process. Yet it is also constantly challenged and always surrounded by controversy, for it prompts further questions such as how much and what sort of actuality might remain after the creative treatment.

We probably need to maintain our genre differentiations (however flexible) in order to maintain our ethical distinctions – allowing, for instance, digital manipulation to happen in fiction, but not in documentary. Yet ironically, the influence of technology leads us to question the task of maintaining definitions, making it into an interpretative burden. Of course, the application of an aesthetic has always been influenced by technology. For many years, within the history of documentary, this acted as a constraint that dictated methods for the creative treatment of actuality. Lack of portable sound equipment made reconstruction necessary, while heavy cameras needed to be mounted and film stock's insensitivity to light meant that an abundance of lights had to be used.

Meanwhile the growth of television as a new medium influenced the shape of documentary as well, with journalism becoming an important influence on documentary style. When the BBC first established a documentary unit, it was inspired not only by some of the more factual and less poetic documentaries from the Griersonian tradition, such as *Housing Problems* (1935), but also by CBS's *See It Now* (1951). The launching of this extended news feature series by CBS was in turn influenced by the cinema's single-issue newsreel series such as *March of Time* (1935), as well as by radio formats. As more television series were established with documentary styles, the flexibility of TV's factual scope emerged. Films could be topped and tailed with studio discussions, and used to craft a new form of television journalism that was both pictorial and talk based (Winston 2000: 21; 2008). The historical compilation format, pioneered in Russia in Esfir Schub's 1927 *Fall of the Romanov Dynasty*, also became a television staple, with series like NBC's *Victory at Sea* (1952–3), CBS's *The 20th Century* (1957–70), and the ABC/ BBC series based on Churchill's war memoirs, *The Valiant Years* (1961). During the 1960s and early 1970s TV current affairs and documentary departments were responsible for some ground-breaking and politically influential classics such as *Harvest of Shame* (CBS 1960) and *The Selling of the Pentagon* (CBS 1971).

The introduction of 16 mm lightweight cameras and portable sound recording enabled documentary makers to film without elaborate preparation, and with a journalistic ethic of observation and non-intervention which became known as Direct Cinema, or 'fly on the wall'. This approach was further aided by the adoption of video from the 1970s onwards, and later by camcorders and digital, miniaturized equipment. Now capturing the event took precedence over the creative treatment of actuality as the combined influence of technology and television made a clear mark. However, documentary at the time never really achieved the mass audience appeal that was to come later – towards the end of the 1990s. In fact, having made its mark, television documentary became a victim of ratings-obsessed scheduling, finding itself relegated to late night or high summer.

Outside of television, some filmmakers believed that cinematic truth could be better achieved if production techniques were (at least partially) revealed on screen in a self-reflexive way. Thus Cinema Verité challenged Direct Cinema's claims to non-intervention by revealing that sequences were set up where necessary, even if the aesthetic techniques of long takes using hand-held equipment and the available light gave the same 'fly-on-the-wall' feel. Television evolved its own version of 'Verité', adding long, naturalistic takes to the existing repertoire, while also endeavouring to adhere to the Direct Cinema ideal of non-intervention. Sometimes conventions were interpreted as meaning that film editors were required to adhere to the order of events filmed, rather than re-arranging them. In fact, classic Direct Cinema did not always achieve this. With television the categories of Direct Cinema and Cinema Verité became confused. The hand-held camera triumphed, the interview remained, but reconstructions, commentary and music were frowned upon as inappropriate interventions. A form of TV journalism remained, with the idea that events should be recorded with only minimal interference, and the filmmaker should be ignored. When it came to definitions, confusion had set in.

Documentary on television was to come under attack during the neo-liberal Reaganite 1980s, leaving it vulnerable to the point of near destruction in the US. In 1984 the Federal Communications Commission abolished public service guidelines for programming: commercial broadcasters were effectively let off the hook. With no requirement to maintain public affairs programming, the networks no longer needed the documentary departments that they had sustained for around 30 years. Cable and the extension of competition were blamed for documentary's television demise. Neo-liberalism's challenge to the regulatory environment proved to be crucial to the fortunes of documentary.

In the US, the reactionary attacks during this period undermined the funding base for any public service documentary subjects that appeared to be left wing. Those films that survived, such as the history of the Civil Rights Movement, *Eyes on the Prize* (1987), were to attract attention out of all proportion to their audience viewing figures (Winston 2000: 49; Zimmerman 2000). In place of documentary, Reality TV became the new saviour of the US networks and 1990s cable channels. Reality TV coaches participants and artificially creates conflict in order to inject drama into the situation being filmed. 'The focus on presenting the audio-visual evidence as much as "the story" is one of the features that distinguishes reality TV from earlier attempts to "catch the real"' (Fetveit 1999: 794). This has influenced the style and content of the documentary that survived. While more traditionally styled documentaries found a 'duty' slot on cable, although not so big an audience compared to network TV,[4] a new form of documentary called 'docuglitz' has come to the fore, compromising both the Griersonian tradition and the serious current affairs film: Carlton's 1993 series *Hollywood Women* tackled topics such as sex and success, glitz and glamour, asking some of Hollywood's most famous stars to contribute – Roseanne Arnold, Raquel Welch and Lauren Bacall among them. The format is dominated by a constant soundtrack and studded with snappy sound-bites.

Grierson aimed to use documentary to foster a sense of citizenship within the community, a laudable goal which was, unfortunately, to be achieved by everybody understanding their place in the bigger social scheme of things. While Winston (1995; 2008) has called for a rejection of this tradition, and formulated an alternative definition,[5] it was Hartley who first attempted to construct a wider critique of the role of 'the knowledge classes' within cultural studies, with his analysis of Grierson's film *Housing Problems*,[6] in which the working-class subjects are unable to be proactive because of their reliance on so-called 'experts'. The deepening reaction against the Griersonian tradition seems to be reflected in the style of contemporary documentary, exemplified by the current trend towards more reflexive films (examined below in Chapters 3 and 6). Gone are the 'defining moments of documentary history, those moments when an expository realism seemed to resonate at least partially with a public, democratic rhetoric of reform and progress' (Corner 2002: 265). But there is still sufficient demand and need, without even starting to list the documentary tradition's significant box-office successes, for a genre that uses the word 'documentary'. As Grierson said, the term is clumsy, but we have to use it. Although documentary's claim to the real may be imperfect, there is a considerable demand amongst the public for its kind of treatment of so-called 'reality'. Our exploration of documentary issues in the pages that follow should be undertaken with an awareness of both the problems that this poses and the diversity of the genre.

The public sphere in many countries used to be serviced by public service broadcasting (PSB) with a 'duty' to provide quality documentaries. In Britain, Grierson had wanted to influence audiences but never achieved mass viewing via the cinema and other alternative venues such as schools, factories and village halls (Winston 2000: 41; 2008). Nevertheless, his ethos was combined with the Reithian non-profit approach into a PSB ethic by the BBC (Chapman 2005: 150–1). Documentary was given a serious mission: its role in encouraging citizenship within the public sphere was proclaimed, but in the context of a social democratic ethic that was at the time under severe challenge from incipient fascism. An educated and informed population, aided by documentary, was central to the 1930s and 1940s idea of social cohesion.

In order to reach television audiences, journalistic news values were integrated with educational values. If the concept of education is construed in its widest sense of both children and adults acquiring knowledge based on the real world, then it is clear that within a PSB context, journalism and education are intertwined. The words used for documentary and factual programmes within the institution of television point to the hybrid effect: documentary appears as 'reportage', in current affairs, arts and other categories. British documentary survived the first wave of attack on the principles of PSB during the 1970s, when it was considered an essential mark of public service quality, although not necessarily attractive to TV audiences (Kilborn 1996: 143). Likewise, during the more recent global neo-liberal onslaught on the principles of PSB, when it was under attack in the US, television documentaries were winning new audiences in Britain, albeit some would say at the cost of what has been called the 'discourse of sobriety' (Nichols 1991; 1994). A British version of *An American Family* (1973) led the way for improved ratings for other observational series on the police, vets, driving instructors, and for a host of docu-soaps. These offered a cheaper way of retaining audiences than did popular fiction, while simultaneously damaging traditional definitions of documentary as a 'duty' genre .The trivial, the titillating and the sensational are now considered the panacea that will attract wider television audiences and ensure survival.

Documentary on television exists within a territory populated by a range of formats, including docu-drama, chat shows, surveillance and undercover video, drama based on fact, factual magazines using fictional techniques such as reconstruction, and so on. Mockumentary, the satirization of documentary, and Reality TV have both impacted on the truthfulness debate. Very often the space occupied by such formats is partly fictional and partly factual, with the onus to detect authenticity likely to fall increasingly on the shoulders of the viewer, as digitalization challenges Direct Cinema's claims that the camera cannot lie.

Documentary images can have a range of functions – illustrative, symbolic, evidential – and there is an unresolved tension between the iconic on the one hand, and the indexical on the other (Fetveit 1999: 792). The relative importance of each has varied throughout documentary history. In the 1930s, the illustrative and symbolic function dominated, but after the Second World War, the evidential came to the fore as actuality took preference over dramatization, and lightweight cameras and synchronous sound recording in the late 1950s also gave support to the evidential. This led to 'objective', fly-on-the-wall techniques with an emphasis on observation. Reality TV is an extreme form of the evidential and indexical, while digital imaging tends towards the illustrative and iconic.

Cinema, television and 'docu-soap'

From time to time, documentary has had an impact on cinema audiences. The early success of *Nanook of the North* (1922) was continued by documentary features during the Second World War. In the postwar period nature films such as Disney's *The Living Desert* (1953) and more recently *March of the Penguins* (2005) and *Earth* (2007), together with sports features such as Riefenstahl's *Olympischespielen* (1938), *Hoop Dreams* (1994) and *When We Were Kings* (1996) have all been successful. Voyeuristic works such as *Mondo Cane* (1962) and the mainly secretly shot social feature *On the Bowery* (1957) have found a place, as have Direct Cinema rock documentaries such as *Don't Look Back* (1967) and *Lonely Boy* (1962), in addition to other Direct Cinema classics such as *Primary* (1960).

During the 1960s the critique of Hollywood[7] and the importance of war reporting on TV both provided a context that encouraged commercial documentary, while more recently Michael Moore's esoteric but politically challenging films have provoked further optimism about documentary's future appeal within the theatrical field of distribution. Wildlife films and climate change are proving fruitful content for the cinematic appeal of documentary on the big screen, and activist films are thriving on the opportunities provided by the Internet for enhancing the reach and life of a film through audience participation and informational support.

Documentary today is influenced by TV formats that have no regard for the discourse of sobriety, preferring titillation and fascination. Subjects for investigation include human sexuality, entertainment profiles and sport. Direct Cinema techniques have been used to invade privacy and to encourage voyeurism: the legacy from Direct Cinema seems to be a move to domestic subject matter. In Britain the phenomenon of 'docu-soap' on television reached a peak between 1996 and 1999, having a considerable influence on the entire broadcast factual landscape, including traditional documentary, which subsequently became more entertainment based. The serialized format with long-running storylines uses the techniques of observational documentary (fly on the wall) combined with drama style editing to portray social actors selected for their ability to perform their real roles – as employees of airports, hospitals, rescue services, cruise liners, police forces, driving instruction schools, etc. – as if they were professional actors in a soap opera. They too could become stars.

Although fly-on-the-wall camera work seems to resemble Direct Cinema, in fact there is a big difference in terms of how far things are set up. Direct Cinema and observational filming traditionally aimed not to influence events, whereas in docu-soap everything is prearranged for the camera on the chosen mediated, performative stage. Ratings for the early docu-soaps were remarkable: *Airline* (1998), for example, on Britain's ITV network, won a 50 per cent audience share at 8 p.m. on a Friday night (Dovey 2000: 135). The 'docu-soap' hybrid has two influential features: it foregrounds the individual experience, without usually presenting any argument (and so becomes free publicity for the enterprises featured), and it frequently focuses on personal traumas and the intimacies of everyday lives which would previously have been considered best kept private, if only because they involve details of boring domestic trivia. Examples on UK TV included *Wife Swap* (2003), *Neighbours from Hell* (1998–2004), *Nannies from Hell* (1998) and *Babewatch* (1998), about the private tribulations of new recruits to modelling.

It is possible to argue that television's move towards mundane personalization of the kind found in docu-soap is but one manifestation of neo-liberalism's propensity to encourage the commodification of every aspect of culture. But since docu-soap, like drama documentary, can be defined as a separate hybrid, it will be dealt with in this book only in terms of how it impinges on regular documentary.[8] The point here is that docu-soap subject matter is indicative of a change in thinking by TV producers about what constitutes an interesting topic for documentaries, as observational techniques shifted from 'official' institutions to everyday, domestic contexts. There was also a stylistic crossover worth noting – by the 1990s TV documentaries had become a packaged product with an emphasis on performance as well as narrator commentary.

Documentary tends to make an argument about a shared, public world. To this extent, the influence of docu-soap represents a retreat from the public sphere. Sustained social enquiry in a documentary form is no longer fashionable on TV. The most damning argument against docu-soap's influence concerns its two-dimensional quality – the fact that no questions are asked. This precludes the possibility that what is recorded can be subject to change, in the way that historical, cultural, economic forces change. The format depends almost entirely on narrative, and the absence of argument undermines the discourse of sobriety. The influence of docu-soap and docuglitz meant that regular documentary became more sensational, at a time when budgetary constraints meant that fewer resources were being allocated to serious, labour intensive research, and social documentary in a traditional style was becoming an endangered species. Reality TV sounded the death knell for the latter, while deregulation also ensured that the TV industry became casualized in a way that made the development of serious subjects as a labour of love increasingly difficult for practitioners who needed to make a living from documentary making.

Mindful of this, Nichols (1991) has called for a more serious attitude towards documentary, a 'discourse of sobriety'. Reacting against such discourse, Renov (1993; 1999) wants documentary theory to adopt an 'aesthetics of delirium' (AoD). MacLennan and Hookham (2001) identify AoD as a position that favours the irrational rather than the rational, within the tradition of thinking espoused by Nietzsche, who analysed the conflict between the aesthetic and the rational.[9] In the context of television, the discourse of sobriety has long been in decline to a point where it is now threatened with extinction by what Corner has called a new 'lightness of being', prompted by a level of instability in the market for factual programming (Corner 2002: 264). This aspect of documentary's fluidity points to a need to revisit the fundamental definitions of fiction and non-fiction.

Definitions of fiction and non-fiction

The need to supply an adequate definition of documentary has had a consuming appeal for interested parties over the years.[10] It is an ongoing task, because the genre is founded on shifting sands. Documentaries can serve a function of reminding us that an event, such as the Holocaust, actually happened. Usually, however, they go further than merely acting as a pointer; they create meaning through the ordering of sequences, the nature of the soundtrack, the context of the shots, and various other production devices. Nichols (1991; 1994) categorizes documentary into 'modes', each with their own type of audience and institutional support. However, this may be too formulaic, and some good films defy categorization, or else fit into several categories. One alternative starting point is to try to define what documentary is *not*: for example, it is not news, which tends to consist of narrative segments, whereas documentary provides more of an in-depth treatment of its narrative, usually based around ordinary people rather than spokespeople or leaders.

Documentary also positions itself in relation to fiction: 'The gamble is that documentary will appear more real because it is less fictional' (Ellis 2002: 116).

In fact, theories of fiction and of non-fiction share an interest in the status of the image, the way it is represented, and the way film can be used to communicate historically. Both also share concerns about screen language, narrativity and issues of performance. And there are elements of fiction in non-fiction such as the way a character is created in documentary (Nanook, for instance, has an on-screen persona), or how music, structuring and close-ups are used for dramatic effect.

In other words, just because we apply a non-fiction label to a film, that does not mean we should ignore its fictive elements. It may be true that in an observational documentary the event or subject that happens to be filmed would have taken place anyway. But the presence of the camera is likely to give it a different inflection, resulting in a level of performance by social actors which indicates that the camera has an influence, if still within the parameters of real life. Nevertheless, the situation has an existence outside of its filming – the institution or organization featured will continue beyond the period of filming, whereas a fiction is created by the script and has no such independent existence in the real world. Notwithstanding this difference, Renov argues that all discursive forms, including documentary, are 'fictive' because of their recourse to tropes or rhetorical figures. For Renov then, the difference is relative, depending on 'the extent to which the referent of the documentary sign may be considered as a piece of the world plucked from its everyday context rather than fabricated for the screen' (Renov 1993: 7).

Although fiction and non-fiction can be seen as two domains that 'inhabit one another' (Renov 1993: 3), documentary can still be defined by its refusal to use some fictional devices such as a shifting viewpoint and the representation of an inner life for characters. In a documentary, the behaviour of social actors is all that the viewer sees and hears, whereas in fiction the script tends to provide other indicators of motivation. Although documentary usually has a narrative, the aim will be to examine an aspect of life rather than present a finely tuned story; thus documentary will not be structured as elegantly as a fictional film, where the drive is eventually to deliver a closure to the narrative – which may not happen in such a complete way with a documentary. Although the style of shooting appears more spontaneous, less prepared and groomed than in fiction, some fiction now emulates the raw documentary feel, with hand-held camera work, for example.

Fictional techniques, however, remain problematic within any attempt to define documentary. 'Fiction is orientated towards *a* world, non-fiction towards *the* world', says Renov (2004: 220); but it is not necessary to see the difference between fact and fiction as an either/or. Roscoe and Hight prefer to see documentary as 'existing along a fact–fictional continuum, each text constructing relationships with both factual and fictional discourses' (Roscoe and Hight 2001: 7). The same toolkit is available to both documentary and fiction filmmakers, and elements of interchange between the two have been discernible right from the beginning of documentary history. In *Nanook of the North*, the director Flaherty changed the name of the title character and replaced his real wife and baby with more photogenic social actors. More recently, the phenomenal success in cinemas of *March of the Penguins* reiterates the intersection of techniques. And, interestingly, since the marketing campaign for *Être et Avoir* (2002) gave no indication of its genre, some cinema viewers went to see it without realizing that it was a documentary (Austin 2005: 5).

Is there an obligation on filmmakers to make the distinction between fantasy and reality clear, or should we abandon this principle? A blurring of the boundaries between fact and fiction, real and unreal, is further enhanced by artists who use a documentary style in their films, without necessarily calling the project as a whole 'documentary'. This phenomenon seems to appeal to artists who want to engage with reality through their own highly personalized line of enquiry. The approach has been described as 'the coming together of the artist's seemingly unorthodox and self-motivated approach to events, set against the stolid documentary format. . . . In short, the documentary style slides somewhere between straight documentary filmmaking and contemporary art' (Muir 2003: 79).

According to Gregory Currie: 'To be worthy of the name, a documentary film has to be made up of a preponderance of documentary shots, but the shot's status as documentary depends on the documentary status of the film it is part of' (Currie 1999: 292–3). It is interesting to assess the marketing terminology used for some recent fictional films in the light of Currie's statement. We need to ascertain what is *not* documentary as well as what is; a look at *Death of a President* (2006) will help serve that purpose in this study.

Case study: *Death of a President* (2006)

Gabriel Range and Simon Finch adopted a manipulative tactic in creating their fictitious docu-drama *Death of a President*. The film uses a large cast in what is called a retrospective 'investigative documentary' set years after the assassination of George W. Bush in Chicago – as seen through the eyes of various security guards, news reporters and political analysts. The film won the International Critics Prize Jury (FIPRESCI) at Toronto for the audacity with which it distorts reality to reveal a larger truth. It also won a BAFTA TV Award, an Emmy Award, and an RTS Award.

The date is 19 October 2007. The opening scenes in Chicago show several points of view, representing people shoving through a protesting crowd waiting for the Presidential procession. A security official's voiceover describing the event accompanies the following interior scene, in which the President is filmed from several angles greeting loyal supporters, and the tension mounts until the moment a sniper shoots him. The shock is real and raw as he silently folds to the ground – security guards bundle him into a car, and the supporters panic.

The film then segues into the FBI's hunt for the assassin. Several people are questioned but only one, a Syrian national, is arrested and charged with murder on slight circumstantial evidence ('probable cause'). He is put on death row. However, a subsequent report is made which finds compelling evidence that another suspect, Al Claybon – a 1991 Persian Gulf vet, one of whose sons had died in Iraq – had planned and carried out the execution. Claybon kills himself and a suicide note to his other son is found which reads: 'Everything I stood for and raised you to stand for has turned bad. There's no honor in dying for an immoral cause. For lies. I love my country, but I love God, and the sons He gave me even more. I must do the right thing by you and by David. George Bush killed our David, and I cannot forgive him for that.' After the discovery of a top-secret itinerary in Claybon's house showing Bush's planned Chicago trip down to the minute, the film ends with the surviving son visiting the family grave. The filmmakers announce that the Syrian is still on death row and that the head of the FBI Chicago office has resigned. Another statement tells of the implementation of US Patriot Act III since Bush's death, allowing investigators unprecedented powers of surveillance and detention and granting 'further powers to the executive branch'.

The film is an intelligent, well-researched piece of drama, though the political sympathies of the filmmaker Gabriel Range are obvious. But what is the film exactly? Made for TV, it was marketed as a real documentary – a fact which clearly highlights a complex question of how such films are sold to the different institutions of cinema and TV. The overall impression of the film as a 'documentary' exercise is further undermined by a closer look at individual techniques and the filmmakers' intention to market the film as a documentary when it is clearly fiction.

Production values for fiction and documentary films are usually different: fictional films make use of inventive plotlines and have a script – a rare occurrence in documentary. *Death of a President* is clearly not a real documentary since it uses actors to portray an event that hasn't yet happened. Neither does it present an authoritative hypothesis in the same vein as Peter Watkins' *War Game* (1966), in which he asked real scientists to provide empirical evidence about what would happen to the human body in the case of a nuclear attack. In using a line up of famous faces and voices in addition to the extensive cast and extras, the makers of *Death of a President* hope to add authority and cachet to their fictional film. Some footage of President Bush on walkabout is real, but the close-ups of him near the security guards (who are actors) and being assassinated in the midst of his supporters (also actors) are produced using digital trickery. Furthermore, most of the cast are credited in the end titles, as is everyone in the huge technical crew – including key grips, stunt co-ordinators, set builders, weapons handlers and costume designers, who are not normally part of a documentary film crew.

It is the marketing of the film as a documentary that is problematic. The distributors Newmarket paid £1 million to screen the film on US screens in 2009 (Spiegelman 2006), thereby playing upon a deeply felt US historical paranoia and obsession about Presidential assassinations (Lincoln, Garfield, McKinley and Kennedy) and numerous assassination attempts. It also serves to feed the desire that some elements in US society had to see the Bush Administration finished off in a brutal manner. The film was screened on the UK TV's More4 channel on 3 November 2008, on the eve of the Presidential election. In this context, it took on an even more chilling prescience given the recent foiling of a plot by white supremacists to assassinate then Presidential candidate Barack Obama in October 2008.[11] At best, *Death of a President* acts as a practice-run should such an event ever happen, at worst it represents the manipulative distortion of the facts. Either way, it is not a real documentary – a fact the filmmakers make clear in the disclaimer at the film's end: 'None of the real people, companies or organizations that appear in this film are affiliated or associated with the film, or its producers in any way. Nor have they approved its content. This film is fictional. It is set in the future.'

Genres, categories and uses of documentary

Since the 1990s, and the fall from grace of Direct Cinema, the range of documentary possibilities and the hybrids that have emerged offer potential for academic analysis. They also demonstrate the existence of an extended range of cultural opportunities, such as subtitled films and community programmes on British and European TV. Corner distinguishes four main uses to which documentary has been put that may help with a definition: exposition, testimony, observation and diversion. With these in mind, he further identifies the functions of:

1. 'Democratic Civics': promotion of dominant versions of citizenship, often funded directly or indirectly by official bodies, such as Grierson's films in 1920s and 1930s Britain.
2. Journalistic exposition: documentary as reporting, the most common use of documentary on television.
3. Alternative interrogation: mainly within the independent cinema, but still surviving within some national media cultures, and sometimes emulated by broadcasters such as Channel 4 in Britain as a critical perspective or alternative artistic expression.
4. Documentary as diversion: emerging as a category in its own right from the institution of television, but borrowing fictional techniques for a primary viewing activity of onlooking and overhearing as intensive or relaxed diversion rather than in the service of exposition, propaganda or analysis. Very often examples are not specifically made as a documentary project, but rather use documentary styles combined with others in a format that uses elements of the game, the 'challenge', or the 'experiment' (see Corner n.d.).

It is genre convention, and in the case of television, channel and programme style, that help us to discern the status of a media recording – so, for instance, we have certain expectations about the veracity of news pictures. Hollywood has been the great developer of generic genres (Ellis 2002: 102), yet Hollywood people have been reticent in proclaiming them. Nevertheless, new combinations of Hollywood genres have kept the interpretative community in business for many years, with each new example or trend within a genre causing a repositioning of the entire category. In contrast, television is up front when it comes to defining categories of programming, taking the line that viewers need to know what they're getting. Audiences tend to respond by quickly accepting new hybrids that selectively merge, mix and combine, as with docu-soap.

However, there are limitations to the usefulness of the genre approach in contributing to an understanding of the medium. The way television recombines tends to be horizontal, across genres: for example, when it first came out, *Hill Street Blues* (1981–7) was defined as a mix of crime show, soap opera and documentary. It is precisely this trend which causes complications for documentary definition, as drama borrows from documentary, and vice versa. Within television, the complication is not confined to documentary versus entertainment: leisure programmes more generally have developed in the space between talk shows and documentary, and have had a considerable impact on the latter.

Non-fiction film offers the ability to document, persuade, promote, interrogate, analyse and express a point of view (Muir 2003: 79). Within the documentary genre, sub-genres have emerged. Observational documentary, using portable cameras to capture current events as they unfold, has survived, but there has also been a fusion with the soap opera into the new phenomenon of docu-soaps, called by Winston 'a bastardisation of television's usual verité bastardisation' (Winston 2000: 55). Popular factual TV has come to consist of a variety of sub-genres. Until recently, Britain's commercial Channel 5 organized its factual department into a number of sections with category labels that illustrate the range: Popular Documentaries, Features, Popular Factual Television Series, Reality Formats, Formatted Manipulated Documentaries, Experiments/Stunts/Events, and Contemporary Biography (Hill 2005: 43).

Throughout its history, the documentary genre has been constantly challenged: reflexive films with their self-conscious reference to generic conventions and those with a performative influence that challenges the boundary between fact and fiction both rely on dramatic techniques such as parody and irony, which serve to question the genre (Hill 2005: 20). Mockumentary has also relied upon fiction techniques, taking a 'fictive stance towards the social world, while utilising documentary aesthetics to "mock" the underlying discourses of documentary' (Roscoe and Hight 2001: 44). Hybrids challenge our definitions; take, for instance, the BBC series *The Ship* (2002). This recreated Captain Cook's 1768 journey along the north-east coast of Australia, using ordinary people and fly-on-the-wall style filming. Had these people been carrying out the experiment anyway, irrespective of whether the cameras were present, the series would have fallen within the documentary category more plausibly than it did, but the event was staged specifically by the broadcaster for the purposes of television. Hence *The Edwardian Country House* (2002) and its sequels were classified as reality history shows rather than documentary, although they too used documentary filming techniques. Documentary can also be distinguished from Reality TV because it offers explanation, rather than simply turning the audience into crude witnesses.

The journalistic documentary

The observational approach can be viewed as a form of journalism. The values are journalistic – liberalism underpins Cinema Verité in the US,[12] and support for an enquiring and critical press is central to this political value. The rise of journalistic documentary was facilitated by technological developments:

> [New] technology (mobile and versatile cameras and synchronous-sound recorders) not only enabled the filmmaker to capture on film social problems hidden from public view, but it also allowed the subjects of the films to speak for themselves . . . The implicit assumption here is that if right-thinking people become aware of the way things 'really are,' they will take steps to correct injustices and inequalities. The advocacy of a specific program of change is not the filmmaker's task; it is enough to reveal the 'truth' of a social situation to the viewer.
>
> (Allen and Gomery 1985: 233–4)

Documentary as a form of visual journalism, which involves a quest for the real facts or information behind the headlines, became especially popular in the 1960s and 1970s on television, within series formats such as *World in Action* (1960–98) in Britain, and the long-running *60 Minutes* (1968–) in the United States. These days, documentary journalism has leaned towards providing an argument. With this style, visuals may be chosen and arranged in support of the argument, or to create a source of internal tension between two versions of the 'truth'. But the unrehearsed, captured moments can also confront us with 'reality'. Either way, the apparent objectivity behind the old adage that the camera cannot lie can also become a powerful weapon of advocacy, for journalism's traditional 'objectivity' has become unfashionable amongst documentary makers. This factor, combined with the attractions of using the Internet as a distribution platform that also acts as a recruitment platform and channel of communication for a plethora of forms of activism, has led to further challenges to documentary definition that will be examined in Chapters 2, 3, 5, 7 and the Conclusion.

Realism

Issues of realism are connected to the bigger debate about the boundaries between fact and fiction – a longstanding issue which has been viewed from different perspectives over the years. Documentary can be defined by the existence of a pre-filmic reality – past or present – with which the film engages. That reality is replicated for purposes of evidence and argument as well as for entertainment, which leads into an ongoing debate about the nature of representation using film. It has always been the quest for verisimilitude as the purpose of documentary that has caused trouble for theorists of the genre.

Although the aesthetic, mediated nature of documentary production, and the position of audiences in relation to this, has prompted a complex discourse, the attempt to achieve 'realism' in artistic creation can be a function of fictional and well as factual genres. Both can be questioned, for as Nichols reminds us, 'We believe what we see and what is represented about what we see at our own risk' (2001: xii). The special responsibility of the documentary maker towards this 'caveat emptor' carries an ethical dimension (see Chapter 8).

The fidelity of an image to what it aspires to represent is as critical for a Hollywood movie as it is for video surveillance footage: it is the usage that differs. 'Even though we may agree that documentary representations are as constructed as fictional ones, the stance that documentary takes toward the social world is one that is grounded on a belief that it can access the real' (Roscoe and Hight 2001: 8). Yet there is an intrinsic irony inherent in the nature of the moving filmic image. The documentary genre has always been predicated on perceived authenticity, yet if one pauses to analyse how its moving images are constructed, one sees it is from individual still-frames. The fascination of Muybridge and other early film inventors (who considered themselves 'scientists') for experimentation was based on a study of how to reassemble these frames in order to recreate the sensation of movement. Muybridge carried out an experiment with the movement of horses (Chapman 2005: 124). Movement in real life had to become indistinguishable from filmic movement. In this way it is action, or movement – the panacea of all directors ('if it moves, shoot it!') – that lies at the heart of the recreation of reality/verisimilitude problems.

This reality problem, then, has to do with the very nature of film as a medium. Why not just write off the issue as an inconvenience that has to be accepted? Why do we chase our tails when discussing it? After all, technology has succeeded in persuading us of its effectiveness. Not only can technological devices in documentary making be used to increase our perception of reality, they also appear almost to guarantee the authenticity of the documentary image. If a camera operator has used a lens or produced a grainy image, or if the hand-held camera movements are shaky because the event being captured is fast moving, we can be easily convinced. More precisely, such techniques create an impression of fidelity to the pro-filmic event that is in fact being constructed and interpreted by the very act of recording.

But perceptions of reality will change according to period. The authenticity of Direct Cinema seemed greater at the time of its introduction because it was a new trend. Yet after a period of 'de-familiarization', technical approaches that were originally seen as realistic may become 'automatized' by repetition (Hall 1991: 44). Repetition then makes them seem conventional, such that eventually Cinema Verité's restless, hand-held camera work and blurred, grainy visuals appear in Hollywood movies, television commercials and music videos as standard practice.

At one time, for example, Eisenstein's *Strike* (1925) was held up as a good example of how realism could be achieved (Nichols 2001: xi). But after the Second World War, realism gradually became an essential tool for documenting the daily experiences of ordinary working people in a way that – because it was embedded in real life and not fiction and involved location filming rather than studios – would bring middle-class filmmakers closer to the social reality of their subjects. Long takes, for instance, were evidence of lack of mediation and hence taken as a sign of authenticity. The British Free Cinema movement, works by the French New Wave and from the National Film Board of Canada, were all influential in this way of thinking. But by repeating such techniques, contemporary filmmakers conventionalized the innovations of Cinema Verité until they became clichés that would eventually be satirized. For example, in *This is Spinal Tap* director Rob Reiner used the by then classic tracking shot of a music star walking on stage, emerging from the dark to blaring sound and dazzling light (first used to present J.F. Kennedy in *Primary* and later, memorably, for Bob Dylan in *Don't Look Back*) (Nichols 2001: 45). Later, new kinds of realism appear – Reality TV and films based around surveillance footage, for instance.

The concept of realism has itself been much debated: MacLennan and Hookham refer to a differentiation in the past between 'naïve realism', 'where the film is deemed to offer an unmediated relationship with reality', and what they call 'irrealism, where the emphasis on the mediating properties of the film was such that reality itself was called into question' (MacLennan and Hookham 2001: 1). Corner makes a similar distinction when he identifies two sorts of realism used in documentaries: observational realism, which is a 'set of formal markers that confirm to us that what we are watching . . . is a record of an ongoing, and at least partly media-independent, reality', and expositional realism, which is a 'rhetoric of accuracy and truth' most commonly seen in television documentaries (Corner 2001: 127). In both cases, the audience is expected to acknowledge the observational techniques, such as the hand-held camera work, or how the argument is developed by the way the evidence is interpreted.

The contention over documentary and realism thus centres on two main aspects: first, the relationship between the film and pre-filmic reality, and second, connected to this, the role of filmmaker as an agent in relation both to themselves and to the people about whom the film is being made. In addition, it could be argued that the real problem with realism concerns the interface with audience perception, and the kind of assumptions that may be encouraged by the sense that we are witnessing an almost real situation. For Christian Metz, who distinguishes between whether an event is narrated or not, the problem for cinema in general arises from 'the fact that films have the *appeal* of presence and of proximity that strikes the masses and fills the movie theatres' (Metz 1974: 4). It can become more of an issue when a documentary consists of a narrated event rather than an event that is presented as it unfolds, live at the time, and with the outcome still unknown. A retrospective story will involve more intervention, or control by the filmmaker, such as reconstruction.

Realism has been attacked from many quarters, and the debate within feminist film has been an interesting one related directly to production techniques and practice amongst those who wanted to use film to bring about change. The 'essentialism' of women's realist documentary has been criticized – that is, the assumption that there was a specific power in the individual female body, and that low-budget, raw propagandist films, using hand-held cameras, fast grainy stock, and shock editing, were automatically effective as organizing tools. But since an image of a poor woman does not automatically lead to political awareness of the need to equalize the distribution of wealth, the 'documentary filmmakers were misguided in returning to the 18th century notion of art as capable of simply imitating life, as if through a transparent glass, and in believing that representation could affect behaviour directly' (Kaplan 1982–3: 55).

From 1962, work done by the American Newsreel Collective epitomized the drive to use realist techniques to publicize the plethora of radical events at the time, ranging from Vietnam protests to strikes, student sit-ins and occupations, and activities by the women's movement. But could these codes that were used explicitly for activist left politicization – exemplified by Newsreel's *The Woman's Film* (1971), dealing with the exploitation of working-class women by capitalist private enterprise geared up to the accumulation of individual wealth – actually change consciousness? The argument was that the styles of camera work, sound, *mise-en-scène* and editing connected with realism were no different from existing forms. As Eileen McGarry argued, to not take into account the 'manner in which the dominant ideology and cinematic traditions encode the pro-filmic event is to hide the fact that reality is selected and altered by the presence of the film workers, and the demands of the equipment' (McGarry 1975: 51).

Questioning such as this prompted a move away from didacticism and propagandist approaches to practices that focused more on forms of representation and cinematic techniques. In fact, the change in thinking represented a wider move in progressive film's theoretical base away from an exclusively Marxist analysis based on structuralism and an interest in the workings of social institutions, and towards the underlying signifying practices on and through which we base our awareness of reality and the social environment. The new thinking was influenced by theories of the unconscious developed by Freud and Lacan. Furthermore, semiologists denied that any conscious reality existed independently of discourse derived from the signifying practices prevailing within a culture.

Armed with a combination of semiology, psychoanalysis, Marxism and structuralism the internal critics of feminist realism such as Claire Johnston and Laura Mulvey took up the mantle with their own avant-garde films, mixing documentary and fiction. They focused on the cinematic process in order to involve the spectator, by using techniques that would rupture the fantasy of presenting 'reality' and separate the spectator from the text in their exploration of female subjectivity and the signifying practices of representation itself. Yet it may well be that the problems feminist documentary has faced are those attached to the effectiveness or otherwise of activist cinema more generally. Audiences can derive pleasure from recognition (of, for example, women similarly exploited) or, or as in later feminist films, pleasure from cognitive processes of learning, points which will be developed in Chapter 7.

Arguments about truth

As Muybridge demonstrated, the camera is incapable of simply delivering an unmediated reproduction of truth: the camera itself is by definition an instrument of visual mediation, and today there are a host of other techniques connected to mediation in production. Part of the problem with debates about fact and fiction, reality and truth, is that the contested discourse has evolved from a heritage of film theory, not specifically from documentary theory. Yet documentary's vision of depicting the truth is complex; it can tell *a* truth, but not *the entire* truth. This fact does not diminish its importance: most documentaries are still concerned with retaining a relationship of some sort with the 'real', and the 'truths' that 'matter in people's lives but which cannot be transparently represented' (Williams 1993: 13).

Historical events presented on film or video do not guarantee agreement over meaning. As Renov says: 'The nonfiction referent's "historical status" is arrived at through a complex set of relations among perceiver, material, signifier, signified, and referent rather than awarded a priori. This status is neither fixed nor absolute and can be remanded on the basis of subsequent knowledge' (Renov 1993: 193). There are no absolute truths or definitive answers, according to relativists such as Butchart who argue that the only permanent and enduring truth is that which resides in the visual perception of the documentary (Butchart 2006: 445). Similarly, Dovey adopts a sceptical view of truth within a television context: 'the production of documentary "truth" on TV is subject to specific political economies in which fact is a flexible commodity used to deliver audiences through complex narrative strategies' (Dovey 2000: 11). Add to this the economic pressures stemming from declining ratings and audience share, as well as the technological issue of digitalization's capability, and documentary truth seems to be in trouble.

Williams has argued that it is possible to select relative and contingent truths without throwing the baby out with the bathwater, that is, without abandoning the ideal of the real just because it is complex, and without consigning documentary to a category of fiction either (Williams 1993: 14). Using the example of Errol Morris' *The Thin Blue Line* (1988), Williams argues that Morris' use of fictional techniques does not represent an abandonment of documentary's truth claims: they may not create an image of truth, but they are used as a strategy to help the viewer discern the truth from the body of the film as a whole.

It has been said that the fundamental problem for a Morris film is 'how to extract a situation's truth without violating its mystery' (Gourevitch 1992: 46).

But how can we talk about documentary truth when elements of dramatic reconstruction are used, and when the director himself states: 'I've always thought of my portraits as my own version of the Museum of Natural History, these very odd dioramas where you're trying to create some foreign exotic environment and place it on display' (Gourevitch 1992: 44). His pioneering techniques in *The Thin Blue Line* have been hailed as revolutionary, and Morris himself rejects the idea of objectivity as 'anti-artistic'; but, as discussed in Chapter 3, truth and objectivity are not necessarily linked. As a result of *The Thin Blue Line*, a dramatized documentary, the conviction of Randall Adams, who was wrongly accused of murdering a Dallas policeman, was overturned. The filmmaker maintained that he wanted to make a movie about the fact that the truth is difficult to know; and in order to prove that Randall Adams, who faced death row, was innocent, he adopted highly self-conscious, stylized and experimental techniques that questioned reality.

By abandoning Cinema Verité realism in favour of very expressionistic re-enactment, slow motion and self-reflexivity, Morris got nearer to the truth. 'There is no reason why documentaries can't be as personal as fiction filmmaking and bear the imprint of those who made them. Truth isn't guaranteed by style or expression. It isn't guaranteed by anything' (Morris 1989: 17). It is worth noting that Morris could have used fiction techniques to demonstrate the truth, but he adhered to silent docu-drama re-enactments that show only what each witness *claims* happened. His stylization never maintains that this is what actually happened.

These days it is fashionable to say that documentary's previous claims to be revealing the truth of events were naïve. When Cinema Verité aspired to attain this, the movement effectively, in the words of Carroll, 'opened a can of worms and then got eaten by them' (Carroll 1983: 7). A description of the work of Albert Maysles exemplifies the approach as 'one in which ethics and aesthetics are interdependent, where beauty starts with honesty, where a cut or a change in camera angle can become not only a possible aesthetic error but also a "sin" against Truth' (Blue 1965: 22). Within a decade, documentary theorists were denouncing Cinema Verité as a 'transparent purveyor of ideology' (Hall 1991: 26).[13]

Another expectation of documentary's inherent veracity is provided by the increasing availability within the public domain of surveillance and amateur footage. Raw video footage can reveal crime situations with hidden cameras, for instance, and this has formed the basis of a proliferation of Reality TV formats. However, even amateur footage, unedited, is still open to interpretation, as George Holliday's tape of Rodney King being beaten by Los Angeles police indicated (see Chapter 3). Nevertheless, we must acknowledge what Nichols calls the 'authenticating trace' that connects the documentary film to its real referent (Waldman and Walker 1999: 11), for it constitutes the space where truth can be scrutinized.

What happens when that space is violated – something that digital manipulation makes easier? The implications for journalistic truth-telling when the use of modern technology is combined with a clear didactic and activist motivation become clear in three films made by the 9/11 denialist, Dylan Avery, entitled *Loose Change* (2005), *Loose Change 2nd Edition* (2006) and *Loose Change: The Final Cut* (2007). The arguments for veracity are made by the counter-documentary *Screw Loose Change* (2006). The latter acts as a documentary version of the debate on truth, journalistic standards and definitions of documentary that draws our attention to the implications of not adhering to documentary's 'mission impossible' of truth-telling.

Case Study: *Loose Change* (2005), *Loose Change 2nd Edition* (2006), *Loose Change: The Final Cut* (2007) and *Screw Loose Change* (2006)

Loose Change is a diatribe that accuses elements of the US government of orchestrating the destruction of the World Trade Centre and Pentagon on 11 September 2001. The first edition made in 2005 started as a fiction film project, and was 'transformed' in its second edition into a documentary, with Avery's voiceover accompanying free usage of film clips, photographs and news reports, and hip-hop and other urban music, all in support of his conspiracy theory. The filmmaker attracted both criticism and writs for using copyrighted material from other films. Understandably, the makers of these films objected to their work being aligned with Avery's views and filmmaking style (see the discussion of activism in Chapter 7).

Mutable truths, changed storylines and misplaced 'evidence' are the norm in Avery's trio of so-called documentary films. First, in making three versions, Avery compromises his claim to truthful documentary filmmaking. Blogger Mark Iradian criticizes Avery's need for second and third editions of the film – he suggests that perhaps filmmakers who resort to this strategy (see also Jones 2007) are not happy with their truths. 'It seems that 9/11-deniers have to revise the truth every now and then. I never heard of the truth requiring a second edition or a final cut. Must

be a fad for the new kids' (*Screw Loose Change*, 2006).

Second, Avery changes his storyline – the *2nd Edition* removes an accusation, present in the first film, that the aeroplanes were in fact drones (remotely controlled missiles) flown into the towers. In another scene comparison, the first film states that Flight 93 came down in a field in Pennsylvania, but in the second version Avery changes his story and asserts it was flown to and landed at Cleveland Hopkins Airport (more later). Likewise in *The Final Cut*, Avery is equally cavalier about his 'facts' as to whether Flight 77 actually crashed into the Pentagon, having said in the previous two films that a missile hit the building.

Third, sources are manipulated to fit Avery's theory. He uses 'evidence' of official flight records stating that the aircraft the drones replaced are still in active service, though he admits he doesn't know what happened to the passengers. In the second edition, Avery pursues his theory further (and refutes his own original findings) with constant revisions, a tactic which removes trust in him as a reporter of a true story. Journalist George Monbiot focuses on the people called upon to give evidence, and questions the filmmaker's 'complete absence of scientific advice'. He expands:

At one point, the presenter asks: 'So what brought down the twin towers? Let's ask the experts.' But they don't ask the experts. The film-makers take some old quotes, edit them to remove any contradictions, then denounce all subsequent retractions as further evidence of conspiracy. The only people they interview are a janitor, a group of firemen, and a flight instructor. They let the janitor speak at length, but cut the firemen off in mid-sentence.   (Monbiot 2007)

The Internet permits ordinary members of the public to comment constructively on films. Iradian was so irritated with Avery's *Loose Change* and *Loose Change 2nd Edition* that he made the film *Screw Loose Change* and published it on the Internet. Iradian highlights the problems of defining what *Loose Change* and its sequels represent in documentary filmmaking. He corrects Avery's entire film with a running subtitled commentary, criticizing it for sloppy sourcing and changing versions of the truth. For example, Iradian points out as wrong Avery's assertion (at 2 hours 3 minutes into the film) that Flight 93 landed at Cleveland, using an image of the Air Traffic Control log to prove it. In fact the controllers had become confused in the crisis and later announced that another aircraft had landed there, a Delta 1989 unrelated to the day's events. Iradian states that by the time the Delta touched down, according to Avery's own documents, Flight 93 had crashed into a field one hour earlier. The passenger lists for both aircraft are also at variance – the Delta held 60 passengers and Flight 93 circa 200. At no point has Avery checked or revised his information in the subsequent five years.

Avery also uses shots of other crashes as evidence to disprove expert findings in this particular case. Avery claims that footage of wreckage in a mountainous area of Greece, showing sheered fuselage, allows him to dispute that Flight 93 crashed at all. Indeed, he relies on a one-stop approach to trajectories in order to define how a crash develops and affects its environment. Iradian says that 'context and attribution are essential to understanding if the quote is relevant to the issue being discussed, something a "real documentary" would do' (*Screw Loose Change*, 2006).

The 'truths', plot twists and presented evidence are so enmeshed in conspiracy that they defy sense and categorization as a documentary. In fact Avery's films are agit-prop devices – they are the shop-front on his website for recruiting activists to a cause dedicated to overthrowing the Bush Administration. On every aspect of the film's discussion about the reasons for 9/11, Avery distorts the facts to fan the flames that promote an impression of a terrifying, tiny, controllable world.

The peddling of a perverted 'realism' against the political controllers exposes what Monbiot sums up as the film's greatest flaw:

the men who made it are still alive. If the US government is running an all-knowing, all-encompassing conspiracy, why did it not snuff them out long ago? There is only one possible explanation. They are in fact agents of the Bush regime, employed to distract people from its real abuses of power. This, if you are inclined to believe such stories, is surely a more plausible theory than the one proposed in *Loose Change*.   (Monbiot 2007)

Conclusion

In 2007 a YouGov survey, carried out for Britain's Edinburgh Television Festival, confirmed a number of previous polls, and also the research of Annette Hill (2005), on the subject of audience trust of documentary. More than half (59 per cent) of the 2216 people asked felt that documentaries are 'generally truthful but with some distortion at the editing stage' (Media Guardian 2007). This, of course, is an understatement of the issue of trust that, as Chapters 1, 7 and 8 discuss, is far more complicated because connected with expectations of truthfulness and perceptions of reality. Any suggestion that documentary provides an unmediated reflection of the real world should be challenged: images provide evidence of the real world as a subjective interpretation in the same way that a painting or piece of writing does, and audiences are close to realizing this, as the above survey reference to editing suggests. But maybe it is possible to retain an overall concept of documentary as aiming to portray truth if we view it as 'a set of strategies designed to choose from among a horizon of relative and contingent truths' (Williams 1993: 14).

2 Representation
Problems, Purpose and Perspective

Summary

Documentary is representative: it represents, and is representative of, certain cultural and social phenomena. This chapter analyses the wider context within which representational considerations operate, looking at the implications of different methods in more depth, and assessing continuity or changes in balance of emphasis. Representational strategies are important because documentary has a potential referential quality – we can become curious about what lies behind or beyond what we see on the screen. Do types of representation in documentary film reflect notions of connection with society, especially in personal, group and public terms? Would it be fair to argue that all representation is influenced by institutional and environmental factors and by thinking during the period in which the films are made? The documentary maker needs a fine-tuned political awareness of the implications and readings that are likely to emerge from various representational choices (the adoption or rejection of public, group and personal agency) and an appreciation of current social values and potential audience reactions. Thus the study of representation entails a contextual awareness in addition to the understanding of particular films as texts.

The documentary producer has to be aware of the potential readings that will emerge from the varying representational choices that are made during the production process, for each form of documentary carries its own burden of representation (Chapman 2007: 7–8, 58, 85–91, 110–11). There are problems inherent in the representation of history, for the past can never be adequately replicated: the filmmaker chooses a strategy from a palette of imperfect colours. Equally problematic, the representation of 'other' carries a political dimension that requires sensitivity. Does ethnographic film, for instance, use Euro-American conventions to document the practices of other cultures?

Even the representation of traumas such as war, rape and human rights violations is influenced by institutional and environmental factors, and by the kind of thinking prevalent at the time the films are made, although it is also the case that some of the best filmmakers, such as Rouch, had a vision that was clearly ahead of their time. There are continuities of style and approach, but representation in documentaries is influenced by broader ideological shifts. One such contextual influence has been a gradual move away from the representation of collective causes – even if these are presented through the stories of selected individuals – to a focus on personal agency that evokes an emotional response.

Introduction

Representation is not simply about capturing 'reality': a documentary seeks to persuade, which means that representational issues are central to its inherent ideology. 'Through the assertive stance taken towards its representata [*sic*], it [the non-fiction film] expresses and implies attitudes and statements about its subjects' (Plantinga 1997: 38). Although a documentary will claim that the affair it covers is actually happening, or has actually taken place, the film may also examine abstract ideas or concepts. To this extent, what appears on the screen is 'a complex transaction between a variety of contending interests' (Nolley 1997: 268). As such, there is never one ideal form of representation: it is never definitive, but always ongoing and historically contingent. In fact, this influence of the historical period is peculiar to each and every film. In this regard, Walter Benjamin proposes a theory of the 'aura' in a work of art, by which he means the traces of history that guarantee its authenticity and uniqueness; or, as Horkheimer put it: 'the greater a work, the more it is rooted in the concrete historical situation' (Horkheimer 1941: 291).

'Representation' can be construed in three different ways: as a photographic or aural likeness of something; as a way of standing for the views of organizations, groups or agencies; and as making a case or proposition for some aspect of the real world. A documentary can do all three, and there will be some overlap between them. A documentary might adopt a variety of representational strategies in relation to expressive sound, editing, photography and structures for the ordering of information, including narrative and rhetorical approaches. On the content side, factual films offer representations that communicate a subject matter by three means:

- *Testimony*, which offers a first-person perspective on experiences.
- *Implication*, where the viewer becomes involved in the process of a lived experience through specific social actors, in a way similar to that of a Hollywood fiction.
- *Exposition*, where a third-person narration explains the situation, behaviour or experiences of other third persons. This will tend to create empathy rather than direct identification on the part of the viewer, although audiences may well ask themselves how they would have felt or acted in such a situation.

The evolution of film as a medium gave us the ability first to judge the representational framework in purely visual terms, then in terms of an accompanying commentary, and finally in relation to synchronous dialogue. By the 1930s, the exploitation of this last technique allowed for a convergence of means, rhetoric and social strategy that ultimately influenced the forms of representation to such an extent that it established the myth of the 'documentary tradition'. This has been challenged in subsequent debates which have underlined the requirement to first appreciate the political and economic climate within which a film is made.

Viewed historically, the 'documentary movement' can be seen as a response to a moment of social and economic crisis during the 1920s and 1930s in Western Europe and the United States. This was also a crisis of representation, a struggle to understand social identity and the social experience. Thus John Tagg – referring to Roosevelt's reformist 'New Deal' programme in America and to the more oppositional Griersonian social documentary movement in Britain – claims that the 'documentary tradition' never existed. Instead, documentary's roots were embedded in specific institutional sites at a time when the genre was used to accommodate specific political needs:

> It was entirely bound up with a particular social strategy: a liberal, corporatist plan to negotiate economic, political and cultural crisis through a limited programme of structural reforms, relief measures, and a cultural intervention aimed at restructuring the order of discourse, appropriating dissent, and re-securing the threatened bonds of social consent. (Tagg 1988: 8)

Thus Tagg sees documentary as an extension of the history of centralizing, corporatist reform from the mid-nineteenth century onwards. During this pioneering period, photography was appropriated for social regulation within the fields of surveillance, training, record keeping, discipline and reform.

> If there is continuity, then, it is that of developing systems of production, administration and power, not of a 'documentary tradition' resting on the supposed inherent qualities of the photographic medium, reflecting a progressive engagement with reality, or responding to popular demand. (Tagg 1988: 10)

More recently, the so-called 'documentary tradition' appears to have been further challenged worldwide by an eclectic diversity of representational strategies –all of them a function of the political and economic context in which they are produced. As Theodor Adorno said:

> The task of criticism must be not so much to search for the particular interest-groups to which cultural phenomena are to be assigned, but rather to decipher the general social tendencies which are expressed in these phenomena and through which the most powerful interests realise themselves. Cultural criticism must become social physiognomy. (Adorno 1967: 30)

Representing history

The ability of film to overcome spatial and temporal limitations is due to the power of representative symbolism within the medium, but this is more complex for documentary than for fiction. The good news is that the filmic form, whether fictional or non-fictional, can help us to explore and resolve social contradictions through narrative strategies that allow the audience to experience social or political tensions – tensions which in real society might take years to resolve or to work through.

There are, however, numerous problems in depicting the past. On the visual side, there is a narrative to construct, perhaps with paintings, locations, artefacts, or using visual symbolism and actors. It is the way such elements are brought together that presents a challenge for the study of representation. Documentary representations of the past often use visual iconography and familiar signs, such as bullet holes in walls or sites of mass destruction. But how can an empty battlefield express the horror of the past for great numbers of people? Narrative forms will help to integrate the elements but, as with the empty battlefield, there is still the challenge of how to create an awareness of *magnitude*. Documentary is almost always dealing with the past as a reconstruction or re-enactment of another time or place in history. Even with an observational film following a person's activities at a given moment, that moment becomes historical and pre-recorded by the time it is presented to an audience. Although people may act as the agents of history in a documentary, there is an inherent problem with representation: we can never reconstruct the full extent of people's contribution, or the numbers involved, hence the complications inherent in representing the reality of the past. According to Nichols, history is what exceeds documentary rhetoric: 'always referred to but never captured . . . History awaits us outside the text, but aspects of its magnitude may be discovered within.' Representation can never do full justice to what he calls 'a body too few' (Nichols 1991: 142, 236, 230–3).

Documentary's dependence on individual personalization in the form of narrative profiles, testimonials and witnesses can have the effect of creating exemplary figures that carry a burden of representation as icons. In the case of celebrities, there is a danger that they will become myths: once made in to a symbol, a stereotype is created. Photographic clichés then obstruct the real history – Che Guevara and Marilyn Monroe spring to mind. More generally, the most significant representational issue for documentary involves what to do with actual people, both living and dead. In the case of the latter, the filmmaker is faced with a number of representations of a person, but not the person her or himself. How can that representation ever measure up to the actual person when he or she was alive? Even when a historical personality is brought to life by an actor, she or he is a mediator, and the very appearance of a performer illustrates the gap between the life that is being represented and the text, for the actor poses as an intermediary. The limitations are similar to those imposed by language on our ability to express what we really think or feel – there is always a difference between a representation and whatever is being represented.

A good example of these representational dilemmas emerges from the criticisms of *The Life and Times of Rosie the Riveter* (1980). Director Connie Field interviewed over 700 women before selecting the ones to feature as profiles of women at work during the Second World War, yet even in this case, use of testimony could only ever present a partial truth (Chapman 2007: 62). Field's choice of Jewish, black and Asian-American women has been criticized as not being typical: most of the women recruited tended to be white ethnics from northern cities or else southern white Protestants.

The documentary maker tackles the challenge of representing historical movements involving many people in a different way to a fiction film that attributes subjectivity to a fictional character. Documentary will produce its own version of fiction, which can vary in effectiveness and will be open to criticism in terms of choices made and methods used. But documentary presents an additional and unique layer of complication: we are confronted with an encounter between real people and a filmmaker that presents two levels for interpretation: first the world of social actors that we encounter in everyday life; second, the narrative structure that the documentary maker builds around the depiction of that world.

The historical documentary film places a tension on the shoulders of its participants or witnesses, who do not appear as social actors from within the field of historical engagement, but from somewhere outside of it, recollecting or commenting on it. The fact is that the person featured has acted as an agent of history, rather than being merely part of a filmmaker's narrative. Archive footage, of course, can help to locate the people featured in a past event, but the contributors are called upon to make real the contradictions and complexities of an historical moment, and in their on-screen appearance, they appear to do so for the first time. A poignant example is provided in Claude Lanzmann's *Shoah* (1985). Amongst the many recollections of the Holocaust presented in this film, there is one from a former diplomatic courier. He breaks down in front of the camera when asked to explain his experience of entering the Warsaw ghetto. This painful contribution provides a specificity located in the moment of filming, rather than in the past. In this nine-hour documentary, Lanzmann makes an actual and metaphorical journey to meet concentration camp survivors. There is no archive film; the marathon work consists entirely of specially shot footage about the Holocaust.

The unpredictable results that emerge from Lanzmann's encounters with collaborators, former SS members and other witnesses have provoked a variety of opinions about the filmmaker's emotional and passionate on-screen prompting, questioning and cajoling of testimonies concerning the extermination process. Michael Renov, for instance, argues that *Shoah* is a media-specific work of mourning. 'As film, it shows as much as it tells. The words of the witnesses reveal only a portion of a complex and subterranean drama. Nonverbal signs abound – the casting down of a glance; the shifting of body weight; the uncanniness of one survivor's mask – like facial expression, part smile, part grimace' (Renov 2004: 128). Yet these are revealed by the camera, and as Tagg says: 'Like the state, the camera is never neutral. The representations it produces are highly coded, and the power it wields is never its own' (Tagg 1988: 63–4).

Trains are central to the symbolism in the film, and the reality of the endless, multiple journeys; this draws our attention to the contradictions between the potential of representation and its limitations. Lanzmann aimed to re-live the experiences by re-tracing the victims' steps with a restless, constantly moving camera to support the testimonials. This approach can be seen as an antidote to previous more conventional Holocaust documentaries that depended on archive footage as a way of representing the Nazi atrocities. Lanzmann's personal quest to delve into the facts and uncover the evidence comprised 350 hours of film shot over eleven years in fourteen different countries with four years of editing, yet there is no closure or sense of completion, for the film stops short of representing the moment of final extermination.

Simone de Beauvoir compared the viewing experience to a musical composition: 'with it moments of intense horror, peaceful landscapes, laments and resting places, what *Shoah*'s subtle construction calls to mind is a musical composition. And the whole work is punctuated by the almost intolerable din of trains rushing towards the camps' (de Beauvoir 1985: iv). Hence, the filmic representation connects style with subject as the camera becomes a tool of re-enactment, exemplified by the occasion when it is mounted on a horse and cart to evoke a walking pace. Jump cuts, rapid zooms and pans are avoided, in favour of painfully long takes reminiscent of the heavy, purposeful discomfort of *Night and Fog* (1955).

Thirty years on, Lanzmann believed that audiences had become immunized to the black and white Holocaust archive footage (in contrast to Spielberg's decision to make *Schindler's List* in black and white because that is how we remember the Holocaust [Rabinowitz 1994: 104]). Whereas *Night and Fog* juxtaposes present colour shots with past shots in black and white, in *Shoah*, witnesses are forced to re-live their excruciatingly painful experiences in the present. In *Night and Fog* the evocative, poetic, yet expositional narration speaks on behalf of the dead. In contrast, *Shoah* consists entirely of interviews with living survivors, although Lanzmann relentlessly compels his witnesses to speak on behalf of the dead, insisting that the visuals are not literally representational. A former concentration camp barber talks of having to cut the hair of naked women and children inside the gas chamber, but the camera shows him cutting a man's hair during filming, since to have staged the scene with a woman would have been 'obscene', unacceptably literal, according to the filmmaker (Lanzmann 1985: 97).

Shoah is not the only example of a deliberate decision to withhold certain literal forms of representation, such as archive film. A more oblique symbolism is also taken to an extreme in the film *Human Remains* (1998). In this black and white documentary about Hitler, Mussolini, Stalin, Mao and Franco, a technique of going to black is used instead of visuals of suffering. By leaving out any visual representation of evil, the film actually draws attention to the nature and object of visual meaning. The predictable is not included.

The period during which a film is made and its context play a role in determining choices as to what to include or not include. When earlier Holocaust films were made, we needed to be reminded of the archival images – since then, they have become clichés. Although they represent reality, our compassion-fatigue calls for a new method of representation, but this is only one possible choice where representation is concerned. There are others. Contemporary art house director Karl Nussbaum, for instance, combines Holocaust references with fantasy by using a technique of personalized visual collage (Chapman 2007: 11, 32, 139). Although Lanzmann resorted to 'the imaginative recuperation of memory through the spoken word' (Rabinowitz 1994: 15), historical representation can consist of 'showing not telling' by foregrounding aesthetics to give an impressionistic feel. The work of experimental landscape filmmaker William Raban blends structural film with documentary, usually with very little voiceover commentary or synchronized dialogue. In *Thames Film* (1986), Raban documents a landscape that is soon to disappear with the large-scale Docklands redevelopment, itself a clearly visual theme. He explores the formal qualities of image and sound, based on an aesthetics which uses poetic codes. There is rhythm, rhyme, metre, punctuation and resonance, but this does not mean that the political message is necessarily sacrificed; what emerges is 'a form of visual polemics minus the heavy didactic symbolism' (Green n.d.; see also Chapman 2007: 8, 59, 91).

Historical documentary brings together character, icon and social agent in a way that can be problematic. With all of the above examples, a tension emerges between representation and historical referent. This is further exacerbated if the filmmaker opts for a form of reflexivity with a presenter or mediator as an on-screen presence. Attention is then drawn to the nature of discourse, which can detract from the sense of realism, or even foreclose it altogether, as in Trinh Minh-ha's *Surname Viet Given Name Nam* (1989).

Ethnography and pioneering democratization of representation ▪

Equally problematic is the way in which ethnographic film has created a memory by recording the lives and cultural practices of 'disappearing' communities worldwide. Usually, the camera allows the audience to be present because the ethnographer is present, which has prompted critical analysis of the concept of representation by others. The influence of mainstream representations means that ethnographic film tends to document the practices of other cultures within a medium that relies on Euro-American conventions. This kind of approach was first identified in the now famous quotation from Karl Marx's *The Eighteenth Brumaire of Louis Bonaparte*: 'they cannot represent themselves; they must be represented'. The question arises as to whether a filmmaker from one culture can ever represent another culture in a way that avoids stereotyping, and without the film becoming a form of 'visual imperialism'.

Edward Said's *Orientalism* (1978) was a major formative influence on this debate, and within documentary studies the issue is well illustrated by the classic *Nanook of the North*, a film that has been described as relying on a 'taxidermic' mode of representation. Ethnography is here set against 'a picturesque past innocent of, rather than in fierce, complex struggle with, the spread of Western capitalist society'. As with all forms of representation, there are political connotations:

> the premise of the inevitable death of the Native, moreover, allows the physical and cultural destruction wrought by the West to appear ineluctable, and such films, albeit with pathos, implicitly provide ideological justification for the very colonial and economic conquests that brought filmmakers like Flaherty to the Arctic. (Rony 1996: 196)

In Winston's scathing assessment: 'the film systematically misled us about the reality of Inuit life in the early 1920s, recast Inuit family structures in inappropriate Western mode, proposed a Western exploitative relationship with the land and did nothing to ease the burden of Allakariallak's short life' (Winston 2000: 154; 2008). Yet these days *Nanook of the North* is also viewed as a useful historical document for the Inukjuak community among whom it was filmed, because of the valuable shots of their land and ancestors (even if they laugh at the obvious staging of the seal hunt).

The idea of ethnographic film as a scientific 'tool' for anthropologists has involved a variety of different documentary styles designed to tackle this central issue of visual imperialism, exemplified by the observational work of John Marshall, Timothy Asch and Robert Gardner. Films such as the latter's *Rivers of Sand* (1974) rejected the conventions of didactic narrative film by not explaining the images or providing much by way of information or contextualization for the audience, leaving the meaning to emerge from the images rather than from a textual rhetoric. This restrained style involved long takes, slow pacing, seamless editing and often synchronized sound.

The films of Jean Rouch are also presented with a sensibility that causes the audience to question assumptions about inherent visual imperialism. *Les*

Maitres fous (1955) confronted the colonial framework of Africa's Gold Coast, where it was filmed – the 'masters of madness' of the title referring to both British colonialists and to Hauka cult members whose trance ceremonies are contrasted to their everyday lives as labourers within the system. Whilst recognizing their 'explosive potential', Rouch represents these possession ceremonies as harmless and therapeutic for the participants because these activities provide them with a way of dealing with 'the psychoses that accompany the colonial situation' (Cooper 2006: 34). This kind of sensibility is difficult to achieve, given the inherent imbalance of power between filmmaker and participants. Devereaux notes that few films achieve it, Basil Wright's *Song of Ceylon* (1934) being a notable exception, for it 'reflects an ecstatic experience, an epiphany. It was, Wright said, "the only film I've made that I really loved, and it was in fact a religious experience"' (Devereaux and Hillman 1995: 240).

Although the documentarist can never totally replicate another person's experiences, both *Song of Ceylon* and *Les Maitres fous* come across as a celebration of the filmmaker's sensibilities in encountering another society. A Western view shapes non-Western images in most anthropological and travel films, and it is impossible to avoid the presence of the narrator appearing as a controlling influence in the production. For ethnographers who wish to avoid this, such as Rouch, the effect of domination is minimized by internalizing aspects of the lives of others and then reproducing them in the first person through the camera. With *Les Maitres fous* this entails 'a double-edged portrayal of master madman and mad masters in which neither blacks nor whites occupy a comfortable position of mastery, least of all one over another' (Cooper 2006: 39). One solution to the potential for representational imbalance has been to introduce a level of reflexivity. When Rouch and Morin put themselves on screen in *Chronicle of a Summer* (1960), the relationship with the 'tribe' in Paris was manifested differently (see Chapter 6).

Ethnography and the 'other'

When the culture that emerges from the pro-filmic content is different to the filmmaker's culture, then a politics of difference – ethnic, class, gender – emerges from the production process in a way that can either change or confirm a given personal consciousness. The expression of this within the documentary forms part of the politics of representation. This has a number of different manifestations.

Traditional representations of the 'other' in cinema have usually meant presenting the identities of other cultures in an oppositional role to the mainstream. As Nichols says:

> The 'Other' (woman, native, minority) rarely functions as participant in and creator of a system of meanings, including a narrative structure of their own devising. Hierarchy and control still fall on the side of the dominant culture that has fabricated the image of the 'Other' in the first place. Monsters, aliens, Indians, and killers . . .
> (Nichols 1991: 204)

Narrative structure can act as a constraint, for it has its own method, which is in fact an inhibiting factor: often the need for closure in the storyline will tend to bring us back to the dominant role of the Western, white, middle-class male, relegating the minority 'other' to a subordinate role. The conventions of narrative seem to create a need to explain changes between the beginning and the end of a film, terminating with a form of closure that in itself has representational implications.

Ethnography has enabled the filmmaker to move beyond these inhibitions in order to explore other cultures from the inside. But even here, a society's dominant discourses and accepted practices can still structure any enquiry. Such limitations are almost inevitable. In the late 1960s two anthropologists, Sol Worth and John Adair, carried out an experiment in ethnographic documentary making which involved giving some Navajo youths film cameras, in order to see whether, freed from the constraints of Hollywood conventions, what they filmed could provide any insights into their way of seeing the world. However, the anthropologists brought with them their own assumptions about technique, which had cultural implications; at one point Worth became so frustrated at the way Maryjane Tsosie was filming her grandfather sand-painting that he grabbed the camera away from her. His anger was prompted by the fact that she would not go in for a close-up. She exercised restraint by keeping her distance. This could have been due to a discomfort emanating from her own background: as a child she had been sent to boarding school as part of a US government measure to assimilate North American natives into white society, in order to forget their language. It is also likely her reluctance represented a form of reverence for an elder, prompting her not to encroach on his space.

Ethnography's treatment of the 'other' does not necessarily mean studies of geographically distant tribes, as *Chronicle of a Summer* demonstrated in the Parisian setting. Similarly, *An American Family* brought upper-middle-class Santa Barbara to the screen as a distinct social grouping. More recently, theorization of how to listen to the 'other', the representation of 'other' stories, and the development of a reciprocal text as a way of correcting the imbalance between filmmaker and subject, have all been given a higher profile by the 'new ethnography'.[14] A recent trend at festivals and in student screenings is for domestic ethnography with an authorial subjectivity, often about eccentric or aging family members, with their lives depicted as a means of offering insight into the filmmaker themselves. A prime example amongst many is artist Su Friedrich's *Sink or Swim* (1990), a family history which goes beyond its domestic parameters to consider universal aspects of family attachment and tension (Renov 2004: 219–22). This is also the case with Gwen Haworth's *She's a Boy I Knew* (2007), a film in which Haworth uses her personal crisis and her family's reaction to it to raise questions relating to the difficulties involved in conforming to society's expectations.

Case study: *She's a Boy I Knew* (2007)

Narrated by Haworth, the film documents the filmmaker's journey of gender reassignment, from male to female, through the voices of her family and friends. A deeply personal account of self-empowerment through self-representation, Haworth's film charts the challenges she faced in being accepted as a transsexual by society and at home. In using her friends and family to frame responses to her sexual and social realignment, Haworth extends the form of personal diary into an enquiry about wider social questions on sexual identification.

The change from married male into a female is traumatic for her family, to whom she was lost as a treasured only son. The filmmaker uses cartoons to document a further complication: that she is lesbian. Her family and friends explain their confusion and difficulty, but eventually accept the status quo. Haworth tries to represent concepts that are difficult to film by resorting to cartoons as a rather simplistic device, almost a comic relief. One animated section of the film shows Haworth's transformation from male to female form: out of which there then bursts a stereotypical image of a butch lesbian, accompanied with popping noises. Haworth's cartoon metamorphosis highlights issues that are not easily explained in conventional film, conversation or voiceover – so the combination of animation and voiceover fills the gaps in a memorable sequence.

In making her private psychological and actual transformation (then confounding expectations) through filming, Haworth relies on the form's mildly politicizing effect to gain our sympathy towards her outsider status. Documentary representation enables her to achieve recognition and hence social satisfaction. The film includes several scenes in which Haworth attempts to integrate her sexuality into the mainstream. The most interesting of these is when she describes her battle with her (female) doctor, who has consistently refused to refer Haworth for transgender surgery. The filmmaker provides evidence of letters and telephone calls to the chosen hospital whose surgical team never received any referral. Eventually, Haworth realizes that her doctor does not approve, and relates her despondency and consequent decision to find someone who will help her.

In another scene towards the end Haworth films herself bruised post-surgery and expresses her hope that the film will highlight the difficulties many transgender people face being accepted in society. A short clip focuses on her commune-dwelling, independent and openly gay younger sister, the acceptance of whose sexual identity by her family and community Haworth quietly celebrates, in contrast to the battles the film documents.

Institutions, minorities and identity politics

The self-reflexive questioning of the process of production and representation within ethnographic film has been paralleled by criticisms of the Euro-American media representation of marginalized peoples, who have also been attempting to gain improved access to mainstream TV and film production.

Pioneer representations have influenced black documentary making. In the United States these include *Black Journal*, a black television news magazine series from 1968 to 1970, and *Eyes on the Prize* (1987), Henry Hampton's award winning series about American Civil Rights in the 1950s and 1960s. In the case of the use of documentary to portray the lives of individuals from African-American communities, film and video has inherited a cultural tradition that incorporates spirituals, folktales and slave narratives, characterized by the way it 'fills in for the absence of conventional historical records by creating alternative accounts of black life' (Thompson 2003: 492).

In his research into cultural difference as represented in British film, Stuart Hall has discerned two broad stages in the representation of black people: the earlier stage was influenced by the realism of the first black filmmakers of the 1970s, who used the documentary tradition to 'tell it how it really is', and to 'correct' black stereotypes that were prevalent in the mainstream media (Mercer 1994), in a reversal of oppositional differences (Hall 1988: 444). The second movement, exemplified by documentaries such as *Handsworth Songs* (1987), marked a shift to 'new ethnicities' with an emphasis on internal differences within the category 'black'. This has the effect of deconstructing 'the logic of racism by exposing its basis in representation and therefore the position from which it speaks' (Procter 2004: 127–8). *Handsworth Songs*, for instance, uses documentary footage from the (largely white) mainstream media in a fragmented cut-and-paste mode of representation as a form of quotation that highlights differences in how notions of 'black' are constructed. The effect is 'a recognition of the relationship between representation and power while seeking to contrast those powers by revealing the fictions on which they are based' (Procter 2004: 127).

Hall works with and through a series of often irreconcilable critical positions rather than progressing from one to the next. The effect is to reveal that, as a consequence of the emergence of heterogeneous societies, representation of the multicultural remains an unresolved, contradictory question (Procter 2004: 135). Hall argues that contemporary society is characterized by difference and that the multicultural is an 'inevitable process of cultural translation' (Hall 2000: 6). Although Hall's ideas emerge from his study of the representation of British blacks, his theorizations can be applied to the use of documentary as an expression of cultural difference elsewhere.

Documentary is regularly used by Aboriginal Australian TV, North American tribes and Inuits, who all see methods of self-representation as linked to national cultural politics and their relationship to state bureaucracies (Devereaux and Hillman 1995: 4). Not only are representational issues central to the reactions of marginalized cultures towards mainstream media, but this also acts as a motivating force for generating indigenous documentary production. When indigenous or marginalized communities are dissatisfied with the way they are represented in the mainstream, the obvious alternative is to present via documentary new and better role models than those usually offered. Minorities have often adopted a pragmatic approach, epitomized by a representative of the Inuit Broadcasting Corporation: 'the history of the Inuit people is a history of adaptation; to climatic change, to cultural threat, to technological innovation. Television had clearly arrived to stay; a way had to be found to turn this threat to our culture into a tool for its preservation' (Devereaux and Hillman 1995: 266).

Anthropologist Faye Ginsberg poses the dilemma as follows: if Third World indigenous groups take up First World technology, the process can change their cultures beyond recognition (Devereaux and Hillman 1995: 259–60). Some argue that this dilemma represents a no-win contract with the devil, and point to the predictions of the Frankfurt School, who were amongst the first theorists to critique mass culture for not being genuinely radical. In particular, Herbert Marcuse, in his influential 1964 analysis *One Dimensional Man*, argued that technology has fuelled a synthesis of business, state, the media and other cultural institutions under the absorbing hegemony of corporate capital, and that this has led to a trend towards one dimensional thought and politics that threatens the preservation of cultural diversity.

Certainly the way that the media and political establishment supported 'Reaganism' in the 1980s seems to illustrate Marcuse's argument, although he and other Frankfurt School writers were also optimistic about the liberating potential (including of technology) hidden in the oppressive social system. Marcuse ends *One Dimensional Man* with a quote from Walter Benjamin: 'It is only for the sake of those without hope that hope is given to us' (Marcuse 1991: 257). Hence others believe more optimistically that Faustian bargains between Third World minorities and First World technology may by used in ways that increase indigenous community influence and self-expression, foregrounding alternative forms of representation.

Escaping the clichés of popular culture is not easy: 'Instead of learning about the meaning of historical symbols, stories, images, and myths through the traditional channels of tribal communication, North American youths imitate movie portrayals of Indians; life imitates art' (Leuthold 1997: 728). Within the wider context of representational practices, Hollywood conventions and production values have an inevitable influence on culturally specific film and video, enforced by the need to compete for an audience, and by the demands of advertising, packaging and distribution (Devereaux and Hillman 1995: 4).

Similarly, it has been argued that television formats such as docu-drama have portrayed history in a way that can actually have the effect of erasing memory, hence challenging the political culture of minorities to such an extent that they are falsified for the sake of entertainment. In this situation, non-fiction film without dramatization, made by and for marginalized peoples, can present historical truths whilst also representing a more accurate form of contemporary life. Yet even here there are compromises and dilemmas over forms of representation, and not always visual ones. North American Indian languages, for instance, are under threat and need to be preserved as a form of historical authenticity and cultural identity: 'However, the preservation of native languages may conflict with the desire of native directors to reach young Indian and non-tribal audience members who do not speak the language' (Leuthold 1997: 734). On the one hand, historical documentaries remain an attractive form of communication to many indigenous producers as a vehicle for portraying native realities through local history, in contrast to what they see as the distortions and stereotyping of the Hollywood productions. On the other hand, they recognize that the global nature of electronic media can undermine indigenous experiences and histories. It is no surprise, therefore, that part of the politics of representation involves encouraging institutions such as mainstream television to change, and to increase their representation of minority communities.

Much of the support for exploration of multiculturalism and cultural diversity has been provided by public service broadcasters, whose survival and funding is under constant threat in many parts of the world (Chapman 2005: 252–7). Furthermore, social mandates for minorities, as pioneered by public broadcasting, are essential for documentary's survival in attractive schedule slots in the face of competition from other entertainment programming. In these television environments, documentary producers have had to balance the need to cater for mass audiences with their social mandate at a time when the broadcaster response to this inevitable compromise has been to conjure up formats that bear out a more general trend to 'mainstream the margins'. This trend has had implications for the representation of minority communities, who are not represented for and by themselves, but often appear as 'exotic others' served up for a mainstream audience.

A study of a New Zealand PBS series entitled *Immigrant Nation* (1999) concluded that a tension had emerged 'between communities being presented as having assimilated and made a positive (and acceptable) contribution to New Zealand society, while also maintaining their "difference" and hence "exotic-ness" for the mainstream New Zealand audience' (Roscoe 2000: 257). This often came from community groups themselves, who spent time discussing how well they had assimilated to New Zealand society whilst simultaneously highlighting the ways in which they were different, which emphasized a contribution based on their uniqueness. The broadcaster wanted to demonstrate assimilation, reinforcing a unitary nationhood in the country, whereas the communities themselves desired greater representation based on their diversity. As broadcasters and documentary makers are increasingly motivated by market competition to find new ways in which to represent the social world, such compromises will continue.

There are other caveats, for instance that the insider/outsider issue will always be present to some degree. The existence of an insider native director does not necessarily 'authenticate' the images used, although it may provide for a higher level of social understanding. Conversely, the communities themselves may be divided over how certain aspects of a documentary should be represented, and an outsider director may have a different sort of relationship with the pro-filmic subjects. Such tensions will ultimately be reflected in forms of representation. Research on ethnic minority producers at the BBC, for instance, has revealed that they feel a 'burden of representation' because they need to challenge stereotypical negative representations and to present their communities in a positive light. Their professional interactions and their programme making experiences were coloured by the perceived need to speak on behalf of their community (Cottle 1997). The burden on black media workers is thus twofold – to depict their community positively but also to use representation as a form of delegation (speaking for the rest of the community). According to Hall, there is a certain tension between these two facets (Hall 1988: 441), and this will be a consideration for any form of representation that seeks to challenge society's hegemonic values.

Representing collective struggle

Many of the most famous documentaries in the canon are motivated by profound convictions shared by both the filmmaker and the subjects filmed. This was particularly the case during the 1970s when Emile de Antonio, along with Third World directors, pioneered political and activist documentaries. The aim of committed documentaries is usually to empower the hitherto disempowered by making visible the hitherto invisible, or by using the medium to expose or declare oneself by 'coming out'. During the Thatcher/Reagan period of neo-liberal conservatism in the 1980s, many documentary films went against the current by giving a voice to minorities. Cultural representations continued to have political agency, even in the face of severe de-funding. Films with a strong impact such as *Roger and Me* (1989) and *The Thin Blue Line* (1988) challenged the prevailing ethos (Chapman 2007: 21, 80).

When advocacy replaces objectivity in the rhetoric of political documentary (see Chapter 3) it is common for representation to foreground sexual, class, racial and gender differences. This means that the audience is positioned at a point within history and located in a way that essentially remakes the relationship of truth to ideology (Rabinowitz 1994: 7). This positioning becomes a function of political context. As Kaplan says of feminist filmmakers in Britain such as Mulvey, Johnston, Cook and Wollen, who critiqued realism in the mid-1970s: 'The directors are concerned with demystifying representation so as to make women aware that texts are producers of ideology, and that we live in a world of constructions rather than of solid essences' (Kaplan 1982–3: 58).

It is interesting to note how representational strategies for depicting striking workers can change according to the political climate. For instance, highlighting a strong individual protagonist in their struggle within the union and against management will serve to reduce the collective significance of the actual political organizations in conducting campaigns on behalf of an entire body of workers (Rabinowitz 1994: 27). In fact, the way a documentary makes representational claims about larger collective historical movements is always likely to be open to challenge. In 1976 Barbara Kopple presented a radical, sympathetic image of a dramatic union struggle in her Academy Award winning film, *Harlan County USA*. She followed this up with a second film in 1990, which also won an Academy Award for its examination of contemporary unionism. Over the years, forms of representation had changed, but so had the times. By the late 1980s class politics had been ruptured by a combination of the Reaganite assault on unions, recessions and corporate mergers in an age of deindustrialization and structural adjustments to the economy.

In the 1990 film, *American Dream*, the image portrayed of the strikers (who had received a 23 per cent wage cut) was complex and contradictory in its questioning of their tactics, with the result that the film was criticized by many local union activists for a failure to convey the culture that grew up during the period of the conflict. Footage supporting the striker's criticism was cut out, destined to lie as unused footage in the University of Wisconsin's archives. When compared to Kopple's earlier film, the second documentary, involving a large cast whose loyalties and identities are less clear cut, seems to imply a more balanced treatment. Yet Kopple was accused of a sell-out in her representation of the strike breakers, or 'scabs', by giving them a platform and too much airtime. These men, who invited audience sympathy by shedding tears on screen over the pain of crossing the picket line, worked with the UFCW leadership to weaken the strike and replace the existing union with their own 'trusteeship' union. But they are allowed to explain their decision to strike-break more fully than those strikers who, through solidarity, remain on the picket line.

By allowing sympathy for the tears of the scabs, the filmmaker seems to have changed allegiances: '*American Dream*, unlike *Harlan County*, slips the veil of sentimentality over the wrong faces' (Rabinowitz 1999: 60), but we are left wondering whether Reaganomics has influenced this challenge to the virility of the traditional working-class image: 'Kopple undercuts the rhetoric of the labor documentary by thoroughly inscribing the sentimental, using men's tears against their modern origins to tell a post modern tale still unfolding around us' (Rabinowitz 1999: 60).

Representing trauma, women, children and human rights

Issues of representation have become central to sexual politics. The camera's gaze traditionally dictates that women should be looked at as objects of desire. Female representation is a spectacle, whereas male characters become objects of identification because of their active roles. Documentary, with its heritage of association with social movements, has long been championed as an alternative representational practice for women, although at first discussions about the representation of women in film were confined initially to other genres – perhaps because there issues of representation could be more neatly defined. But during the late 1960s and the 1970s, feminist anthropologists were searching for new methods and new practices to tackle the sex–gender system. Laura Mulvey's seminal 1975 essay, 'Visual Pleasure and Narrative Cinema', expanded and brought into focus a theoretical approach to the visual image arguing that within the Hollywood genre, men look, while women are there to be looked at.

The attentions of feminist theorists were centred on 'readings' of films rather than on the political economy of the film industries: a study of the latter would have highlighted the contributions of women to film production and culture through their increasingly significant employment in jobs such as camera and sound operation, editing, directing and producing, marketing and fundraising, festival organization, writing and lecturing. In fact, a documentary history from this period notes that the 'arrival of scores of women filmmakers' was the 'single most conspicuous development in the seventies' (Jacobs 1979: 516). Frequently, feminism relied on cultural performance to explore politics. In 1968, for instance, the New York Newsreel Collective filmed the Miss America Pageant, where members of the women's liberation movement staged a counter-event – the first, it is claimed, at which bras were burned. The spectacle further included a rubbish bin for disposal of high heels, girdles and other garments of constraint.

Regrettably, many of the 1970s 'feminist realist' documentaries have been lost, due in part to piecemeal distribution and lack of interest from academics (Waldman and Walker 1999: 11). Thankfully, however, there are also some continuities between the pioneering feminist films of the 1970s and the present, exemplified in the US by the work of Margaret Lazarus and Cambridge Documentary Films, for instance. Research into media images and the cultural conditioning of women started during this period with *Killing Us Softly* (1979), and was updated in 1987 with new work on the social construction of femininity in advertising with *Still Killing Us Softly*. In 2000, the critique of the media was broadened to reflect the changing nature of consumer reaction to the power of the image, especially amongst young girls, in *Beyond Killing Us Softly: The Strength to Resist*.

The role of ideology in the representation of women, both as motivator for the films and as subject matter for this series of documentaries, is clearly articulated by Lazarus, who hopes that the films will 'generate new forms of activism that will both hold the media accountable and encourage the production of alternative images that ultimately render the mass produced images of women outdated, reactionary and irrelevant to women's lives' (Lazarus 2001: 249).

Only more recently has the inevitable overlap between the representation of women and other subject areas been addressed from a feminist standpoint. *Mother Ireland* (1998), despite bans and censorship, was still screened at an international level[15] – perhaps because it addressed universal issues about forms of representation, gender and nationality, demonstrating some of the very ambiguities on which documentary thrives. The film deals with the myth of 'Mother Ireland', as illustrated by historical and contemporary material about the 'mother country' and the role of women in this depiction. Yet it also includes a critique of this idea and its means of representation, which leads us to question whether 'Mother Ireland' is a representational construct that allows Ireland to continue 'to be violated, exploited and repressed as women have always been' (O'Brien 2004: 206). The stylistic blend of cutaways, film clips and interviews both employs and criticizes the means of representation, but for this interface of feminism and nationalism there is no easy solution, because the issue itself cannot be neatly subdivided: 'It is ultimately irresolvable into discrete contexts of women and/or "women" as a representational construct within nationalism and ideas of nationality, which is where its polemical force comes from' (O'Brien 2004: 206).

In the past, feminist analysis has often been absent in areas of study where gender, race, class, nation and sexuality meet in a more complex way. Women's history as communicated in documentary has become one recorded through gaps and silences, for as Foucault reminds us a document tends to exist as such only once it is certified by those in power. The silences that documentary sometimes addresses can be painful ones. The depiction of personal trauma such as rape is clearly linked to representational issues, examined back in 1975 by Cambridge Documentary Films in *Rape Culture*, a film that applied the then unknown term 'rape culture' to the cultural messages that perpetuated rape and reinforced rapist behaviour.

> What emerged from our exploration of representations . . . was that each image could be broken down into codes of power and control. We asked questions such as who was dominant, who was the active agent, who was the recipient of the action, who was powerless, from whose point of view was the image, who was looking, who was being looked at? Once that 'eye' was opened, it could never be closed again.   (Lazarus 2001: 247)

Since that time, poststructuralist critiques of the issues of abortion and female representation have questioned the whole feminist project, even its name. Yet world conflicts through the 1990s and into the twenty-first century have ensured that the representation of rape has remained an issue. At the heart of the problem of representation of individual experiences lies the problem of how to depict historic experiences for which no visual record exists, especially in light of the poststructuralist argument according to which there is no unmediated access to the 'real'.

In the example of *Rape Stories* (1989), there were two categories of representation addressed by the filmmaker – a materialist, historical reality and a psychoanalytical 'real' which involves a fantasy of retribution. There is a stark contrast between the 'austere and realist rendition' of the rape at the beginning of the film and its later portrayal of the retribution fantasy which is conveyed with a sense of pleasure and 'a subversive smile'. Although the latter invites the potential criticism that violence is being reproduced, with the viewer being made into a voyeur, the film nevertheless offers no spectacle of violence, and there is no visual image of the rape or of any counter-violence fantasy (Hesford 1999: 194, 212).

In the case of human rights violations, there is always a danger that any representation of the crimes will turn the viewers into 'voyeurs of the suffering of others, tourists mid their landscapes of anguish' (Ignatieff 1997: 10). Yet violence is frequently represented in order to generate resistance to it, or simply to draw attention to the suffering. When one considers that it was only in 1996 that rape in the former Yugoslavia was recognized as a war crime by the International Criminal Tribunal at The Hague, and this only after serious lobbying by human rights and feminist activists, then the gravity of documentary testimony and representation can be fully appreciated. Part of the evidence that led to the Tribunal decision was an award winning documentary film entitled *Calling the Ghosts* (1996) by Mandy Jacobson and Karmen Jelincic. If the message of the film concerns the hope for social justice and human rights, it also raises questions about the complex social functions of memories of collective trauma. At the end of the film, one of the women, Cigelj, states: 'The world watches coldly while everything passes through women's bodies . . . When they were killing and raping older women, they were killing and raping living history; when they were raping younger women they were destroying future generations.'

The method of representation in *Calling the Ghosts* highlights women's collective agency, their healing of communities and activism, not the victimization of individuals in isolation. There are group interviews, montages of many women's faces, and shots of piles of photographs of tortured body parts. The film also challenges stereotypical Western ideas of the ways an abused Muslim woman can be depicted: the main characters are not crazed peasants but two middle-class professionals – one an attorney, the other a civil judge – who had been childhood friends, and who were captured and tortured by former neighbours. In one scene, a woman who had been in a death camp watches a television news report that contains her own testimony, and a denial by the commander who tortured her. Ironically, both the woman and the perpetrator of physical abuse appear equally calm and authoritative: it is only in the wider context of the film that the aggressor's guilt becomes clear. Meanwhile the women change from being victims to being activists as they create support communities to provide legal aid and to gather the testimonials of others. These are political acts of empowerment that 'act as a challenge to concepts of liberalism and its established universalism' (Hesford 2004: 124).

Migrant trauma is a regular theme in some personalized Australian documentaries. In Mitzi Goldman's *Chinese Takeaway* (2002), for instance, we learn that Yen's mother committed suicide after being raped by her husband and suffering a nervous breakdown. The shot of a rope over a beam, followed by photographs of the mother, support a narrative, but this form of text can only act as a limited explanation, in the same way that Lanzmann's interviews in *Shoah* provide a text which is incapable of signifying the original event, only of repeating the claim that it took place (Smaill 2006: 280). But if such films cannot fully represent the trauma, their understatement does not necessarily diminish their potency; rather it provides space for the subject as a form of interpretation, without necessarily diminishing the appeal to audiences.

Thus the representation of trauma can be oblique. Another strategy is to focus the film away from the original tragedy or affliction – but as the following case study shows, this can still be a powerful technique, especially where children are involved.

Comparative case study: *War/Dance* (2007); *Autism: The Musical* (2007)

Andrea Nix Fine and Sean Fine's *War/Dance* (2008 Academy Nomination, 2007 Sundance Winner) shows the fate of northern Ugandan children who became refugees or child-soldiers during the country's long civil war. The children were taken from their families at a very young age, the boys were trained to become killers, the girls became sexual slaves. After the war they were sent to various refugee camps with the intention of their being rehabilitated or returned to their homes. This did not happen.

The film follows the progress of three children in the Patongo refugee camp, all victims of terrible violence and loss, who prepare to enter a music competition that offers them a lifeline of hope. Nancy, Rose and Dominic, a former child-soldier, practise for the contest which provides a welcome respite from the desperate circumstances of their daily lives. The voices are those of the teachers, carers and the children. The representation of previous trauma is oblique and indirect. The music competition represents more than simply a diversion from the children's previous suffering: it becomes a metaphor for the alternatives to violence and loss, a metaphor of hope.

One scene shows the children being interviewed about their experience and their surprise at enjoying partaking in an innocent competition. Fourteen-year-old Dominic tells of his fear and his 'recruitment': 'Life is not good here for children in Northern Uganda.

Here children never stop hiding from the rebels, since they are the target. The soldiers told me if I didn't kill the farmers, they would kill me. [The film shows an image of a smashed skull in a field.] They told me to use a hand-hoe to kill them.' He goes on to say that when he plays the xylophone people like him, and hopes that 'the music will take me to many places'. Rose, a singer in the competition, tells of her parents' heads being stuffed into a cooking pot. She recalls that before her father died, he used to say singing was a great talent. She says: 'whenever I sing I think of him'. The film cuts to Rose dancing and singing. Twelve-year-old Nancy, a dancer, describes her joy as 'songs make me forget what is happening in the camp'. The film shows how the children overcome their brutal history and 'do good things'. They do not win the competition but they gain hope for a possible future not determined by war.

Tricia Regan's *Autism: The Musical* also seeks to represent the triumph of hope over adversity, and won two Emmy Awards in 2008. The documentary follows the six-month rehearsal process of the Miracle Project, in which a group of autistic children write and perform a full-length musical. The film's purpose, according to Regan, is not to present autism as a subject but to show children and parents as people involved in a task where autism is an 'obstacle'. The film concentrates on communication between the children and their families as they go through therapy, school, music lessons and life in general. The five autistic children find making connections to other people very difficult, as is seen in several clips of the children's behaviour, in particular Neal's – throwing tables, shouting and generally being disruptive in times of stress. The parents describe the challenges as extremely trying; Neal's mother tells how she prays to God each day to give her the strength 'just to get through this one bathtime'. She also tells of how her marriage broke up as she grappled with the all-consuming nature of her son's needs.

However the film also conveys a real sense of relationship and represents personal struggles through its coverage of the composition and execution of the musical. The format allows the filmmaker to not only document the musical as an end point but also to act as advocate for a little-understood condition that has devastatingly unsociable traits. In covering autism in this manner, the film avoids a patronizing tone; it serves to demonstrate the power of documentary to re-present and to communicate the voices of a marginalized group.

In *War/Dance* and *Autism* there is a burden of representation: the viewer observes social actors outlined as representational groups of their type. The subject may seem exotic, but, by the way in which the films are edited, a story is told about how a sense of social responsibility and communication brings the social actors within the ambit of normal society. *War/Dance*'s children say they became normal though communication and participation; *Autism*'s participants also overcame the obstacle of exclusion (albeit an inherent isolating trait) to achieve a kind of resolution.

Conclusion

There are powerful documentaries that demonstrate the importance of what is *not* shown. Film may be a literal genre, but in factual examples the content can be so emphatic that visuals are not needed. Sometimes the content calls for alternative strategies. With regard to style and form there is a wide range of choices, each with points in its favour but also a downside. Ethnographic filmmaking first debated what should be filmed, how it should be done, and other multivalent problems that needed to be addressed. The issues it raised have since become equally relevant to all forms of documentary. In fact, the discourse on representation now stretches even further, encompassing feature films, the Internet and the use of stereotypes in visual media such as photographs and advertising. The range of implications for representation is huge, including concerns about idealized or romantic stereotypes, such as the North American Indian's supposed harmony with nature, or the selling of culture as a commodity, or the marginalization of 'other'.

The task of working with a minority culture that has been denied a counter-discourse is best done in cooperation and collaboration with the people who are the subject of the film, in order to determine the most appropriate form of representation. Within the domain of documentary practice, filmmakers and the subjects they depict are always cast in relation to one another, and never in isolation. Thus representation is also about this relationship and its outcome in the finished product – how far the relationship is a negotiated one, involving a sharing of power. Haworth's film is a case in point; her strategy is to take a back seat in front of camera, letting her family and friends respond to the her social and sexual change, while driving forward the editorial slant of the piece. This becomes her method of representing her private self for effect within the public sphere.

Tagg maintains that documentary forms part of a larger institutional and environmental matrix. The examples presented in this chapter demonstrate that the significance of the continuities and changes in representational issues cannot be fully appreciated without at least some consideration to this side of the equation. One contextual change to consider, for instance, is the shift in emphasis from a public representation of causes to a more personal agency that appeals to a reputedly more emotion-hungry viewer who is increasingly becoming more active in response through the Internet. However, greater personal influence in representative forms and an aesthetic that foregrounds the representation of difference (perceived, for instance, by Stuart Hall in cinematic representations of black British as characterized by hybridity, blends and crossover [Proctor 2004: 131]) does not undermine Tagg's thesis. This is equally true of the representation of other issues and themes. The way we use documentary to reflect notions of connection with society is a reflection of the outside world – fluid and constantly changing.

3 Objectivity/Subjectivity Pursuing Truth?

Summary

The subjectivity versus objectivity (or relative objectivity) debate is a fairly complex one, as subjectivity and objectivity coexist in a state of fluidity, or, to use another metaphor, on a see-saw balance that varies according to decisions made by the director/producer, the circumstances during production, and the influence of institutional and contextual factors. The Plantinga thesis is that there *is* such a thing as 'relative objectivity' (Plantinga 1997), while Carroll (1983) defends objectivity by arguing that confusion and abuse of language have led to an imprecise identification of objectivity with truth. Objectivity has become intertwined with notions of balance and bias, and with questions of passivity/ activity on the part of the viewer (see Chapter 7).

The trend over the last twenty years or so has been towards greater reflexivity and subjectivity, with more prominence given to the author/filmmaker. Filmmakers pursue the truth through personal experience, case studies, visual rhetoric and other forms, none of which is easy to categorize. The focus on personal documentary also raises the question of how the documentary genre can be assimilated and hence neutralized by the mainstream, especially television. A documentary's purpose is a critical factor when it comes to levels of subjectivity or objectivity in pursuit of the truth, as is demonstrated by activist documentaries. It is the idea of 'engaged' filmmaking that particularly sparks academic debate about balance and agency. The way that subjectivity is implemented, the level of personalization, and its relevance to issues of importance within the public sphere, all need to be considered.

Although defence of objectivity as a concept has become unfashionable, a degree of objectivity – or at least of the values associated with it such as the attempt to avoid excessive bias – is still largely honoured by journalistic filmmakers who adopt a style of argumentative representation in current affairs documentaries. Yet even here the underlying assumptions and hidden agendas behind the on-screen message need to be questioned. Recent technological advances permit a style of truth-telling that is cheaper, faster, more mobile and extreme in tone than those that came before. Technology such as the Internet has opened up the potential for wider access to audiences. Digital formats and the Internet have enabled contributions to cultural debate from an increasing number of amateurs and a consequent divergence from expert viewpoints. The manner in which society is portrayed can be heavily influenced by individual intention – this has always been the case, but today, with the ease of digital imaging, the camera can be made to lie more easily. The notion of documentary truth that audiences still associate with the genre is thereby challenged, for postmodern truth is a 'truth which, far from being abandoned, still operates powerfully as the receding horizon of the documentary tradition' (Williams 1993: 11).

Introduction

The creative impulse seems to mitigate against impartiality, for it involves an element of personalization. Science does not have to justify truthfulness by claiming objectivity, because its experiments are capable of repetition without authorial influence, whereas documentary involves a non-repeatable human factor. 'Real time, real events are fairly chaotic, and there are usually a million opinions about whatever the issue is that is being discussed, and once you are in the process of constructing a film and editing all of that chaos, you invariably start to shape it to your own view' (Su Friedrich, quoted in Jeffries and Idlet 1997: 23). There is a constant tension between subjectivity and objectivity, which has emerged in different ways throughout documentary's history. Here we will examine just a few examples that demonstrate its fluidity.

Dziga Vertov was the first filmmaker to tackle the issue of objectivity head-on, during the 1920s. In *Enthusiasm* (1920, also referred to as *Symphony of the Donbas*), he proved that subjectivity, and conversely objectivity, are present in every aspect of production by the way he used sound to make a political statement. The film provides a valuable reflection on the recording process (Christie 2006: 88). When synchronized sound was first introduced, filmmakers feared that it would threaten the survival of montage editing by forcing the adoption of a more linear style, but Vertov argued that the same principles applied, with the added advantage that sound gave more options. *Enthusiasm* furnished him with the ideal opportunity to return to his original interest in experimental sound, combining it with a celebration of one of Stalin's first big 'Five Year Plan' projects: the rapid expansion of the Ukrainian Donets Basin coal and steel development. Using both synchronized sound and his experimental practice of deliberately *non*-synchronized sound to enhance the iconic 'montage' visual style, Vertov took the audience on a stunning trip through the drama of underground drilling, overhead railways, coal conveyor belts, and steel production using bulky machinery.

What seems fair at one point in history, to one person or regime, may seem biased to another. In 1927, Vertov had predicted that 'Radiopravda' would develop alongside his celebrated 'Kinopravda' newsreel. As both aimed to extend the newspaper *Pradva*, does this make the now classic film propaganda? As Christie (2006) points out, Chaplin – who had his own reservations about the introduction of 'talkies' – publicly hailed Vertov's industrial symphony, and emulated its style in his own *Modern Times* (1936). Chaplin was subsequently branded a 'communist' during the McCarthyite period and never worked in the United States again.

Part of the obfuscation that enshrouds the question of subjectivity and objectivity is rooted in the early claim that the camera does not lie. Linked to this is the traditional notion that a documentary is in pursuit of truth, enhanced by the influence of observational and journalistic methods that have both, from very different perspectives, combined to constrain the impact of subjectivity.

Philosophically, non-fiction film has always been influenced by the scientific project of the Enlightenment. The European intellectual tradition has grappled with the differences between subjective and objective knowledge since ancient times, and a dualism between the two has been evident since the mid-nineteenth century. Ruby blames nineteenth-century positivism, which encouraged the social scientist to try to be detached, unbiased and objective towards his object of study and to withhold all value judgement (Ruby 1980: 161). Only more recently has the balance between the personal and the 'objective' been challenged more blatantly, although within the field of ethnographic studies there has long been a critique of the objective quest to preserve authentic endangered cultures in remote places. Debates on the nature of truth-telling are fuelled by the various constraints involved in the divergent schools of documentary making. According to Winston, Direct Cinema is part of the problem, for the movement reasserted the claim that Francois Arago had made 130 years earlier with respect to photography – that it represented 'an instrument of scientific inscription producing evidence objective enough to be "judged" by a spectator' (Winston 1995: 151, 154; 2008).

Although French Cinema Verité admitted a role for the personal and subjective, there is no place within either it or its American counterpart Direct Cinema for the third-party outsider as intermediary. Instead, the omnipresent camera becomes a silent ally of the people who are being filmed, for the filmmaker is a chronicler of what is happening, in every detail, no matter how boring. This is how the truth is reached – and the Verité filmmaker argues that the approach is objective because it does not mediate or manipulate, maintaining 'a fly-on-the-wall reserve as it gleaned supposedly deeper, more intimate perceptions filtered out by conventional reporting' (Arthur 1998: 75).

Sometimes the terms 'Cinema Verité' and 'Direct Cinema' are used interchangeably, although they are in fact separate aesthetic categories. The former originated in France, and is exemplified by the work of Jean Rouch, who saw the camera as a psychological participant in the unfolding of events, so that the filming situation will sometimes draw us nearer to the truth. In contrast, Direct Cinema was a type of observational documentary practice developed in the United States and Canada from c.1958 and throughout the 1960s. Pro-filmic events were recorded as they happened and allowed to unfold in front of the camera without intervention by the director.

In fact, with both these documentary forms, subjectivity arises in other ways: in the selection of people and subject matter to film in the first place, and in the later editing, when difficult choices have to be made in order to reduce the enormous amount of footage into a much shorter finished product. At worst, tabloid values can be at work in the selection of dramatic incidents, or the exclusion of more complex, subtler issues that arise during filming. At best, Verité can be relatively uncritical because of the in-depth attention given to the people who are featured. But the style is no more objective than its television enemy, the journalistic documentary. Yet myths persist in filmmaking as much as in the real world. One of these is that Cinema Verité and Direct Cinema somehow moved nearer to the truth because of their lack of intervention at the point of filming. They captured 'reality', even if it was juxtaposed or edited down later.

Statements such as that of Robert Drew, that 'the film maker's personality is in no way directly involved in directing the action', have contributed to a general impression of objectivity due to non-intervention that has its roots in the scientific heritage of photography (Winston 1993: 53; 2008). However, studies of *An American Family* (1973), for instance, focus on the numerous ways in which subjectivity seeps in to the filmmaking agenda, even if unacknowledged at the time (Chapman 2007: 94).

From verité to television current affairs

In Great Britain and other countries with a history of strong public broadcasting systems, documentary has always found a place on television, even if this is vulnerable today. In contrast, the documentary presence on the major TV networks in the United States is weak. Although the structural and historical reasons for the relative financial weakness of PBS in the US are outside the remit of this chapter (see Chapman 2005), there is one episode in American documentary history that is highly relevant. The tension between journalistic objectivity and more subjective artistic expression that emerged during the 'Golden Age' of television documentary in 1960s America split the documentary movement, causing the demise of a mass media genre that had so much potential for serving democracy. Film documentary did grow thereafter, but mainly in art-house and urban areas.

This was a period when the citizen viewer became a 'consumer viewer', and television documentary producers had to work under network constraints, at a time when there was also unprecedented cooperation between government persuaders and corporate media managers. Pressure was exerted to use television as a means to promote American foreign policy while simultaneously restoring credibility to the medium after the TV quiz-show scandals that had rocked the country (Chapman 2005: 223). In response, in 1960 the Federal Communications Commission (FCC) Chairman proposed that each network devote at least one evening hour a week to informational, educational or cultural programming. However, by the mid-1960s the television networks had replaced political documentary with personality-driven, cheaper news magazine shows that were easier for them to control and provided simpler factual viewing.

In the early 1960s Robert Drew and his group of filmmakers brought the influence of Direct Cinema to bear on television, moving in and out of projects commissioned by competing television networks, the government and corporations. The Drew group produced documentaries for the ABC network, until members began to resent editorial interference and sponsorship concerns. ABC executives became increasingly involved in rejecting footage that they feared might offend audiences or sponsors. Although all three US networks were proud of their documentary units, bosses were 'nervous about a genre with a mission to go beyond the facts into interpretation. As a result, they never gave documentary makers the independence or autonomy they needed to produce work that reached important conclusions. They made *cautious* political documentaries and the audience sensed this timidity' (Mills 2008: 9–10).

The executive producer of NBC's *Angola: Journey to a War* (1961) ordered the producer Robert Young to remove evidence that the Portuguese had used

American-manufactured napalm bombs to suppress an African uprising, in case the Russians used the information against the US (Barnouw 1992: 227). Television documentaries analysed by Michael Curtain during the period 1960 to 1964 reveal a tendency to neglect representation of everyday life in communist countries in favour of stereotypical 'pure' political extremism so characteristic of the sort of Cold War depictions that only polarized rather than educated the public (Curtain 1995: 41).

In 1963 CBS and NBC lengthened their newscasts to thirty minutes, with the result that the public was exposed to more images of riots, fighting in Vietnam and crime. Race relations became a major national issue and documentary makers, working in the same newsrooms as news journalists, turned increasingly to domestic themes. Edward Murrow had set the pace with *Harvest of Shame* in 1960, but later TV documentaries did not draw the audiences needed for prime time, and in fact, as the genre attracted controversy, advertisers rejected it. 'Through mazes of controversy, newsmen walked a tightrope labeled "truth", forced to qualify by saying "on the other hand" over and over again' (Barnouw 1992: 227). Meanwhile many local affiliate stations, especially in the South, refused to air documentaries on civil rights and anti-war protests, and TV critics began to question whether some subjects merited a full hour of airtime. Out of this criticism, the news magazine series *60 Minutes* was born in 1968.

By this time TV was beginning to focus more on live news events: with race riots, the assassination of Martin Luther King and the Apollo space mission, inter alia, there was plenty to cover. Now government persuaders were more concerned with diverting audience attention away from Vietnam than they were in educating them on American foreign policy, at a time when filmmakers were setting themselves up independently, outside of the declining Hollywood studio system and television. Although some documentary makers such as Frederick Wiseman and others found a home on PBS, by rejecting the less timid artistic documentary, 'networks robbed audiences of valuable context and perspective in documentaries that allowed them to see committed interpretations of a story' (Mills 2008: 21).

Cinema Verité and Direct Cinema's persistent claims to impartiality and access to 'truth' were particularly challenged by the American documentaries of the 1970s. The work of Emile de Antonio recognized the camera's undeniable subjectivity (Chapman 2007: 115; Waugh in Nichols 1985: 234). Hitherto there appeared to have been a clear differentiation between documentary's subject and the processes of production. Despite such challenges to the original style and thinking, elements of influence from the Direct Cinema heritage were carried forward elsewhere – especially the belief that raw video images somehow have more authenticity and hence objectivity than professionally produced documentary material.

This was the assumption of filmmakers in communist China, after so many years of being given doctored versions of the truth. It is interesting to note the place of the objectivity/subjectivity issue within the developing fortunes of documentary in that country. Independent or underground documentary began in the 1980s with a preference for Cinema Verité, but added an interview style as a reaction to the dominant address of the Party 'voice of God' commentary on official news and documentary programmes. Verité requires good access, time and money, which was difficult to find. Chinese filmmakers therefore supplemented the 'pure method' with pragmatism in the form of extensive use of interviews, which allowed individual testimonies and witnesses to substantiate their truth claims – again, a way of challenging official authority. However, attempts at impartiality led the filmmakers to place all their trust in interviewees to tell the truth, allocating inordinately long takes to what became excessively tedious, unmediated interviews. Self-erasure led to misplaced objectivity.

Within less than ten years, the fashion in China had shifted to a more personal approach. One of the pioneer independents, Wu Wenguang did not even know what documentary was until he attended the Yamagata Festival in 1991 (Zhang 2004: 119). Thereafter concepts like 'Direct Cinema' and 'Cinema Verité' began to circulate amongst the small community of filmmaking rebels, with Wiseman becoming a role model with ideological and aesthetic appeal. Aesthetically, Wiseman's images seemed direct, close and hence nearer to the 'truth'. Ideologically, his engagement with a critique of institutions through individual people foregrounded the personal rather than the political, an approach which was new in China.

Most independents in China have been amateurs learning on the job, who turned technical weaknesses such as grainy images and muddy sound into a positive feature, the way 'Imperfect Cinema' had done so previously. But at least one filmmaker considers the early products 'cheap, unsubstantial and unimaginative' (Lu, 2003: 88–9). Now in China, a fashion for amateur Digital Video, partly influenced by the younger generation's desire to record ordinary people's lives, is defended as being more individualistic and truthful and therefore more likely to provide 'unofficial texts' to help understand Chinese society (Zhang 2004: 131).

But it is erroneous to believe that amateur video shots are automatically reliable, and therefore objective. The beating of Rodney King captured on amateur video led to a high-profile court case in the United States, during which the footage was scrutinized and used subjectively by both defence and prosecution. The video had been shown on television, but in such situations shots need enhancement before they can be transmitted effectively, and that requires selectivity, as of course do the camera angle and choice of position for shooting. The trial verdict, and the arson and insurrection that followed, were prompted by rival interpretations of images that were assumed by all to be unambiguously 'real', even though their meaning was contested. Yet people were wrong to believe that the images spoke for themselves; we know now that this is not the case. Ironically, while the Los Angeles TV station paid George Holliday $500 for the video, the aftermath of the whole episode – the arson and riots – resulted in $700 million worth of property damage (Renov 1993: 8).

Objectivity and the journalistic documentary

Objectivity presupposes a community of people who agree in some measure about the terms and conditions that underscore this distanced presence, although different communities will assign different meanings and definitions. The journalistic documentary has evolved a rhetoric of objectivity as part of a 'professional' approach to observation, to be found amongst documentary makers, journalists and reporters who share a belief in the seriousness of social purpose, which demands evidence as the basis for their enquiries. Such people are employed by TV networks, news agencies, government and other institutional bodies, all of which supply a continuing flow of facts while overtly avoiding forms of interpretation which could be construed as propaganda, persuasion, ideology or editorializing. Carroll defines the practices of such discursive communities as 'patterns of reasoning, routines for assessing evidence, means of weighing up the comparative significance of different types of evidence, and standards for observations [and] experimentation . . . shared by practitioners in [the] field' (Carroll 1983: 15).

Television's institutional constraints can mean that the need to make truth claims actually serves to disguise any partisan tendencies on the part of the reporter. Furthermore, in some circumstances, such as TV current affairs programmes, the claim to be presenting an objective view seems to be needed in order to obtain the trust and intellectual/emotional engagement of the viewer. Even when rhetoric is employed, opposing views cannot be peremptorily or blatantly dismissed, otherwise the filmmaker will be accused of propaganda. Agencies such as television networks seek objectivity as a legal protection against libel. Within this culture, reporting objectively is the job of news and factual departments who use documentary approaches for 'specials' and investigative reports. The objective communication of what happens in the real world by other institutions (including the state) then becomes a means of differentiating such departments from others within the organization, such as those producing fictional programmes. As a means of self-defence where necessary, the reporter needs to be able to claim objectivity by having presented verifiable facts; hence accurate description is required, rather than explanation or interpretation. In a documentary situation, a realistic style of observation, with any reporting effectively effaced, will eliminate accusations of bias by appealing to the authenticity of the witness.

Journalists are trained to present the complexities involved in the diverse perspectives on a given issue, yet ironically many filmmakers blame the growing dominance of journalistic influences on television documentary for the 'myth' of objectivity, the other factor being the misleading nature of Cinema Verité and Direct Cinema. To back up their claims to be reflecting the world, mass-market broadcasters needed a new aesthetic approach – a 'naturalism' capable of generating an impression of objectivity. However, by the 1970s, observers had come to challenge naturalism's claim to authenticity with the realization that subjectivity still applied in the selection of the people and topic to be filmed and in the editing process. At the same time, some if not all Direct Cinema techniques became assimilated and partially used by others in different ways, especially in television documentaries.

Nevertheless, the logic of documentary, even outside of the journalistic mode, still demands that ethics and fairness accompany observation, as is illustrated by certain generally accepted practices. The documentary maker's dependence on real people, places and events rather than fictional constructs means that the claims and interpretations of others need to be documented accurately, as in an investigative film, for instance. Failure to do so might result in litigation.

Filmmakers have to respect the standard practices of the media industries, such as the use of captions for archive film clips and the requirement to verify facts. The convention in current affairs television, for example, is to include different or opposing perspectives, to choose interviewees who are representative of communities or from established institutions, and to consciously avoid extreme viewpoints. Such conventions, however, do not apply to all non-fiction films, some of which adopt other criteria. The personalized video diary, for instance, will have a different agenda. This means that, since not all documentaries adhere to the ethic of objectivity, it cannot form part of a universal definition – indeed the effect of trying to make it so, according to Plantinga, is detrimental to certain categories of the genre: 'making objectivity central to non-fiction film unjustifiably marginalizes subjective and expressive films' (Plantinga 1997: 200). Nevertheless, conventions such as fairness, impartiality and balance encourage a certain discipline in the representation of individual topics, for objectivity in the context of television journalism concerns the manner of presentation.

Complexity seems to be the key to avoiding allegations of propaganda. According to filmmaker St. Clair Bourne:

> I think what you can do if you want to be impartial is to view both or many sides. Once you choose one vision, you're no longer impartial, you're no longer objective. It's not necessarily a great characteristic to be impartial, but I would say it is a virtue to show complexity as opposed to one viewpoint.
>
> (quoted in Thompson 2001: 36)

In situations where different points of view do not emerge from a particular documentary, television broadcasters will often follow the transmission with a studio discussion that gives airtime to alternative perspectives. Alternatively, broadcasters may argue that their responsibility towards the audience is maintained over the course of an entire series by the presentation of other programmes that present differing perspectives.

The History Channel in the US was criticized for irresponsibility towards its audience in broadcasting a documentary called *The Guilty Men* (2003), which claimed that Vice President Lyndon Johnson was complicit in the assassination of President John F. Kennedy. The allegations came from a book, but none of the people under the spotlight were alive to defend themselves. However, the History Channel argued that the allegations (as opposed to facts) were presented as being only one point of view and formed part of a total of eleven hours programming about the assassination in a series, *The Men Who Killed Kennedy* (2003), which looked at many, often contradictory, conspiracy theories on the event (*New York Times*, 5 February 2004). Such debates continue as a vital part of questioning the veracity of reports and opinions, and examining perceptions of the finished product.

By not admitting to the presence of the subjective and the ideological, claims to objectivity create their own problems and inconsistencies with regard to their purpose. According to Nichols, there are three obvious manifestations of the impulse towards objectivity: 1) The adoption of a third-party rather than first-person viewpoint. However, a detached 'voice of God' narration can coexist with relatively subjective camera positioning. 2) A disinterested form of representation that seeks to avoid all personal bias. However, there are always in-built assumptions that can be questioned, such as institutional outlooks and cultural assumptions (representations of terrorism on Anglo-American television are very different from those on Al Jazeera, for instance). 3) Where objectively is the underlying aim, a film will probably leave it to the audience to make up their own minds on an issue. But yet again, ideology will always lie somewhere below the surface, as stated in point 2 (Nichols 1991: 196).

Institutional influences

A documentary text will influence its audience by virtue of the knowledge-related claims it presents; there is, however, usually an assumption on the part of the audience about the so-called self-evident nature of the facts contained in the film and of the necessity for forms of representation that involve rhetorical. All of these elements are based on a standard of objectivity with embedded political assumptions. Concepts such as professionalism, impartiality and balance can themselves be used to conceal bias and issues of power, and have inevitable political implications insofar as they contribute to the power of the media in society.

Institutions move slowly: in one case it took the BBC twenty years to finally agree to transmit a drama documentary that had been commissioned and made in- house in the first place. Peter Watkins' powerful film about the results of nuclear war was considered too horrifying for television viewers. Although the fortunes of *The War Game* will be further analysed in the next chapter, at this point it is worth noting how allegations about a lack of objectivity were used by the BBC (backed by civil servants) as an excuse for a television ban, declaring that the film was 'not objective enough' and an 'artistic failure' despite the fact that it was nominated for a Hollywood Oscar as best documentary feature. The project was carefully scrutinized during post production, resulting in criticisms that the final film had not turned out as anticipated. Hugh Wheldon, then Head of Documentaries, had checked the script, but stated that he was disappointed because he 'had understood, in particular, that the varying points of view about the deterrent would be presented with equal force – and this had not been done' (BBC 1965: WAC T56/261/2). Suggestions were made for minor changes, including the insertion of some explanatory captions. The intention was to correct the 'imbalance' by the device of a studio-based follow-up discussion after the film. In the event, this did not happen.

Both Wiseman with *Titicut Follies* (and observational documentary about a US psychiatric institution) and Watkins with *The War Game* went into more detail in their films than was considered comfortable at the time. For Wiseman, fairness entails a lack of manipulation by the documentary maker of the people being filmed. His approach renders matters of 'balance' irrelevant:

> If you're going to be fair to the people working in these institutions, it seems to me you have to present them on their own terms. I'm not interested in simplifying more than I have to in the interests of some narrower political analysis. I think the effort is to provide a political analysis, but in my terms and not someone else's. Because the final film does represent a theory. The structure of the film is a theory about the events that are in the film.   (Sutherland 1978: 82)

Thus, subjectivity comes through the structure. We never see Wiseman and there are no formal interviews; in fact he has never asked a direct question in a film or voiced his opinions with narration. He does not need to put himself on screen.

How does Wiseman introduce his subjective political ideas in relation to softer subjects? Take, for instance, a zoo. In his film *Zoo*, the subtlety of the political message still comes from the structure. Wiseman has a tendency to depict institutions (a high school, a hospital, a science research establishment) as versions of a corporate bureaucracy. To this end, the zoo study is divided into three parts, observing first the animal spectacle, second the everyday work involved in maintaining the zoo, and third the organizational oversight with its internal wrangling, assiduous pursuit of sponsorship, and trading in 'specimens' with competitor zoos. This structure by itself invites a reading of the film as 'an allegory for the workings of post-industrial capitalism' (Arthur 1998: 78). No further elements of subjectivity are needed.

The conventions of the journalistic documentary were severely tested in Britain and Eire during the 1980s until the mid-1990s. The institutional pressures that documentaries and other television coverage about the conflict in Northern Ireland experienced can be appreciated through a closer analysis of behind-the-scenes dealings over two films: *Real Lives: At the Edge of the Union* (1985), and *Mother Ireland* (1998). Documentaries on Northern Ireland at this time were expected to merely inform, and include only 'neutral' comment on the crisis, as if they were news items. Yet arguably documentary is at its best when it is impassioned as well as informative. Despite the fact that it was also customary in the media for leaders of the paramilitary forces to be demonized, *Real Lives* gave them a human face, while *Mother Ireland* gave their women leaders (on the Republican side at least) an intellectual, cultural and political history.

In the Republic of Ireland, a ban introduced in 1971 under section 31 of its Broadcasting Act (1960, amended 1976) prevented broadcast interviews and reports of interviews with members of a list of proscribed organizations including the IRA and the UDA. It was not withdrawn until 1994. In Britain, a broadcasting ban was introduced in 1988 which prohibited the broadcast of authentic words spoken by anybody from eleven named organizations, including Sinn Féin – even though the latter already had one MP, Gerry Adams, and over fifty elected local councillors in Northern Ireland. Of course, there were other ways of transmitting what the spokespeople actually said, but subtitles, dubbing or reporting the words over silent footage were clumsy alternatives. As a result, coverage of their views was inevitably reduced.

Real Lives was probably vetted by more top management in the BBC than any other programme in its history, while *Mother Ireland*, made for Britain's Channel 4, suffered long delays and a huge number of cuts before it was eventually broadcast. *Real Lives* featured 'at home' interviews (a new departure for current affairs documentary at the time) with two leaders of proscribed organizations: the IRA (Irish Republican Army) and the UDA (Ulster Defence Association). The BBC governors decided it should be banned, but then withdrew the decision after a strike threat from staff (see Chapter 4). One of the governors articulated concern over the domestication of the IRA, with the film showing them as 'lovable people with babies'. The producer Paul Hamann was criticized for his 'soft questioning' of Martin McGuinness, the IRA leader featured (BBC 1985). The criticism was that the film lacked objectivity because of the apparent sympathy for its subjects, which seemed evident from the choice of location, the title and the absence of aggressive questioning.

In the case of *Mother Ireland*, which focused on the role of women in direct political action on behalf of the Republican struggle, producer Anne Crilly was asked why she did not include any Unionist women. Her answer reflects the dilemma:

> [It] was something we discussed at the time and actually considered at a very late stage, but I just decided that it wouldn't be balanced, that it would just be tokenism, and that it was perfectly alright to have a subjective point of view documentary. So when people came up to me and said that the programme wasn't balanced at all, I'd say, 'You're quite right, it wasn't balanced at all. . . . I was hoping that there would be a programme made about the history of Protestant Unionist women in Ireland, and I even developed that myself, but it never was made . . . as a balancing act to *Mother Ireland*, it would have been good.   ('M.T.' n.d.)

This is the response of television executive producers to criticism of lack of balance in current affairs programmes – that any imbalance in one documentary will be corrected by another from an opposite point of view later in the series.

Television impartiality and balance

Public service broadcasters frequently fall prey to criticism concerning their impartiality. The issue tends to remain always either just above or just below the surface, because of their government funding, regulatory frameworks, accountability to politicians and civil servants, and obligations to national populations. But for every action there is a reaction. CBC journalists in Canada construed an ombudsman's ruling on bias in 1993 as an attack on freedom of expression. Their anger sparked a change in policy towards the corporation's future purchasing and screening of documentaries that do not offer a 'balanced' view. The straw that broke the camel's back was a three-part series entitled *The Valour and the Horror* (1992), which was deemed to have contravened the network's standards of objectivity and balance by portraying the Canadian Second-World-War effort as 'inept and Canadian bombers as murderers' (Jenkinson 1993: 49).

Previously the management of the corporation would vet documentaries for balanced coverage of both sides of an issue before transmission, but a new policy was introduced permitting executives to select any documentary for transmission, even if 'biased', so long as it was factually correct and not funded by any organization with a direct interest in the content. However, some sources at the time attributed this change in the rules to an economic motivation, since it is cheaper to purchase documentaries off the shelf from independents than it is to commission new productions in-house. The problem was that most independent products did not meet CBC's stringent definitions of 'fairness'. The issue now became: who decides what is factually correct and by what criteria?

A focus on a single angle may well be thoroughly researched, providing the viewer with ample information. In Britain the long-running current affairs television series *World in Action* (1963–98) gained a reputation for its social agenda and ways of telling and showing, backed up by rigorous inquiry. This approach, programme makers argued, made any further requirement for balance superfluous. However, the regulator, the Independent Television Association (ITA), disagreed, resulting in a long-running battle. Senior figures within Granada television made public pronouncements regularly throughout the 1960s and early 1970s against what they branded as censorship (Goddard, Corner and Richardson 2001: 80).

The idea that television current affairs should be impartial, hence balanced, is well ingrained within the media psyche. But 'balance' depends at what point along the political spectrum the scales are placed. Inevitably the fringes tend to be omitted, with editorial conclusions veering towards the centre in order to make the point that both sides have their faults, but that a compromise (that is, middle ground) is possible. 'Balance' can end up appearing wishy-washy and impartiality can result in either sitting on the fence or centrism.

In 1985 the American PBS series *Crisis in Central America* was hailed by reviewers as 'a great leap forward for integrity and objectivity in television documentaries' (Bakshian 1985: 48). This praise was justified mainly on the grounds that, with four hours allocated to the subject, thoroughness was possible, and that this was achieved by using a range of sources, rather than one main point of view. But such an achievement is more difficult given the shorter running time in more traditional documentary making. The visual and aesthetic nature of the medium necessitates the creative use of shots which both make a statement and also suggest a value judgement.

How do filmmakers go about their task of promoting the truth fairly, especially when their enquiry is focused on issues that invite extreme partisanship? Issues become particularly accentuated in the case of war coverage, which introduces an added pressure of the requirement to be 'patriotic', as well as the increased possibility of censorship. Some practitioners defend their professionalism by arguing that it is possible to combine both objectivity and patriotism:

> I think it's possible to be objective, if not neutral. It's a subtle distinction, but an important one. I'm not neutral about the outcome of the war. I want America to win, I'm not rooting for Iraq, but I remain objective in that I hope to maintain the ability to sift through information honestly presented and give people the most accurate picture we can on what's actually happened.
>
> (Andrew Heywood, president of CBS news, quoted by Reedy 2003: 88).

However, not everything that happens is reported. When it is, are the biases in the reporting of the television station Al Jazeera any worse than those of Fox News? Assessment of bias, like that of balance, depends on the individual's starting point. There are no easy answers, as Jehane Noujaim – who filmed inside Al Jazeera as the director of *Control Room* (2004) – told a festival audience. She embarked upon the film with curiosity and ended up with more questions than answers (Klein 2004: 55), yet she has been accused of bias. But the documentary maker, almost by definition, has to be a destroyer of myths: 'High on the list [of hidden agendas and myths] is the myth that we now live in an "information age" – when, in fact, we live in a media age, in which the available information is repetitive, "safe" and limited by invisible boundaries' (Pilger 1998: 4). Memorable documentaries often break those boundaries.

Forms of subjectivity

Released from institutional constraints, subjectivity tends to become tied up with rhetoric and argument. The American Academy of Motion Picture Arts and Sciences perceived both *Roger and Me* and *The Thin Blue Line* as being too subjective or personal to satisfy their definitions of documentary. Subjectivity comes in various forms. The subjective voice can take the form of personal testimony, but a person appearing in a documentary is always mediated and therefore their subjectivity is inevitably fragmented, no matter how hard the filmmaker tries to make the contribution appear as an independent expression by another person. A different form of subjectivity comes into play when the film is viewed – the spectator's subjectivity will be discussed in Chapter 7. Subjectivity is a product and a quality of the text. The filmmaker's perspective adds another layer of interpretation. Thus different levels of personal influence affect an understanding of documentary films that represent actual events, and do not 'fake' it.

Issues relating to both subjectivity and objectivity in culture and works of art were discussed by members of the Frankfurt School in their analyses of the way creativity is influenced by social factors. Horkheimer on several occasions took up Kant's argument that an element of common humanity, of shared hope for the potential of mankind, informed every aesthetic act (even a subjective one) (Horkheimer 1941: 291). Similarly, Adorno returned several times to his argument that absolute subjectivity renders a work subject-less and objectified, hence estranged from itself, assuming 'the dimensions of objectivity which expresses itself through its own estrangement' (Adorno 1967: 262). Thus subjectivity and objectivity are two complex sides of the same coin, requiring us to examine a range of varying manifestations. In documentary, the most obvious subjective voice is that of a first-person discourse, and this may also centre on a lead character around whom the narrative turns. Yet subjectivity in films is not confined to these two strategies: 'A film can involve the subjectivity of its subjects, the viewer, and the institutional or individual filmmaker in compound ways' (MacDougall in Devereaux and Hillman 1995: 222–3).

Case study: *Tarnation* (2003)

Jonathan Caouette's *Tarnation* (2003) tells the story of his life and his relationship with his schizophrenic mother Renée through a compilation drawn from a twenty-year period of hundreds of hours of old Super 8 footage, VHS videotape, photographs and answering machine messages. After his mother overdosed on her medication Caouette is faced with a stream of family memories of rape, promiscuity, abandonment, psychosis and addiction. In order to cope with this terrible legacy, the filmmaker cuts and pastes together a selection of images, sound-bites, film clips and music in order both to illustrate his own life and to trace his fragile but continuing bond of love with his mother. Initially made for a total budget of $218.32, using free iMovie software on a Macintosh computer, the final version of the film eventually cost over $400,000 after music copyright royalties were paid that boosted the budget. *Tarnation* won many awards, including Best Documentary from the National Society of Film Critics, the Independent Spirits, the Gotham Awards, and the LA and London International Film Festivals.

Though the film focuses mainly on

Fig. 3.1 Jonathan Caouette's *Tarnation* uses a montage of film material in an emotive reconstruction of his difficult relationship with his mentally-ill mother.

Caouette's relationship with his mother, his questions and viewpoints link his experiences to his subjective creativity in a way that sometimes has a manipulative effect. One scene shows a video clip of the eleven-year-old Caouette filming himself improvising the role of a battered woman giving evidence in court, where she is on trial for shooting her alcoholic, drug-fuelled husband 'Jimmy'. Caouette gives his character a name (Hilary Chapman Laura Lou Gerina), a background, and convincing mannerisms to add colour to his act, explaining that she has a two-year-old daughter, and outlining the violent treatment meted out to her by her husband over the years. Finally, his character describes to the 'court' the night when she had had enough and shot Jimmy. The effect of this scene is a complex one as it becomes only too clear to the viewer that the boy has knowledge of domestic violence, victim psychology and court procedures. In addition, the subjective nature of the scene is somewhat compromised, since it is acted out as if representing a made-up world, but is clearly based on the boy's own observation of real events.

Wholly subjective films like *Tarnation* could not have been made by attempting to adopt an objective stance. This documentary *is* an example of how the use of seemingly disparate material can establish a truth – in this case, Caouette's love for his mother – that is not easy to describe in film. It is the manner in which he arranges his paean to love's survival that overrides any claim of a negative agenda on his part.

Audiences and activism

Is the way a filmmaker intends a documentary to be received by the audience part of the subjectivity/objectivity equation? Subjective identification on the part of the audience can be induced by the representation of a filmed character's desire, or by the structure of the film, in both narrative and non-narrative documentary forms. A classic example would be how, in watching *Nanook of the North*, we desperately want the hunt to be successful. This manipulation of our point of view by the filmmaker is a form of subjectivity.

Even more crucial is the context within which a film was made. In the case of *Hour of the Furnaces* (1968), filmmakers Solanas and Getino considered the problems of subjectivity and objectivity to be red herrings introduced by the First World (i.e. Hollywood) model (the 'Second World' model being that of European art-house, 'auteur' cinema, which, so they claimed, was equally prone to bourgeois misconceptions). The hegemony of the former is underpinned by its (imperialist) institutional structures, against which underfinanced film industries in countries like Argentina cannot compete, even within their own markets. In 1969, Solanas and Getino published *Towards a Third Cinema*, a radical manifesto arguing for a collective cinematic practice based on documentary and dedicated to decolonization. This was a follow up to their seminal three-part film which had been made partly under clandestine conditions in conjunction with parts of the Peronist movement, with the negative being smuggled out to Italy for completion. The two filmmakers wrote:

> We realized that the most important thing was not the film and the information in it so much as the way this information was debated. One of the aims of such films is to provide the occasion for people to find themselves and speak about their own problems. The projection becomes the place where people talk and develop their awareness.   (Quoted in Chanan 1997: 373)

One critic sums up the circumstances in which the film was produced as being 'in the interstices of the system and against the system . . . independent in production, militant in politics, and experimental in language' (Stam quoted in Burton 1990: 253). Yet, as Solanas maintains, his film's 'analysis of reality, of the enemy and of history still holds [true] . . . anyone who wanted to make political documentaries after *The Hour of the Furnaces* has had to see it' (Fusco 1988: 59).

There are works derived from the experiences of marginalized people under colonialism, or during the process of decolonization, which push at the boundaries of subjectivity. The films of Alvarez, for instance, can be better appreciated with a wider understanding of the historical role of film, and of documentary in particular, within decolonized and developing sectors, where documentary has frequently acted as the social conscience of a country. The South African anti-apartheid documentary movement was inspired by Solanas and Getino's Third Cinema theory. During the late 1970s and early 1980s a particular narrative of this divisive political system and the resistance to it was presented without any regard for objectivity. Documentary works were necessarily selective with respect to specific processes, people and events. The Third Cinema concept was subsequently elaborated in relation to films by marginalized groups in other parts of the world, including in relation to black cinema in Britain during the 1980s (Maingard 1995: 657–7).

Documentaries can act as a record of indigenous people's history. Supplementing oral histories in this way can serve to revive fading local histories and provide a sense of community. Native North American documentaries relating the story of the vanishing Indian with historical images are often accepted by indigenous communities as being more objective than the written statements of outsiders. Historians working with tribes use rare footage and photographs to encourage an 'objective' understanding that counteracts the underhand way the Native Americans were treated by European settlers who would deliberately distort or break treaties. Over a 400-year period, 50 million indigenous people died from disease, war and hunger (Leuthold 1997: 730–1). Not only can historical records be seen as an 'objective' way of presenting forgotten histories, native video also enables communication and control. *Wiping the Tears of Seven Generations* (1992), for instance, records a horseback ride by 300 Lakota in the bitter cold to mark the end of a period of mourning for the people killed during the massacre of Wounded Knee – an event that still serves as a powerful symbol of the native past.

The women's movement politicized the personal, enabling race, ethnicity and sexuality to become issues of 'identity politics'. This is exemplified in Margie Strosser's *Rape Stories* (1989), a feminist autobiographical film about the trauma of rape, and further difficulties connected with its representation, which presents its own kind of objectivity. Strosser, as the filmmaker and victim, recasts herself by the end of the film as the victor, through a revenge fantasy which challenges images of the helpless female. 'I wanted to keep . . . the facts straight, what I did and didn't do.' She uses direct address, hand-held camera work and head shots to convey a realistic sense of an historical truth. Her fantasy of taking revenge on the rapist can be construed as a psychological truth about her subjective views on rape and victimhood (Hesford 1999: 194).

Presenting the personal

By 1990 filmmakers from diverse cultural backgrounds were increasingly record- ing the historical world by using forms of self-inscription. The tendency was to acknowledge that subjectivity provided the frame through which to communi- cate a particular version of representation to audiences. This emerges through tone, style and authorial voice rather than through an external, third-party authority. Renov argues that during the period of Direct Cinema, filmmakers, being generally white, male professionals, could shun self-reference from a posi- tion of power 'with the ease and self-assurance of a birthright', whereas many of the current generation of what has been called 'performative documentarists' are representative of hitherto marginalized groups within mainstream society (Renov 1999: 94).

Since the personalized perspective is now so common, what requires analy- sis is not the presence of subjectivity, but its effectiveness and the multiple and contradictory levels at which it exists. The self-reflexive, openly personal 'auteur' film, as well as the essay documentary, both give greater prominence to subjectivity.

Subjectivity and the essay form

Lightweight cameras made the video diary approach much easier and the use of the first person in narration more natural and logical. The form does not have to involve an on-screen presence – it can take an essay form. This particular sub-genre of documentary offers scope for both aesthetic and intellectual originality and is well established. Resnais' *Night and Fog* (1955) is hailed as the pioneer, along with Rouch's *Les Maitres fous* of the same year, and Chris Marker's *Letter from Siberia* (1957).

The personalized film seems to represent a reaction against the apparent but elusive objectivity of Cinema Verité on the one hand, and journalism-dominated current affairs documentary on the other. Whereas a written academic essay may be relatively objective, the documentary equivalent is often more controversial. Pasolini's fifteen-year-long filmography (1961–75) contains several different non-fictional formats, often conceived as intermediary projects, as a sort of dialectical but transitional celluloid notebook. Although some of his factual material was envisaged as a preliminary to fictional projects, *La Rabbia* (1963) was conceived as a documentary, consisting of newsreel clips and archive photos combined with a soundtrack of Pasolini's writings, all presented in response to the question 'Why is our life dominated by discontent, by anguish, by the fear of war, by war?' In one scene, Pasolini's poem on the death of Marilyn Monroe is read in voiceover together with a series of photos and archive film of her life, to the music of Albinoni's *Adagio*. 'The combination of montage and poetic commentary turns Monroe's suicide into a haunting symbol of refusal and resistance against the co-opting machine of the culture industry' (Vighi 2002: 500).

Although ample evidence of personalized self-indulgence exists within the essay form, so does a wry minimalism, characterized by stark and witty observation, and carefully arranged scenes. Harun Farocki, for example, has been branded as a 'maverick among mavericks', but simultaneously hailed as 'Easily the most accompanied essayist' (Arthur 2003: 62). In films like *Still Life* (1997), *How to Live in the German Federal Republic* (1989) and *The Appearance* (1996), Farocki gets into the crevices of corporate life, of advertising, stripping, midwifery, conflict resolution, photography, and a host of other corners. Significantly, he does so with a nuanced observation that is not egotistical, but is political without explicitly saying so in voiceover. Conversely, Michael Moore's *Bowling for Columbine* (2002), for example, can be criticized for its lack of subtlety and plurality, but it does fulfil other basic definitions of the essay form, as outlined by Arthur, by offering a 'discernible subject and a segmental, discursive line of enquiry'. Nevertheless, 'it lacks the will to view itself as not just part of the solution but as part of the problem. That is, it avoids the intuition of its own complicity common to exemplary works in the genre' (Arthur 2003: 62). This is a potential problem for the subjective approach.

Activist subjectivity

Recent activist journalistic documentaries highlight problems of conflict between truth-telling and propaganda. One such case, focusing on the resistance to globalization by regional and environmental groups, concerns India's NBA (Narmada Bachao Andolan or 'Save the Narmada Movement'), as charted by two documentary films – Anand Patwardhan's *A Narmada Diary* (1997, with Simantini Dhuru) and Franny Armstrong's *Drowned Out* (2002) – dealing with the Narmada dams controversy. India is the world's third most important dam builder, and consistent mass protest against construction of the 3,200 Narmada dams in this enormous river valley has continued for almost twenty years. *A Narmada Diary* is shot as a video diary cataloguing five years of ongoing struggle at a point when the construction of the Sardar Sarovar hydroelectric dam threatened to drown over 37,000 hectares of fertile land, including many homes. The aim of both films is clearly to increase support for the protest movement, although opposing views are not excluded. In production terms, actuality footage is used to develop a narrative that catalogues a story of triumphs, defeats and confrontations with power elites. Armstrong's *Drowned Out* takes over chronologically where *A Narmada Diary* left off, demonstrating that in the long and wearisome struggle not very much has changed: there are still broken promises from the authorities, indigenous people suffering, and little alternative for the adivasi inhabitants whose culture, livelihood and lives continue to be threatened by environmentally damaging and economically unsound dam construction.

Campaigners seem to have developed a sense of history, but how far do their most well-known international works conform to existing models of media advocacy? Both films popularized the Narmada conflict internationally, but in the process also championed fresh styles of communication. These two works, through their narratives and styles, have brought a creative and political repertoire of 'engaged' journalism on development issues to mainstream outlets outside of India, allowing us to test the continuing relevance of the subjective concerns of counter-hegemonic discourses (Chapman 2006).

Neither film had an on-screen presenter, and it seems that criticisms of partisanship increase with personality-led films. In 1989 Michael Moore's *Roger and Me* was rejected for an Academy Award because it was considered too personal and biased. Yet there are changes in institutional attitude to be noted here, as boundaries shift on the subjectivity issue. Although both the Narmada films were made as independent productions, *Drowned Out* (renamed as *The Damned*) was screened in the United States on PBS, and *A Narmada Diary* was also transmitted on television stations outside of India, such as Britain's Channel 4. They can be seen as further examples of a shifting attitude towards the presence of subjectivity in documentary films. Indeed, perhaps as a result of such shifts, in 2008 Michael Moore's *Sicko* was nominated for an Academy Award. This film was not made for television but for the big screen, and was promoted mercilessly through the Internet on YouTube and other sites. Moore's cinema-going followers expect his iconic brand of subjectivity, and with *Sicko* this is certainly what they received.

Case study: *Sicko* (2007)

Michael Moore and Meghan O'Hara's film alleges that there is a national conspiracy to defraud the American public of their right to a fair health system. The partisan documentary maker looks at American health care and explores the reasons behind the adoption of a for-profit system, selects individuals neglected by the State, and battles with the insurance companies who have drastically affected their lives. In his trademark combative style, Moore compares the US system unfavourably with free, government-sponsored systems in other countries, as he takes a group of sick Americans to Cuba for treatments they were unable to obtain at home, and even attempts to gain access to Guantanamo Bay, pointing out to the

Fig. 3.2 In *Sicko* Michael Moore interviews a British doctor about the benefits of working for the UK government's healthcare system.

guards through a loudhailer that their prisoners, unlike his passengers, enjoy free health care courtesy of the United States. Moore's hectoring manner assists in the promotion of an extremely biased view of the country's health policy – which, of course, can and should be criticized for its inherent weaknesses. However it is Moore's nose for sensationalism that leads him to compare the fate of American citizens with that of the Guantanamo Bay internees. As with *Fahrenheit* *9/11*, Moore uses technology to cut and paste a very fast-paced and brash conspiracy message, but in the case of *Sicko* this undermines his stated concern for his effected group. Moore uses his authoritative voice to promote his point of view while shepherding his flock of invalids around the world, but too frequently lapses into *telling* rather than *showing*. An alternative approach would have been to engage the audience by showing more of Cuba's top quality universal health-care system.

Some critics of Al Gore's *An Inconvenient Truth* say that there would have been more tension and excitement had oil industry or Republican supporters been able to confront Gore (as if advocacy per se is not exciting enough!). He has also been reprimanded for not exploring alternative viewpoints on global warming. If the film had been a television programme, there would have been more of an obligation to maintain a balance, if not within the film, then across a spread of programmes or by holding a studio discussion afterwards, where alternative standpoints could have been represented. Mark Lawson claims that Moore's cinema films and Gore's project 'are defined by propaganda and over-promotion', and that 'Oscar-hunting documentaries remain a branch of propaganda', pointing to the aggressive editorializing in the cinema, where balance is not required (Lawson 2006: 33).

Opponents of the global warming argument, or 'climate-change sceptics', do not have it any easier. Their own documentary, *The Great Global Warming*

Swindle, transmitted by Britain's Channel 4 in March 2007, was criticized by other scientists for distorting facts and views, and for being misleading to such an extent that they argued the film should not be allowed DVD distribution without substantive changes. Thirty-seven experts grouped together to sign a letter to the regulator Ofcom demanding the removal of misrepresentations. The film was accused of taking a very cavalier attitude towards science, and of being as close to pure propaganda as anything since the Second World War. The broadcaster was criticized for not understanding that science is about the arguments, not about the people who make them. The regulator received 246 complaints; but had all the errors been corrected, as requested, the whole premise of the documentary would have collapsed. Critics pointed out that the issue was not one of censorship, but of quality control. 'All this programme did was rehash debates that were had and finished in the scientific community 15 years ago', according to one signatory of the letter (Adam 2007: 6).

Journalist Geoffrey MacNab thinks that changing styles may 'break the unwritten contract between documentary-maker and viewer' (MacNab 2008). There are plenty of examples of recent documentaries that could be used to examine the claim that the bond of trust between documentary maker and audience is being challenged (see Chapters 7 and 8). Alex Jones' style of filmmaking and extremely subjective approach in his *9/11 Chronicles* (2007) offers a particularly good example in terms of the techniques he uses to reposition the audience's perspective on a delicate subject.

Case study: *9/11 Chronicles* (2007)

Jones' enquiry into the fate of the 9/11 heroes questions the official version of the day's events, and continues the tradition of engagement using frenetic editing of image, jagged sound, rhetoric and phatic pause. This approach – designed to provoke an emotional response from his Internet viewers – seems to concur with Umberto Eco's definition of 'cogito interruptus' and how it supports subjective interpretation:

> cogito interruptus is typical of those who see the world inhabited by symbols or symptoms. Like someone who, for example, points to the little box of matches, stares hard into your eyes, and says, 'You see, there are seven . . . ,' then gives you a meaningful look, waiting for you to perceive the meaning concealed in that unmistakable sign; or like the inhabitant of a symbolic universe, where every object and every event translates into a sign of something hyper-Uranian that

everyone already knows but wants only to see reconfirmed.   (Eco 1986: 222)

Jones' subjective style not only exposes the mistreatment of 9/11 heroes but also shows how perspectives on events are skewed, as the film manipulates the catastrophe to reflect Jones' conspiracy theories. His work is an example of how a growing number of people around the world are questioning the official version of events that day. An example of his film expressing his subjective perspective is apparent in an early scene covering the fifth anniversary of 9/11 at Ground Zero. People are shown milling around fencing covered in photographs, while in the background the names of the dead are read out to the sound of a tolling bell. As the scene continues, other individuals gradually appear, wearing black T-shirts with the words 'Investigate 9/11' printed across them. More arrive in shot and eventually the camera rests on Jones himself delivering a speech on the supposed cover up:

he is also wearing one of the black T-shirts. Innocent onlookers are implicated in Jones' impassioned invective against the government, and thus a visual link is made that seems to stand for a general protest by all.

Other parts of the film intercut between different points of view and coverage of the filmmaker door-stepping various politicians making accusations of criminality. Bill Clinton is filmed being asked if he thought 9/11 was an inside job. He furiously responds, 'How dare you!' Jones uses this clip among a slew of others to advance his view that politicians at the top are covering up. In re-presenting a version of the 'truth', he makes use of free association to relocate the viewer towards a new and potentially awkward perspective.

The popularity of locating the self within historical reports centring on the family and/or earlier cultural and geographic identities, combined with the theorizations of Minh-ha (1992) and Gabriel (1982), amongst others, and the contextualization of scholars such as Hall (1996) and Renov (1999), all contribute to the legitimization of the personalized form. Add to this the new accent on diasporic and intercultural cinema (Marks 2000; Naficy 2001), and an important institutional support for the financing of the form by public service broadcasters such as ABC and SBS in Australia, and a critical mass for the trend towards subjectivity begins to emerge (Naficy 2001: 10).

An understanding of the adaptation of the Australian mainstream to minority personalization in certain documentaries requires acknowledgement not simply of the national immigration context, but also of the global influences emanating mainly from the United States and France during the 1960s and 1970s, through movements for feminism, civil rights, gay rights and an awareness of identity politics. These encouraged a growing body of work from diverse cultural backgrounds in which self-inscription becomes the key to revisiting history in some way. Hall points out that such works need to be situated in the context of migratory movements in the post-colonial world, and above all in relation to processes of globalization, since subjectivity is presented as a transnational product of multiple contexts and discourses (Hall 1996: 4).

Non-fictional programmes that discover and/or piece together fragments of knowledge about the past, particularly about travel, family and other aspects of subjective history, are popular worldwide. Their impact obviously depends on their relevance to national audiences, which in the case of Australia has been identified as 'the desire of the viewing audience for a particular depiction of the migrant experience'. One scholar has identified this as being 'a desire for explanatory and originary migrant hardship and trauma' (Smaill 2006: 270, 279). The stories of people who escaped war, poverty and persecution to establish a new life elsewhere is so well recognized by audiences that it has been appropriated by the mainstream and by Hollywood. Arguably, some personalized documentary narratives of migrant hardship not only enhance the pioneer-as-hero myth, they also form part of a wider acceptance of subjectivity as a creative approach for documentary communication. 'In these films subjectivity is no longer construed as "something shameful". It is the filter through which the Real enters discourse as well as a kind of experimental compass guiding the work toward its goal as embodied knowledge' (Renov 1999: 88).[16] But does this approach divert us away from a wider vision? The answer depends on the way subjectivity is implemented and the level of personalization applied.

Mash-up, documentary and the Internet

'Mash-up' is a Web-application which combines information from disparate sources into an integrated product. The term mash-up originated from a trend in hip-hop music where two songs are overlapped to make a new, often dissonant, sound experience. A mash-up editor takes film documentary techniques and digitally remixes films, speeches and music to suit his/her political message and broadcasts it on the Internet. The concept diverges from a traditional single viewpoint to a collection of second-hand representations of a cultural debate. Representation of society is continued, but the manner in which society is portrayed on the Internet is changed by editorial intention to question the status quo. With the mash-up 'doc' the intention is to evoke an emotional response, but the original material is not necessarily created by the maker, and its authenticity as archive is not necessarily respected. Quite the reverse – mash-up documentaries tend to consist of a hard-hitting barrage of questions, images and noise.

Mash-up is essentially a professionalization of an amateur skill combined with a message. Sitting in front of the computer 'grabbing' video clips and mixing them with other material is a powerful tool for getting a message onto sites such as YouTube. These films are mostly uncommissioned, and often the result of a lone 'politico' who seeks to advance his viewpoint on what is wrong with culture and to open up a debate. It is difficult to say whether or how far they consider the potential viewer – when a broadcaster commissions a programme, they will have in mind a target audience, whereas the mash-up artist seeks a mythical common sympathizer: the masses.

Brett Gaylor is the enemy of traditional documentary filmmakers.[17] As an open-source documentary maker he appeals for contributors to comment freely on any topic through the Internet. He attacks traditional film documentaries because he believes they present closed arguments which fail to reflect the evolving cultural debate. Instead he opts for an open-source method – a deconstructed documentary – which invites several voices to contribute to an open, and presumably never-ending digital debate. There is an inherent flaw in this method: if we are to believe Gaylor's claim that film documentaries present closed arguments it could equally be argued that his open-ended approach betrays the weaknesses of over-inclusion and a lack of focus. He conveniently overlooks the fact that he imposes an editorial structure on his mash-up production. Despite the many contributors, it is not objective but remains a personalized account of the 'truth'.

Do we really need to mash up films to prove that they are 'open texts'? According to Umberto Eco 'artworks are texts' that are open to infinite interpretations and re-editions (Eco 1976: 196–200). Open-source originally referred to the act of making software 'source code' freely available, so that anyone could copy, rewrite and improve it. The principle has since then been applied to culture: now there are open-source novels, paintings and encyclopaedias (Wikipedia, for example). On the film side the trend is towards open-source cinema where audiences take an active role in making a film, suggesting plot twists, dialogues, and even mashing up scenes to tell more stories than the filmmaker could ever have imagined.

Gaylor's 'OpenSourceCinema' website is a 'documentary project to create a feature film about copyright in the digital age', according to his manifesto (Gaylor 2007a). Gaylor conducted interviews with remix icons, made a wiki on the film script, and invited any interested parties to remix his material and/or add their own. As he says: 'Please – comment, change, act, create. Changing is not breaking – changing is evolving. Structure is dissolving. Music is revolving' (Gaylor, 2007a). However, even when made by a collective, a documentary can never be wholly objective. Gaylor as the website editor decides ultimately what is or isn't published – there is always a point of view. Alternatively, changes made by contributors could be infinite, as points of view, and the work itself potentially, may never come to an end. The idea of a never-ending documentary project is facilitated by technological advances, but essentially there is still continuity in the structure of question, dialogue and answer, theoretically supporting, in Gaylor's view at least, a more or less balanced view on any given topic.

Furthermore, there is an ethical as well as a creative issue at stake: Gaylor's untitled film (Gaylor 2007b) questions ownership in the digital age, featuring a disturbing mash-up of George W. Bush's State of the Union Speech mixed with John Lennon's 'Imagine' and coverage of bombings in Iraq and Afghanistan. Although it shares more in common with music videos, it nevertheless raises issues about originality, ownership and the re-appropriation of material.

Conclusion

Documentaries can be seen as either objective or subjective attempts at uncovering the truth, and all documentary filmmakers usually strive to achieve a sense of truth in their work. Differences emerge in the style of execution and sense of perception of a film's presentation. Some of the examples in this chapter demonstrate that subjectivity and objectivity can effectively coexist in the same film. Where does this take the debate? Noel Carroll would have us leave objectivity alone, thereby admitting that it *is* achievable, for he believes that film theorists are too quick to take on impractically big premises which cannot be proved either way.

> If you want to do the sort of critical work one usually finds in relation to Errol Morris, why do you have to commit yourself to the view that there is no truth or objectivity in documentary? It might turn out that some documentaries are true and/or objective, and you might be able to say very interesting things about them. People do useful work in that direction. Why in the world do you have to begin with the most exorbitant premises?   (Privett and Kreul 2001)

Carroll points out film theorists were wrong to identify what they saw as a weakness of documentary – the necessity for selectivity during production – with the notion of objectivity. The two are not synonymous. He admits that objectivity is difficult to achieve, but believes that the scepticism about this 'local difficulty' should not lead us to deny its feasibility or desirability (other disciplines such as history and science still retain objectivity as a principle). He demolishes the arguments of Renov who is sceptical about the ideal of objectivity in relation to both history and documentary, and of Nichols whose suspicion also relates to the existence of institutional agendas within a political or organizational culture that may obstruct a documentary maker's objectivity.

Certainly it is easy to make connections between the concept of objectivity and other 'virtues': as noted above, Carroll argues that confusion and abuse of language have led to an imprecise identification of objectivity with truth, which needs to be addressed. Should we abandon any attempt to define standards of objectivity? Only if we continue to believe in absolutes – of fairness, impartiality, lack of bias. Yet every representation is relative to a perspective, which prompts Plantinga to argue for a relative objectivity, fairness and balance which, realistically, could well be the only sort of objectivity available to the journalistic documentary. The Plantinga thesis is that there *is* such a thing as 'relative objectivity'. This approach demands a sense of responsibility which involves both engagement and distance: we cannot abandon the elusive practices associated with objectivity, for they are still ethically pragmatic.

It is just as important to address levels of subjectivity. Plantinga argues for relative objectivity, but one might similarly argue for the relativizing of personal influence. The best documentaries manage to personalize and reveal in a creative way while avoiding excessive exhibitionism or voyeurism. Yet it is creativity – the very essence of the Griersonian definition – which favours art above science, making impartiality elusive, and allegations of bias more likely. What one person sees as 'propaganda', another person sees as meaningful didacticism or an appeal to activists for further support. Television has absorbed the personal at the same time as filmmakers like Moore have broken new boundaries in terms of what might be acceptable, and enjoyable, to cinema audiences. And there is still a demand for themes that encompass the concerns of the wider public sphere, as both Australian and Chinese filmmakers have demonstrated.

It is possible to be both subjective and objective in the same film, but this is dependent on the filmmaker's perspective. Auto-ethnography, for instance, can avoid self-indulgence if it develops an argument. As Marcel Ophuls said: 'I try to express my political views in my films, but empiricism and pluralism are part of my political views. I do get the facts from both sides . . . I do use confrontation of different points of view by means of irony, contrast, and methods like that to finally put across my own point of view' (Peary and Turim 1973: 41–2). Audiences are so well acquainted with the varieties of documentary style these days that the idea of documentary as an inevitably subjective interaction with the world must surely be acceptable. Critics as well as audiences are well aware that subjectivity runs the risk of being accompanied by narcissism, over-personalization through an on-screen presence, over-indulgence in performative techniques, and the encouragement of voyeurism.

The emergence of cheaper and more flexible technology allows anybody to make a documentary, to edit their films quickly, and to promote them on the Internet. In the context of globalization, technological advances also allow documentary makers to use the Internet as a platform to present their views in regard to sometimes distant debates involving not just partisans and activists but an increasingly large and interactive audience. As the platform becomes more truly global, differentiations and distinctions between subjectivities and objectivities dissolve into the ether.

4 Censorship
Whose World Is It?

Summary

It is easier to deplore censorship than it is to understand and locate it within contexts that will inevitably vary from country to country, across cultures and across time spans. Nevertheless, that is the challenge for this chapter. As a deciding factor with regard to censorship, political context can often be more important than the content of the film itself. Forms of indirect censorship are increasingly emerging, with a range of manifestations that are equally dependent on economic and political influences.

Classic examples of censorship from the canon, occurring at particular crisis moments in history, demonstrate that concern about a film's potential meaning for its audience tends to be the main factor behind decisions to exercise control over a documentary. There are points of continuity here: within mature democratic environments censorship is still ongoing as a current phenomenon. Thus the problem is not simply part of documentary's heritage. For instance, control over what the public see, and the way they see it, is a live issue for the coverage of contemporary wars. Equally, globalization and the neo-liberal environment have led to censorship by the market, and to self-censorship – often within so-called 'democratic' regimes. Here we will analyse the shifting balance of power in conventional censorship in relation to the State, institutional practices, politics, audience reception, connections to the so-called 'free market', and self-censorship. The documentary form will be examined through aspects of the support for or the rejection of controls over content. Technological advances offer new ways of both imposing and evading censorship, and elements of both traditional concerns (such as a film's potential effect on its audience) and of more recent trends (such as use of the Internet and the use of digital cameras to generate DIY footage) will emerge from this analysis of the complex manifestations of censorship. It is a many-headed hydra.

Introduction

Censorship is not simply the opposite to freedom of expression, and it varies in strategy and method according to the system in which it belongs (Darnton 1995: 59) Frequently it amounts to a punitive action taken as a result of some form of institutional disapproval. Hence this chapter continues the emphasis of the previous one on the relationship between documentary and institutional frameworks. As far as regulators and gatekeepers are concerned, censorship is an unfortunate but necessary step when, according to their assessment, a film lacks the appropriate balance between subjectivity and objectivity, or the mode of its representation is inappropriate, or likely to cause undue offence,. However, artistic licence, sometimes coupled with a desire to present a political challenge, can become confused with a filmmaker being given free rein, and this has led many people to question the terms to be examined here. It remains possible to exercise some artistic licence while having only limited freedom of expression, as a result of either regulation, or the presence of a controlling institutional culture, or self-censorship.

To understand sensibilities towards censorship it is necessary to appreciate the potential impact of the documentary form's critique of dominant ideologies in society. Sometimes this arises purely by implication, as when a film presents an aspect of social reality that challenges the outlook of those in power. The process is not new. During the great Depression, a Joris Ivens documentary entitled *New Earth* (1934) looked at the effects of a land-reclamation project in Holland. The workers who have laboured hard on the reclamation subsequently discover that the 'grain is not for food, but for speculation' and that 'there is too much grain and not enough work'. The film was banned from exhibition in a working-class suburb of Paris on the grounds that the reaction of many poor people living there would be to march on City Hall demanding bread (Rosenthal and Corner 2005: 399). This example raises two themes that will be examined later: first, the importance of political context when analysing reasons for censorship (hunger marches, for instance, were common during the Depression of the 1930s). Second, the importance of attitudes towards historical memory (in France, for marches in demand of bread date back to the 1789 French Revolution, and even earlier).

Censorship tends to provoke emotion. In 1997 an Iranian filmmaker received a standing ovation at the Cannes Film Festival simply for attending. Abbas Kiarostami's film *The Taste of Cherries* (1997) had been granted permission to enter the competition at the last moment after a dramatic escape from censorship problems, grounded on religious objections to the subject matter which centred on a pre-occupation with suicide (Maslin 1997: 13). But Censorship is not confined to so-called 'repressive regimes'. In 2004, French filmmakers protested that a new and severe form of censorship was being applied in their country. Their protest formed part of a wider discontent demonstrated by a petition with 16,000 signatories, including publishers, musicians, architects and actors, complaining that the government was waging a financial war against the creative professions – despite the fact that the French state has spent the most in the world per capita on subsidizing culture over the last fifty years (Johnson 2004).

Censorship always forms part of a wider historical context. At the time of writing, documentary makers have played an important role in bringing the uncomfortable realities of life for the Iraqi people to the attention of a wider public. Institutional support can help such films see the light of day. For decades in Iraq, no television or film production free of government control was possible, but in 2004 when the climate for creative production was still dangerous and insecure, the Independent Film and Television College was established in order to encourage young Iraqis to express themselves. Some of the documentaries that have emerged depict a stark reality. *Blood of My Brother* (2005), for instance, directed by Andrew Berends), and screened in London by DocHouse,[18] tells the story of an Iraqi family's struggle to cope after the killing of their eldest son by American troops. In a short, *Omar Is My Friend* (2005), directed by Mounaf Shaker, a student at Baghdad University works as a taxi driver to support his wife and four children. He reveals his aspirations as he manoeuvres his tired old vehicle around tanks, traffic jams and checkpoints.

Censorship is usually inextricably linked to contentious issues such as politics, finance and religion. Most countries have regarded censorship, together with propaganda, as a legitimate practice in times of war. The subjects of censorship fall in to recognizable categories worldwide: social and political threats to law and order; offence to mainstream religious or political ideas; the depiction of sexuality and violence. Film's experience of censorship has of course been relatively short compared to that of print. The Catholic Church's *Index Librorum Prohibitorum* (Index of Prohibited Books) existed for 407 years from 1559, 'whereas Danish film censorship lasted a mere 53 years (1907–1960) and had thus been and gone by the time the *Index* was abolished in 1966' (Jones 2001: 797).

Documentary's survival as a means of freedom of expression since 1945 has been influenced by the pressures of international events and movements and by trends in politics and ideology. Thus films have inevitably been judged within a context of power-bloc clashes, withdrawal from colonial empires, the emergence of new nations, military and authoritarian one-party states, and the growth or renewal of religious fundamentalism. At different times in history, and under various regimes, prevailing institutional cultures enforce outlooks that exclude alternative ideas and counter-cultures. There have been some eras in history, such as the period since the 1980s, when forms of containment and restrictions on radical expression have prevailed over resistance and oppositional thought. Mainstream media have been complicit in this process: 'Intellectual freedom of expression is ineffectual when the media either co-opt and diffuse, or distort and suppress, oppositional ideas, and when the image-makers shape public opinion so that it is hostile or immune to oppositional thought and action' (Kellner in Marcuse 1991: xxxi). Clearly forms of both domination and resistance need to be analysed.

Circumventing the State

In Poland, documentary shorts disguised by aesthetic style prospered under communism because they offered a back-door opportunity to challenge the officially sanctioned memory. During the 1970s and early 1980s, Polish documentary makers used the medium to examine social issues, presenting 'metaphorical confrontations with the communist regime' (Skaff 2003: 133), aimed at encouraging political change. An emphasis on the aesthetic meant that documentary could compete successfully with feature films, and contentious content could sometimes escape close scrutiny. Documentaries were, and are still, positioned 'within the limits of arts rather than of journalism and propaganda', which means evaluation in aesthetic terms (Lubelski 2002).

Yet, an end to repressive autocracy may not necessarily mean an end to censorship. It is a common misconception that censorship is confined to authoritarian regimes and only exists in democracies at times of war. Critical theorists from the

Frankfurt School and Herbert Marcuse in *One Dimensional Man* onwards have examined how social contradictions are contained, and possibilities of liberation are suppressed, by a one-dimensional advanced capitalist system. After the collapse of communism in Poland (referred to as the 'Freedom Shock') in 1989, the state-owned and controlled film industry transmogrified into independent studios. Private companies now experienced the double-edged sword of freedom in that they had to make their own financial and production decisions. The subsequent abolition of censorship may have meant that 'hidden archives and victimized dissidents no longer constituted the Polish film landscape' (Haltof 1995: 16), but this was replaced by market dominance, necessitating 'safe' topics and conformism for profit. Specifically Polish or 'difficult' topics would not sell (Kornatowska 1993: 47). The majority of documentaries these days are broadcast on television, and although some manage to attract worldwide audiences, audiences seem to have become tired of political and historical issues which were so common previously.

Freedom from communism has been accompanied by an immense and 'sometimes unbearable sense of responsibility' (Aitken 2006: 1058), for the producer has to exercise self-censorship in deciding what audiences will see. As Winfried Junge, the East German filmmaker of *Die Kinder von Golzow* (1961–), puts it, 'the new situation closes mouths in a different way' (Richter 1993). *Die Kinder von Golzow* is the longest-running documentary film project in the world. Inaugurated during communist rule by the famous DEFA film studios, the project follows the lives of a class of pupils born between 1953 and 1955 in the village of Golzow.

Self-censorship

In many countries, television journalists have frequently been called upon to exercise self-censorship, but other creative people are equally vulnerable. Jean Renoir, who moved to the United States, once told his son that during the McCarthyite period it was better to keep one's indignation to oneself. The great French film director avoided the censors by applying self-censorship; for as he said to the Indian director Satyajit Ray: 'You don't have to show many things in a film, but you have to be very careful to show only the right things' (Bhatia in Sherzer 1996: 60).[19]

Self-censorship can involve decisions by the filmmaker to avoid certain aspects or themes altogether, or it can involve a decision to favour an aesthetic approach which will appear more indirect, or perhaps metaphorical. In France, the Algerian war was a sensitive subject for fifty years afterwards, but mentioning it just a few months later was the risky strategy adopted by Resnais, in *Muriel, ou le temps d'un retour* (1963), Pontecorvo in *La Bataille d'Algiers* (1966), and Marker in *Le Joli Mai* (1963). In the latter, Marker cautiously and subtly forces his audience to face the subject of political responsibility for a war that they would rather forget, and all of this under the guise of an apparently innocent question – the same one that Rouch and Morin started with in *Chronicle of a Summer* (1960) – 'Are you happy?' (Chapman 2007: 16). *Le Joli Mai* was temporarily censored the year before it was released commercially in

1963. In a scene filmed in the Montmartre cemetery, the narration refers to the cult fiction anti-hero 'Fantomas'. The shadow of this classic popular villain, we are told in May 1962, will be cast upon Paris. He becomes the means of signalling repression of the war and a haunting symbol of the need for historical accountability. Yet Marker never admits that his filming is about the country's reaction to the Algerian conflict. The editing ensures that interviewees blame themselves for failing to acknowledge the evils of colonialism such as torture and racism, while responsibility for the war is allocated to an amorphous, apolitical French public.

The problem of censorship becomes more extreme in the context of war, and the restrictions, often of military matters, can amount to self-censorship by the media. Examples abound in the writings of John Pilger, particularly in *Hidden Agendas*, where he calls for more current affairs programmes and documentaries 'which attempt to make sense of the news and which explain the "why" of human events' (Pilger 1998: 58). Self-censorship was evident during the 'terribly superficial and sanitized' US coverage of the 1991 Persian Gulf War (Zinn 2000: 630). Canadian Charles Lynch admits: 'It's humiliating to look back at what we wrote during the war. We were a propaganda arm of our governments. At the start, the censors enforced that, but by the end of the war we were our own censors. We were our own cheerleaders' (in Bell and Webb 1998: 164).

Influences on self-censorship can usually be traced back to a combination of institutional politics and media organizational requirements, implemented by people who 'have usually internalised the constraints imposed by proprietary and other market and governmental centers of power' (Herman and Chomsky 1994: xii). When official censorship regulations are removed, they may be replaced by subtler strategies that still influence levels of reception for documentary. As Britain's leading radical director, Ken Loach, points out: 'so-called liberal and democratic societies have their own means of censorship, more insidious than the bureaucrat in his office' (in Bell and Webb 1998: 281). Coercion is unnecessary; according to Herman and Chomsky, the freer the society, 'the more sophisticated the system of thought control and indoctrination' (Maher and Groves 1999: 139). This amounts, they claim, to what they describe as a 'self-supportive propaganda function' that relies on internalized assumptions to feed a form of self-censorship sustained by market forces. Predictably, 'an advertising based media system will gradually increase advertising time and marginalize or eliminate altogether programming that has significant public affairs content' (Herman and Chomsky 1994: 17). They describe a now famous 'propaganda model' with 'invisible forces' ensuring that the mainstream media act as propagandists. It consists of five news filters that remove all 'undesirable elements' from ever being well publicized: money (corporate concentrated ownership and the dominant profit motive); advertising; reliance on information provided by government, business and experts (as sources for programming and news); 'flak' (as a way to discipline the media); and 'anti-communism' (though these days there are new 'evil empires' [Cogswell 1996: 83]). Although documentary is not Herman and Chomsky's main focus of attention, contextual influences and prevailing political climates will mean it is not immune from their analysis. Clearly the process requires further examination.

The self-censorship of the market and funding

In the environment of the free market, competitor television channels all show entertainment programmes during prime time as a strategy to attract more viewers. Even amongst public service broadcasters, 'serious' programmes have been relegated to what the industry calls 'graveyard slots' late at night. This can be seen as a form of censorship via the market, but without official censors.

The issue is an institutional problem for television and has made for a lively debate in France amongst intellectuals (see, for instance, Jaigu 1990), who criticize the tyranny of opinion polls and 'focus groups'. These can end up reflecting the narrow-mindedness of broadcast executives, forming a barrier to inventiveness which some commentators see as yet another form of censorship. The claim that the main culprit here is the influence of television is best articulated by sociologist Pierre Bourdieu, who argues that the effects of television on journalistic practices, and on cultural production more generally, are far more significant than the influence of popular literature, fiction and newspapers. Advertisers want programmes on television to attract popular audiences, hence broadcasters take fewer risks. Intellectuals, according to Bourdieu, are forced to either play the game – that is, accept the conventions and hence censorship – or be silenced (Bourdon 1998: 235). The range of subjects that sponsors usually find attractive, or at least acceptable, is limited. They are unlikely to want documentaries on television that criticize corporate activities such as environmental malpractices, arms dealing or investment in tyrannical regimes. Barnouw cites an example of an environmental documentary series that failed to procure sponsorship on NBC at a time when companies were spending plenty of money on environmental promotion, including advertising. The reason was that the series suggested corporate failure, in contrast to the company's message of reassurance (Barnouw 1992: 135).

An alternative route for the filmmaker is to go for grant-aided funding (Chapman 2007: 29–31). However, prospects have become more limited. Deregulation worldwide has been accompanied by de-funding for independent documentary, acting as an effective restriction on freedom of expression. 'The concerted effort to de-fund art and media institutions has in reality been a purge of the enemies within to purify the nation not only of difference, but of the nonprofit organizations that provide access to the production and public exhibition of this work as well' (Zimmerman 2000: 31). This process has been monitored in the US context as a form of arts censorship by annual publications such as *Artistic Freedom under Attack* (People for the American Way, 1992–95). The fact that the religious right have lobbied extensively on questions of morality, obscenity, family values and decency has had an influence on the support for and amount of screenings given to independent documentaries on issues such as sexuality, AIDS, abortion, and also race and immigration.

Zimmerman highlights two other trends that emerge from this research in the United States: censorship at local level has consistently increased, and attacks have focused not on the artistic merits or otherwise of creative works, but rather on the infrastructures that exhibit them, targeting schools, film festivals, galleries and museums (Zimmerman 2000: 32). The use of taxpayers' money for the arts is a predictably vulnerable target in many countries. President Reagan's attempts to de-fund endowments in the US led to a 40 per cent drop in financial support for the arts between 1979 and 1989, in a situation where the world's richest nation already had one of the lowest arts-funding levels and the shortest history of arts funding of any industrialized country, spending one dollar per person compared to 20 dollars per person in France and Germany (DiMaggio 1991: 222).

Since the Reagan period, deregulation and the widespread acceptance internationally of neo-liberal economics have created a financial climate in which individual concentration of media ownership has become easier. This climate makes the analysis of Herman and Chomsky into the ways the propaganda system suppresses certain kinds of information – such as enquiries into the role of corporations – all the more timely. Powerful individual magnates such as Rupert Murdoch have been able to exercise corporate censorship within the so-called 'free' market. Robert Greenwald's documentary, *Outfoxed: Rupert Murdoch's War on Journalism*, demonstrates how the system operates on the ground, as we see how audiences are led to believe in highly constructed news articles fitted to a distinctly conservative political agenda. The exclusion of other, more progressive views can be interpreted as a form of censorship.

Case study: *Outfoxed* (2004)

Greenwald's film is a powerful exposé of how Rupert Murdoch's Fox News Channel manipulates news and distorts the truth, misinforming the public and compromising the journalistic integrity of its employees.[20] The narrative evolves into an example of wheels within wheels, or in this case, of censorship within censorship, within censorship. Greenwald's combination of talking heads, artful arrangement of controversial Fox News clips, and photographs of internal memos provides ample evidence (supportive or damaging) of the channel's 'trademark' political affiliation to the far right.

The film is a careful and thorough examination of Fox News' editorial values, using one of the channel's slogans, 'We Report. You Decide' (another is 'Fair and Balanced'), as a departure point from which to raise questions about their style of combined news and commentary and declarations of fairness. Greenwald tackles Fox's managerial system, 'eliminative journalistic' techniques, and production practices as an example of how the channel decides what will be shown to the public and what will not. Both named and anonymous ex-employees (some voices are digitally altered) comment on the culture of fear promoted by Vice President of Fox News John Moody's daily memos to staff directing them what to say and how to say it. In censoring the news, Moody promoted a feeling that the Fox News Channel is not so much a news service as a political campaign for ultra-conservatism. One memo shown, dated 9 May 2003, directs reporters to support the Republican stance on abortion. Moody writes:

> Let's spend a good deal of time on the battle over judicial nominations, which the President will address this morning. Nominees who both sides admit are qualified are being held up because of their POSSIBLE [sic], not demonstrated, views on one issue – abortion. This should be a trademark issue for FNC today and in the days to come.

Supported by the testimony of ex-employees, the film's premise is that Fox News' style of journalism is far from its claim of 'Fair and Balanced' reporting. One interviewee blames Murdoch for Fox News' polarity of opinion. David

Brock, President and CEO of Media Matters for America, says: 'Murdoch wants all news to be opinion because opinion can't be proven false.' John du Pre, a former Fox News anchor, agrees with this view in the film and says: 'we weren't necessarily a news-gathering organisation so much as we were proponents of a point of view'.

Greenwald's film also demonstrates Fox News' censorship of the news in the way in which experts, guests and subjects are treated. 'Eliminative journalism', according to author Robert McChesney, is 'unique to Fox'. The film shows how guests on Bill O'Reilly's comment show are told to 'shut up' when O'Reilly doesn't agree with their views. O'Reilly denies this when accused of rudeness by a viewer. The next section shows a barrage of 'shut-up' clips as clear evidence of O'Reilly's partisanship, and proving him a liar. Experts and guests are selected largely from the right and therefore, the interviewees claim, Fox News is not balanced or fair. The consultants are under contract to say what Fox News wants them to say. Ex-CIA officer Larry Johnson relates that 'facts don't seem to have any effect' on Fox News. Johnson was told to call suicide bombings 'homicide bombings', among other edicts he refused to obey. Fox News stopped using him after only eight weeks. High-ranking commentators assess that 83 per cent of Fox News' prominent guests are Republican, and just 17 per cent Democrat. Invited Democrats also tend to be less well-known and centrist conservative. John du Pre also talks of weak news items being pushed to the fore on Fox News. Stories about Ronald Reagan (who was greatly admired by Murdoch) would regularly make the news. For Fox News, Reagan's birthday amounted to a 'holy day'. Du Pre was sent to cover a celebration of the event attended by a class of fourth graders painting pictures. He points out that since neither Reagan, nor family members, nor any officials were present, this story had no news value. He received a furious call from John Moody who, watching the broadcast, decided it wasn't nearly celebratory enough. Du Pre says he was suspended for few weeks after that broadcast.

Greenwald examines Fox News' coverage of the Bush Administration's reasons for going to war in Iraq. Clips show how Fox promoted the Republican war effort by using fear of the enemy's facelessness and potential power to damage US drives for action into Iraq. Also shown is another pair of Moody's memos concerning casualties in Iraq: 'Do not fall into the easy trap of mourning the loss of US lives and asking out loud why are we there?' Two days earlier, he wrote a memo during US military operations in Fallujah: 'It won't be long before some people start to decry the use of "excessive force." We won't be among that group.'

The interviewees discuss Fox News' use of fast-paced rolling graphics, banners, and slogans as part of the channel's drive to monopolize right-wing America, even using the Stars and Stripes to consolidate their claim to 'Fair and Balanced' reporting as representing the American people's view – all of which makes a mockery of the slogan 'We Report – You Decide.' The case presented is that Fox News adopts an internal practice of political censorship.

The issue of Fox News Channel's partisanship and *Outfoxed*'s charge of extreme political bias encroached into fiction programming. Fictional television drama show *Boston Legal* rewrote an episode, *Let Sales Ring* (2005), centred on the issue of free speech, in which criticism of Fox News had appeared as well as substantial parts of *Outfoxed*. The episode featured a story about Chi McBride, a school principal, who places a 'Fox Blocker' on every television in the school, and accuses Fox News of generating 'hate speech'. Stuart, a student, protests that this action is censorship and takes his case to the fictional lawyers. However, before the episode aired, documentary filmmaker and journalist Rory O'Connor (2005) obtained *Boston Legal*'s writer and producer David E. Kelley's original script and its subsequent alteration, and notes that all mention of censorship criticism, Fox News, and indeed any other channel was edited out from the script. O'Connor published the two versions of the script on the *Alternet* website on 10 March 2005, three days before the programme aired. The re-edited programme aired on 13 March 2005 with all reference to Fox News removed.

It is not known if Fox News objected to the direct juxtaposition of *Outfoxed* clips to the mention of Fox News in the script and the film's implied criticism of Fox News' practices. The fact that evidence of the script change exists suggests that someone at Fox News had seen a preview of the programme and its original script and had perhaps complained to ABC. No official reason for the content removal was issued by ABC, Kelley or Fox News. It is ironic that a fictional programme about censorship should be censored in turn.

In addition, ABC refused to run an advertisement for *Outfoxed* adjacent to the programme. On 9 March 2005, four days before the programme aired, Greenwald wrote on his blog:

> In an effort to spread the word about *Outfoxed* to the millions of people who will be watching *Boston Legal* on March 13th, our distributor, Disinformation, attempted to buy an ad on ABC during the *Boston Legal* episode, about *Outfoxed*. However, they have refused our money, refused to make suggestions to the ad so they would run it, and in short have said no! Now, if they were not airing an episode in which *Outfoxed* is the center of the storyline, it MIGHT be justifiable on some grounds about fear of conflict. But to refuse to air an ad, when the storyline of the show features *Outfoxed* . . . well, it boggles the mind.   (Greenwald 2005)[21]

Institutional practices

Censorship is relative. Bourdon argues, in relation to the period of censorship that applied to French television under de Gaulle's leadership, that although such approaches pose a real threat within democracies, they should not be over-rated. In this case the press and radio could still criticize the regime, and documentaries were screened theatrically. In production terms, especially for current affairs programming on television, threats of censorship or bans sometimes arise from the fact that the film covers one particular aspect in depth, but does not contain a balance of arguments within its discourse. The long-running UK current affairs series *World in Action* was usually assessed in this way by regulators. One film that highlighted the cost of Britain's defence spending in March 1963, and another programme in the same series, from June 1964, focusing on inadequacies in the training of British athletes, were banned by the ITA before transmission (Goddard, Corner and Richardson 2001: 80). Such examples are small fry compared to some other historical experiences of censorship. Bourdon quotes a distinction made by the philosopher Primo Levi in 1976:

> in merchant societies there is too much information and it is hard not be over-whelmed by advertisement; however, those who *want* to know find out the truth; whereas, in Nazi Germany, the rules of the game were totally different, those who knew kept silent, those who did not know did not raise questions, and those who raised questions did not get answers.   (Bourdon 1998: 234)

A documentary maker who refuses to conform under capitalism faces lack of funding and potential limits on distribution, whereas censorship in a fascist or authoritarian regime, and the dangers involved in challenging it, are severe. This is not to say that we should ignore censorship that is subtle and indirect: funding problems and the day-to-day compromises that many documentary makers may have to face within specific institutional cultures often reveal forms of indirect censorship.

A film does not have to be radical in order to face a ban. Marcel Ophuls' film *A Sense of Loss* (1972), for example, faced a refusal by the BBC to transmit it, despite their financial interest in the project, because it was 'too pro-Irish' in relation to the longstanding issue of independence for Northern Ireland (*Sunday Times*, 5 November 1972). The film opposed violence on both sides, but was critical of the Unionist cause by implication. It consisted of interviews with ordinary Protestants and Catholics, politicians and soldiers. Ophuls later admitted that he was in favour of negotiation in the conflict: 'I don't think this comes out in the film, but I am very much in favour of the British army staying there for the time being' (Peary and Turim 1973: 44).

During the restrictions on broadcasting coverage of the Northern Ireland conflict and the 1988 ban on interviews with paramilitary organizations (see Chapter 3), civil liberties groups called such broadcasting activities 'prior restraint censorship' – that is, the State only took action if the ban was broken, but did not become involved in daily operations under such constraints. Broadcasters had to police themselves, subject to a flawed form of 'democratic' control. Documents released in 2005 reveal the political pressure, secrecy and damaging divisions this caused within the BBC. Leon Brittan, Home Secretary at the time, demanded that the BBC ban Paul Hamann's programme *Real Lives: At the Edge of the Union* on security grounds. He was backed by the BBC governors. The move was strongly opposed by the Director General, and by BBC staff, who called a strike, supported by journalists and production staff at other news channels. Within a month the board of governors changed their minds, deciding that the film could be broadcast, with minor changes. Ironically, both sides in the Northern Irish conflict – Republican and Loyalist – were happy with the programme. When it finally went out it was watched by 4.8 million people – a good enough viewing figure – and there were sixty telephone calls from viewers, about average for this kind of programme. Approximately half complained, while the other half could not see what all the trouble concerning the film had been about (Rolston and Miller 1996: 117).

Censorship can arise either through legislation or as a result of statutory regulation, with the relative balance varying between these two tools for restriction. Writing during the 1990s, observers of media law commented that 'the recent history of moral and political censorship in Britain has been characterised by a move from criminal law to statutory regulation' (Robertson and Nicol 1992: 594). They noted that although the amount of freedom from censorship in Britain is better than in most Third World countries, by comparison with the United States, Canada, France, Scandinavia and Australia, it is less so. However, since the early 1990s, a combination of new, 'lighter touch' regulatory systems and the introduction of the Human Rights Act have resulted in much greater freedom from official censorship in Britain.

Television also brings us visual conventions: war propaganda glorifies and turns even mundane images into a spectacle, and this can amount to a form of censorship because debate is restricted by the nature of coverage. It is not merely a question of restricted information. The nature of images also needs to be considered. Zimmerman argues that the State has a productive relationship with the image:

> Whether they be Pixel-vision images from the nose of a missile during the Gulf War, 16 mm film wing-side views of bombs dropped over North Vietnam from B52s, or *New York Times* photographs of weeping Bosnian Muslim women burying their children . . . Despite the different historical and geographic locations of these wars, these images inculcate a fetishistic relation for the spectator, using repetition to annihilate all differences and distinctions and to blunt our senses.
> (Zimmerman 2000: 59)

Such fetishized, state-manufactured images of war function as a spectacle that has the effect of containing or excluding all other senses, because the specific explosion of sight and sound saturates as it overwhelms all other senses, thereby inducing passivity. Hence the possibility for debate is precluded, as is language and speech as a way of talking back. 'The independent documentaries that counter war, then, accomplish much more than the simple dismantling of the spectacle effect, slowing down the image and rethreading it into history. They address the silencing strategies of the image through language and invent new minor languages rich with memory-in-the making' (Zimmerman 2000: 60).

Deborah Scranton's *The War Tapes* is an example of how documentary makers circumvent military censorship. Three US soldiers took up her offer to take a video camera to the Iraqi frontline during 2003–4, to film action against insurgents, and gained unique footage denied to embedded journalists. She also includes film from the soldiers' families as they react to news from the front.

Case study: *The War Tapes* (2006)

Documentary filmmakers wishing to avoid overt military control are becoming ever more resourceful in their attempts to tell a story. Deborah Scranton, Robert May and Steve James' *The War Tapes* tells the story of three National Guard soldiers of Charlie Company, 3rd battalion of the 172nd Infantry (Mountain) Regiment, who served on the frontline fighting insurgents in the Iraqi Sunni Triangle, as part of Operation Iraqi Freedom in 2003–4. The subjects volunteered after Scranton had made the opportunity available – with the permission of the unit's commanding officer – to the whole company of 180 soldiers before deployment to Iraq. Twenty-one men accepted her offer to take a digital camera, five filming the entire period, three of which were featured. Over 800 hours of film were collected, the soldiers communicating via email and instant messaging to brief Scranton on events and to receive instructions. The editor selected the stories of the final three soldiers: Sergeant Steve Pink, Sergeant Zack Bazzi and Specialist Mike Moriarty. The direct contact gained Scranton access to 'hotwash', a military term for an immediate reaction after an event, a reaction often missing from official military reports that results in a softened and professionalized overview of occurrences in the field.

The technology used enabled a sense of immediacy and intimacy to be conveyed in real time, as often two cameras were deployed in a patrol vehicle – one camera mounted on the gun turret, the other on the dashboard. The aim was to make viewers feel more sympathetic to the fate of soldiers serving in Iraq and to describe the 'disconnect' of war and its effects thorough documentary film. Documentary maker Ken Burns, one of the Tribeca award judges, said of the film:

> 'Politics isn't ignored – the film isn't afraid of politics, but it's able to transcend the politics. In the aftershock of the film, people will try to come to terms with their own feelings and their own politics.' He described [Scranton's] ability to direct the film via instant messaging as 'a remarkable accomplishment'.
>
> (Richard Allen Greene 2006)

Only one tape – recording violent and heavy fighting in Fallujah – was held back by the military (the filmmaker substituted stills). Scranton herself said in an interview on the Tavis Smiley Show that she was concerned for the viewer's sensitivities and may not have used that particular tape: 'the story is told in the film itself. I can tell you from my perspective, even if we had gotten the tape, I don't know if I would have used it. There is a line where you want to tell the story, but, by no way, go so far that it's unbearable for people to watch' (Scranton 2006). Such self-censorship is part of the editor's remit to inform the viewer about the realities of war 'from the inside out versus the outside in . . . in a new way of trying to make a documentary', she says (Scranton 2007). This is perhaps a disingenuous tactic on Scranton's part to dispel a sense of revulsion at footage showing horrendous scenes of death and suffering in other areas of the film. The effect of rendering the Fallujah incident in stills depicting scenes of death in awkward juxtaposition with the moving film of live events of dying and death is powerful. This appeal to the story in both moving and still formats performs two functions; it tells an otherwise inaccessible tale and also shows up the fine line between personal and military ideas of censorship and sensibility.

Scranton also shot 100 hours of footage of the soldiers' families as they react to the unit's despatch to Iraq with moving farewells, anxiety for their safety when news reports come in of events over the tour, and tearful reuniting of soldier and family. The whole 900 hours of footage was compacted into 97 minutes and shows a unique perspective as it affects those directly involved in the action. The family responses are juxtaposed in real time with retrospective coverage.

In conclusion, Scranton shows ingenuity in bypassing the traditional routes to finding sources in sensitive zones. The downside is that she is remote from the filming process, but in editing the final returned films from the soldiers and their families, she adopts a flexible approach in order to escape the worst excesses of military control.

Historical memory and censorship by inertia

At times, a filmmaker has to be determined to challenge a kind of benevolent amnesia with documentaries that sometimes carry an uncomfortable message. As the Czech novelist Milan Kundera has said: 'The struggle of man against power is the struggle of memory against forgetting' (quoted in Zinn 2000: 629). Is this challenge exacerbated by the postmodernist condition that acts as an influence, however obliquely, on forms of indirect censorship such as self-censorship? Postmodernism has been construed as damaging or oppositional to the study of history,[22] and this could lead to history having to be justified by the demands of the present, rather than pursued for its own sake. Instead, the present is used to angle the presentation, in the way that McElwee does in *Sherman's March* (1986), for instance. Postmodernism seems to have given us fragments of the past, frequently through memory via the eyes of witnesses living in the present, as in Lanzmann's *Shoah*.

The recording of earlier history in documentaries is further impeded by lack of visual evidence, necessitating recourse to fictional techniques. This could result in indirect censorship for earlier, pre-photographic history at the subject-selection stage. This is especially problematic for ancient and early medieval themes where fewer artefacts exist, or where philosophical stances are important, but do not lend themselves easily to the medium.

Furthermore, it is possible to argue that television and mass-market print publications and films can become a means of repressing popular memory. In such films, according to Foucault, 'People are shown not what they were, but what they must remember having been . . . It's vital to have possession of this memory, to control it, to administer it, tell it what it must contain. . . . And when you see these films, you find out what you have to remember' (Foucault 1989: 92–3). If a documentary presents a memory of an event that has been repressed by official censorship, it can then create an important and powerful counter-discourse. Foucault's comments were made with reference to the depiction of the Second World War and the Resistance in a number of films: 'since memory is actually a very important factor in struggle (really, in fact, struggles develop in a kind of conscious moving forward of history), if one controls peoples' memory, one controls their dynamism. And one also controls their experience, their knowledge of previous struggles' (Foucault 1989: 92).

Marcel Ophuls' *The Sorrow and the Pity* (*Le Chagrin et la Pitie*, 1969) carries an uncomfortable message. It was one of the most influential and important documentaries of the twentieth century, yet was only finally broadcast on French television in 1981. The film was intended to challenge the myth of the glory of the Resistance (propagated widely in public by de Gaulle) that was rapidly becoming standard as the 'official version' of France during this period. In France from the end of the Second World War, right up to 1997 when President Chirac recognized that French history included Vichy, governments all wanted to deny any connection between the Republic and the Vichy regime. The film clearly had radical implications. Reactions to what Ophuls refers to as 'the traumatic discovery of various national majorities' unlimited capacity for treason, selfishness, and corruption in Nazi-occupied Europe' (1980: 6) reflected not only on attitudes and political culture at the time but also during subsequent Pompidou and Giscard years (Bowles 2006: 22). Allegedly, one Gaullist official said in reference to the film's 'anti-patriotism': 'Myths are important in the life of a people. Certain myths must not be destroyed' (Milestone Films 2000: 6).

During 1969–70 several journalists referred to the French public as not being sufficiently 'adult' to be able to face certain truths about collaboration with the Nazis during the German occupation, as revealed in *Le Chagrin et la Pitie*. Jean-Jacques de Bresson, director of the public service broadcaster ORTF, defended the decision not to broadcast the documentary by stating that it 'destroyed myths that the French still need to have' (Seknadje-Askenazi in Camy 2002: 103) – notably the Gaullist myth that the majority of people united around the courageous Resistance. The audience needed to be protected from the wrong sort of messages.

However, it is a common misconception that Ophuls' film was banned by French television for twelve years – the very audience that the producers had hoped to reach. In fact, the film was funded by German and Swiss broadcasters, not by French broadcaster ORTF, from whom Ophuls and producer Harris had resigned in indignation over 'censorship' of student protests during May 1968. In a 1978 *Wide Angle* interview, Ophuls set the record straight:

> Afterwards, the French journalists, who were the co-producers, tried to sell the film to French television, but I don't know why they tried. What they were trying to do was portray themselves as true martyrs and the victims of Gaullist censorship. So they mounted big press campaigns complaining that French television had banned the film. French television hadn't banned the film, they hadn't bought the film! (Milestone Films 2000: Appendix C)

Nevertheless, Ophuls was effectively blacklisted: 'I was marginalised, because people hated the film so much. So I was unable to work in France for a very long time' (Fraser 2004: 34). Ophuls argues that the 'scandal' at the time the film came out 'was less a function of what it showed than a function of what other films were not showing'. He calls this censorship process 'controlled repression, exercised by mass media executives' (Ophuls 1980: 61, my translation). His comments came in the form of an open letter to *Le Monde* and *Le Nouvel Observateur* papers, but they did not publish it, although the film was screened worldwide on television, with ABC buying the network television rights in the United States.

Context and timing are everything. In the wake of May 1968, the fact that the film did not give great attention to the role of de Gaulle would have accounted for the official disapproval. At the time of its release, political comparisons could be made with America's conduct in Vietnam, and that of France in the Algerian liberation struggle. The film held a mirror to cinema audiences: what would they do under such circumstances? The darker side of French collaboration with the Nazis after the fall of France was gradually discussed more publicly as historical knowledge increased and a new generation emerged who were willing to accept a more complex and qualified interpretation of the Nazi occupation.

Using wartime newsreel intercut with interviews, Ophuls tried to stem the erosion of historical memory by presenting in a sober way villains as well as heroes: German war veterans, Resistance fighters, teachers, farmers, politicians, shopkeepers, intellectuals. In *The Sorrow and the Pity*, the French are allowed to judge themselves (James 2004: 5); indeed they were forced to reassess their wartime history. The film examines four years of collective destiny, with its courage, cowardice and commitment, and concluded 'that individual life and politics cannot be separated' (Yergin 1973: 20).

What is it that made this documentary – part essay, part oral history – so popular? The personalized stories are disturbing. Maybe non-French audiences were surprised that Ophuls had been able to capitalize on the moment immediately post-1968, when the middle-aged French bourgeoisie were caught off-guard, when they were able and willing to be more self-critical than usual. The results are also ambiguous: a couple of school teachers do not remember seeing German troops in Clermont-Ferrand, nor did they notice certain pupils disappearing from the classroom. An aristocrat recalls his philosophical attraction to fascism, but his revulsion at wearing the Nazi uniform of the French Waffen SS division. Witnesses are given enough rope to hang themselves, with little intervention from the filmmakers. There is no commentary, instead the interviewer becomes the author. The film has been criticized: 'no female Resistance fighters were interviewed, the Catholic Church emerges unscathed, and the present generation of French leadership is missing in action'. Yet its stoicism has also been noted: there are no tears in this long-form revisionist classic (Doherty 2001: 50, 52). What disturbed the Gaullist myth was the fact that, as one observer comments, 'The authors have placed their spotlight not on the 1940s, but instead on the end of the '60s, after a decade of Gaullist rule' (Rousso 1990: 134, my translation). The emphasis then shifts to fact, and memory of fact, and the disturbing inconsistencies that this involves. So, for instance, a well-known champion cyclist, Raphael Geminiani, states that Clermont-Ferrand was not occupied, followed after editing by Marcel Verdier who declares that there were Germans everywhere. The historical record of events comes not from the State, or official institutions, but from the 'annals of the participants, mainly the victims, leaving for other generations the narrative of their pain and the visual and aural traces of their memories' (Furman 2005: 169, 183). At the time, this approach was new, and its piquancy seemed dangerous.

Political contexts

What may seem logical during one period of history and set of political circumstances may seem irrationally harsh and unreasonable in retrospect. An example is the changing viability of the FCC's 'Fairness Doctrine' in the US, which specified that both sides of an issue should be given airtime. It represented a late 1960s and early 1970s form of regulatory activism articulated by citizens' interest groups, along with worries about violence and the television provision made for children. This was at a time when access to cable and support for the public system was increasing. It was short-lived as a tool to combat bias from broadcasters. In a changing political climate it came to be seen as an unacceptable infringement of commercial broadcasters' freedom of speech, constitutionally guaranteed by the First Amendment (Chapman 2005: 243).

Perceptions of political acceptability and the nature of communication within the public sphere are slow to change, especially when subject matter touches on a severe wound. Alain Resnais' *Night and Fog* (*Nuit et brouillard*) was commissioned to commemorate the tenth anniversary of the liberation of the Nazi concentration camps after the Second World War. However, the collaboration of the State during German occupation was still not discussed in films, at a time when 'national interest' was the primary concern (Langlois in Aitken 2006: 1119).[23] The film was censored until Resnais disguised the uniform of a French policeman who appeared in footage guarding an internment camp, so as not to make any connection between the French authorities and deportation.

At the time, a film censorship board granted visas for both internal and external screenings, a system which was also adopted in India after independence. Some historical examples of censorship appear farcical these days, while others that remain are more insidious. In 1958, legislators in the state of Tamil Nadu in India discussed imposing a ban on the use of rock and roll music in films, but no action was taken because a satisfactory definition of the genre proved impossible! (Jones 2001: 804). India may be officially secular, but legal deference to the sensitivities of Hindus and Muslims has led to censorship of documentary makers who tackle the dangers of religious fundamentalism.

Anand Patwardhan's *In the Name of God* (1992) has won national and international awards, but was initially not shown on national TV, so Patwardhan was obliged to argue in court that the broadcaster Doordarshan had a duty to respect the public's right to information by screening it, and that not showing the film on TV was a denial of freedom of speech, both guaranteed by the Indian Constitution. They finally transmitted it in 1997. Patwardhan has faced almost continuous opposition from the censors. India is one of the few democracies where censorship rules are followed rigidly (*The Hindu*, 9 June 2005), which means that as a documentary producer Patwardhan has had to expend more effort fighting legal battles than he has making films.

The fate of the film in New York City demonstrates that censorship is still on the agenda, even in 'democratic' societies. The American Museum of Natural History decided to screen *In the Name of God* along with Patwardhan's *We Are Not Your Monkeys* (1993) to complement an exhibition as part of the 2002 Margaret Mead Festival in New York. After complaints about their decision, the screenings were quickly cancelled and moved to New York University. As Patwardhan commented: 'The events in New York City also reveal the way Hindutva [Hindu fundamentalism] exploits liberal guilt and the rhetoric of multiculturalism, while showing no compunction about its own record' (Rajagopal 2002: 279). Patwardhan has campaigned for the abolition of censor certificates for national awards and films.[24] Critics construe the attitude of India's Central Board of Film Certification as being censorious of peace. As recently as 2002 the board called for six cuts in Patwardhan's award-winning three-hour documentary, *War and Peace* (2001), that warns of the dangers of nuclear war in the Indian subcontinent. Demands for cuts included a call for removal of all the footage of the prime minister, ministers and other political leaders, as well as a short reference to a corruption scandal which had already received four hours of coverage on prime-time television.

The point of the documentary was to promote peace, which makes two of the other cuts all the more astonishing. The first was the deletion of a song describing the assassination of Mahatma Gandhi. The second was the removal of a sequence in which a neo-Buddhist Dalit leader condemns the choice of the Buddha's birthday as the date for the 1998 nuclear tests. In the light of the fact that the Buddha has always been associated with peace, he also criticizes the use of the Buddha's name in announcements about the success of the explosions. As one writer commented at the time: 'It is a strange world where nuclear weapons are believed to help and prevent war and a film on peace is seen as a potential instigator of violence' (Ammu 2002). For Patwardhan, the issue is wider than his own documentary, or even the contradictions in policy from a film censorship that permits pornography, but bans peace. He believes there are broader implications for the right to freedom of speech and expression, even though these are guaranteed by India's constitution. He refers to 'the near absolute ideological control that is exercised over the global media. The images the world needs to see, the facts it needs to hear, are often doctored or suppressed' (Patwardhan 2004).

The fortunes of *The Gate of Heavenly Peace* (1995), by Carma Hinton and Richard Gordon, demonstrate the elusive nature of the holy grail of fairness. The film has been praised by critics for its impartiality ('Rigorous and critical as to facts and methodology' [Chen 1996: 21]), lack of sensationalism and the way it demystifies the role of students as romantic campaigners for democratic reform during the Tiananmen Square riots in Beijing, China in 1989. The film is not an attack on China's communist government: the filmmakers are veteran Sinophiles who lived in China in the 1970s and 1980s, although they subtly weave in their own view that, in a modernizing country, the shadow of past Maoist language, as expressed by some dissident leaders, will not suffice.

It was the conclusion of the film that was contentious: the idea that extremists on both the rebel and the government sides wanted the Tiananmen massacre to happen. Using an archive of 250 hours of footage, augmented by television material and interviews, the film seems deliberately to embark upon a mission to record history. The central irony is an uncomfortable one: the polarized approach of both sides made the tragedy inevitable. Student leader Chai Ling, in an interview on the eve of the now famous massacre, reveals that she and some others are hoping for bloodshed: 'Only when the Square is awash with blood will China be awakened.' According to one critic, Chai Ling is held responsible in the film for the massacre, by refusing a strategic retreat when in fact she did not have the power to keep people in the Square (Friedman 1997: 582). Again, it is the implications of the message that provoke controversy. 'By using this interview extensively, the film suggests that, had the student leadership been moderate and rational, the massacre could have been avoided, and China's democracy movement might have had a more promising future' (Sheng 1996: 1151).

Chinese student dissidents condemned the film, with Chai Ling attacking producer Hinton in the Chinese press for 'hawking (her) documentary film for crude commercial gain by taking things out of context and trying to show up something new' (Cheng 1996: 90). At first, during 1996, the authorities were half-hearted in their attempts to prevent the screening and the initial report from agents who attended the New York International Film Festival premiere stated that the film was 'not as damaging to us as might have been expected' (Rayns 1997: 25). They had attempted unsuccessfully to persuade the organizers not to include the film. Then, following the death of leader Deng Xiaoping, long-range censorship by a global effort to suppress the film began to occur. Planned screenings in 1997 in both Singapore and Seoul were cancelled after pressure from China. In the former country, there was no protest, but in Korea, there was a full public airing from the press. Meanwhile, the film enjoyed rapid commercial success in Hong Kong, despite, or maybe because of, its long-standing tradition of self-censorship aimed at placating Beijing. Timing was crucial: the screenings came just months before Hong Kong reverted to Chinese rule. In the first five weeks of opening at a Hong Kong cinema, 16,000 people sat through the three-hour programme, with an estimated half of these from mainland China (Gilley 1997: 44). By 1997 the documentary had been show in seventeen countries and at many more film festivals, with Chinese embassies worldwide protesting about the screenings.

Political sensitivities that influence censorship also need to be understood at the level of individual shots. It is precisely the details that sometimes reflect attitudes and context. When Allied troops first entered Nazi concentration camps at the end of the Second World War, they were accompanied by the media (Chapman 2005: 195). Some of the documentary newsreel footage made at the time – originally intended for screening to the German people, to encourage remorse as part of the de-Nazification process, but suppressed for forty years because of political sensitivity – was made into a film, *Memory of the Camps* (1985), and a longer version, *A Painful Reminder*, issued the same year. But the footage of mass graves being dug, then filled with emaciated corps was so harrowing that the British government suppressed the very film that their own Ministry of Information had commissioned. Alfred Hitchcock had been recruited to advise on the construction of the footage, but his intervention resulted in an establishing shot which, according to one scholar, may well have been what clinched the official censorship. Blonde children play before a bucolic Bavarian cottage in an idyllic forest setting. The camera pans through the trees to reveal barbed wire and piles of flesh and bones. This pan tells a poignant story, revealing 'the heart of darkness beating within the German people – more than the footage of the camps alone, which was potentially damaging to the post-war alliance' (Rabinowitz 1993: 120).

Potential audience reception

The censor tries to anticipate all the meanings that audiences might receive from a film once it is exhibited. There may be a fear, for instance, that a film could incite unrest, hence the peace and security of the population have to be protected by a ban. The 'cause célèbre' in the annals of 'protective' censorship was Peter Watkins' *The War Game* (1965). Possible public reaction was the main reason that this BBC drama documentary was not transmitted. In particular, its effect on elderly viewers who might be alone at night was cited (BBC n.d.), and the corporation's managers were mindful of the panic that had ensued in the United States over Orson Welles' radio broadcast of *The War of the Worlds* way back in 1938 (Chapman 2005: 152). However, the political concerns went deeper than this: in content terms, Watkins' film questioned the feasibility of survival after a nuclear offensive: 'In predicting the collapse of social order, moreover, *The War Game* challenged conventional views of British society as cohesive and consensual' (Chapman 2006: 89). Such attitudes are grounded in a specific historical context that has since changed, but the significance here is that there will always be limits to how far an institution can go in allowing dissident voices to surface and challenge established thinking.

Fifteen years later, during a public debate as to whether it should now be broadcast, supporters pointed out that not only had it become an historical document, but it also remained the best attempt to imagine the unimaginable – what effect a future nuclear attack would have on Britain. The BBC was accused of trying to stifle debate on nuclear policy and of wanting to shield the public from graphic illustrations of the horrifying consequences of such warfare. It was finally shown on British TV, twenty years later, in 1985, to coincide with the fortieth anniversary of the bombings of Hiroshima.

Why was it not shown at the time? After all, the film has become one of the most influential anti-war films of the twentieth century, and spearheaded twenty years of CND (Campaign for Nuclear Disarmament) campaigning. Enormous public pressure led to the granting of a licence for limited release to film clubs. It also had a limited theatrical release by the British Film Institute, won the BFI Academy Award, the United Nations Award and the Special Jury Prize. Hollywood gave the film an Oscar for Best Documentary Feature. Was the BBC's censorship of *The War Game* – a film they actually commissioned in-house, made on a shoe-string budget and using amateur actors – an act of cowardice? Defence strategists at the time argued that people could survive, and a country recover from, a nuclear attack. Watkins' film showed this to be untrue. This message was not compatible with the government's plan for a gradual education of the public into acceptance of the inevitability of the nuclear option. Watkins had carried out meticulous research, interviewing scientists and a cross section of interested parties, who warned of the dangers of nuclear fallout and of the hugely destructive potential of firestorms (Chapman 2007: 11).

Events surrounding the controversy over *The War Game* have been discussed at length ever since, mainly because they represent one of the defining moments in the complex relationship between the British state and the medium of film and television. At the time the BBC claimed that the decision to ban the film was made without any pressure from the government, as an entirely internal decision. Watkins resigned from the BBC in protest and launched a vociferous campaign in defence of his film. This was matched by the passionate dedication of peace activists who tirelessly organized screenings in church halls, schools and other venues, in order to ensure that the nuclear debate continued. Thus initial efforts to ban the film only resulted in making it more famous, despite the continuing ban on television screenings throughout the 1960s and 1970s. By the time it was finally transmitted in 1985, it was hailed as a 'classic' by the same organization that had banned it (Cook and Murphy 2000: 132).

In terms of the political climate at the time, support for the peace movement was at its zenith, bolstered by fears in the wake of the Cuban Missile Crisis which had brought the superpowers so close to a nuclear war. Opinion polls suggested that between a quarter and a third of the British public supported CND (Chapman 2006: 79), so Watkins was striking a popular chord. But there were other contrary pressures at the time which should also be taken into account. Much of the press, the Conservative opposition in parliament, and the conservative media pressure group for 'viewers' led by Mary Whitehouse, all exerted pressure on the BBC to be 'professional' (objective/detached). An indication of how audiences still receive the film was provided by one reviewer: 'it is one of the most powerful pieces of television ever made: no one who saw it will forget the grey, windswept, smouldering devastation of its shattered urban landscapes, or the deadpan exactitude of the commentary' (Murphy 1997).

Bourdon, while referring in retrospect to 'an archaic vision of order in politics, society and morality', draws up a list of concerns for the censors of French television in 1960, a period when the country was seriously divided over attitudes to the prolonged and painful decolonization war in Algeria. Even after that date, films that did not adhere to official versions of recent history were not broadcast. The fears of the censors at the time demonstrate the range of issues from which audiences should be protected:

(1) Any criticism against the head of State, the government and public institutions.
(2) Questioning the policies of 'friendly countries'.
(3) Too favourable comments about the opposition.
(4) Too much attention to social unrest.
(5) Allusions to painful episodes of recent history such as the German occupation and collaboration or the Algerian war.
(6) Any topic likely to offend public morality. (Bourdon 1998: 232)

Set in Bridgewater, an institution for the criminally insane in Massachusetts, Frederick Wiseman's *Titicut Follies* (see Chapter 8) was equally if not more disturbing to audiences. Typical was a response from Robert Coles: 'What really hurts is to see the sight of human life made cheap . . . the inmates needlessly stripped bare, insulted and mocked' (Coles 1968: 18, 28–30). In 1967, a Massachusetts Superior Court Justice permanently banned it from public showing worldwide and ordered all copies seized and out-takes destroyed. This was the first American film to be banned for reasons other than obscenity or military secrecy. It was on the grounds of the individual's right to be left alone – or privacy.

   Bridgewater's administrators and employees were pleased with the film until reviewers were so damning of the institution, taking their cue from Wiseman's bold selection of camera movements, that make the institution appear cruel and insane, despite the absence of commentary and contextual facts. The people involved were forced onto the defensive by the reviews. New scandals in 1987 involving inmate suicides resulted in court rulings that the State should make changes in practices. Wiseman argued that if the film had been shown twenty years earlier, some changes might have taken place that would have prevented the deaths, and the attitude towards him might have been different: 'I'm not seen as a pornographic Cambridge lawyer. The *Follies* has been legitimised by time' (Taylor 1988: 98). The case was finally settled in 1992 so that the film could be shown to general audiences. Even today, the film is still powerful and disturbing.

Conclusion

The status of documentary within the public sphere, as it relates to political conditions and threats to freedom of speech, has always been problematic. Documentaries contribute to the never-ending unravelling of secrets from the past, for 'light shed on one area of the past leads us to the edge of another shadow'. A single documentary has the potential to destroy the equilibrium of accepted thought, but in the long run the censor/regulator is fighting a losing battle, for 'Only a temporary equilibrium can be achieved which, in time, will be challenged. It is the continuum of history' (Langlois in Lloyd and O'Brian 2000: 118–19).

   The word censorship shouldn't be used as a catch-all for every problem that documentary faces; we need to be precise. Yet when we analyse specifics more closely, there is clearly still a problem with censorship under a number of different circumstances and guises in different parts of the world. Censorship does not have to be official to be effective. In the future, it is likely that indirect forms of control on expression, such as self-censorship and market influences, will become even more important.

Deregulation and reductions in funding have had an effect on the role of politics, difference and dissent. This has determined which documentaries are made. 'The quest to de-fund the arts infrastructures strips the nation of its histories, its imaginations, its visions, reducing its public functions at exactly the same time that transnational capital seeks to deterritorialize nations' (Zimmerman 2000: 41). Alternatively, technological development and increased audience awareness have combined to make the Internet a popular forum for protest. This has the potential for the dissemination of ideas, but nevertheless, it is still only pressure from citizens that will bring about change: 'Unless far more of us choose to become citizens rather than consumers . . . even the most advanced media technologies cannot, by themselves, engender a truly informed populace' (Zinn 2000: 628). That is the bottom line for censorship and our responsibility to defend documentary within the public sphere. Edmund Burke once pointed out that it is necessary only for the good man (and woman) to do nothing for evil to triumph.

5 Authorial Voice
Editorial and Message

Summary

Documentary viewers engage in the content and editorial approach of the film as well as its style and structure, but is 'voice' connected to aesthetics and approach, or to subject matter? Can a factual film avoid the elements of 'authorial voice'? This chapter looks in more depth at ways in which argument and viewpoint can be expressed as authorial voice and how these interface with a creative approach. In the context of documentary, authorial voice refers to what the documentary is saying – what sort of comment it is making on the world – but the argument presented here is that the message of a film depends on an unavoidable triangle of authorial intention and skills (both aesthetic and technical), subject matter, and audience interpretation.

The power of a documentary resides in the potential challenge that its message or argument may make to accepted views. Stories that examine the complexities of ordinary people's lives can provide an antidote to traditional or stereotypical thinking. The voice of the text is a discursive one which responds to particular historical situations and is conditioned by them, for, as with documentary more generally, the nature of authorial voice is a product of its context. Voice applies to all forms of documentary, and cannot be identified with any one single feature such as voiceover or dialogue. Thus, although Direct Cinema films do not usually offer historical context or an obvious perspective, this should not be construed as a total absence of authorial voice. Authorial voice is even an issue in styles of documentary that appear to have a neutral stance, such as the compilation documentary intended as an historical record.

Digital and non-linear formats make possible a fresh way of approaching authorial voice, because they allow for structures that encompass several different perspectives. However, the traditional narrative style remains a dominant factor in many digital films with a strong authorial voice, for example Alex Gibney's *Taxi to the Dark Side* (2007) and Charles Ferguson and Audrey Marrs' *No End In Sight* (2007). The Internet has made access and audience participation easier. Films such as *An Inconvenient Truth*, made with the intent to encourage participation, offer audiences the opportunity to become involved in a campaign. This can strengthen the cause, the dissemination of the message, and the range of follow-up activities that accompany the film: all of these act as forms of active engagement by audiences.

Introduction

It is not easy to analyse how authorial voice emerges, for it involves both linguistic and visual operations. Historically, fiction film and documentary have developed in tandem, sharing technology, themes and contextual political influences. The much-debated question of the blurring of distinctions between fiction and documentary serves to signal the possible relevance of the theorization of authorship within film studies, which revolves largely around fictional works and how a text is 'read'.

Authorship can always be understood as a historically specific and variable aspect of creation that legitimizes authenticity. As social and political values change, so will ways of expressing them. Authorship does not have to be attributed to one single person as an individual act of creation or origination. This approach is influenced by Roland Barthes' idea that there is no longer much sense in talking about the 'author' of a novel or a film, because the signifying systems, and in the case of cinema the film language, are so powerful that they provide the central focus. Thus meaning is produced at the point of readership/spectatorship: the text offers a position for the spectator by establishing particular methods of address.

This field of scholarship now recognizes that the role of criticism is not to discover the author, 'but to discover the history and the discursive organization which is foundational for the text, and which negotiates its relationship with its historical audience. A theory of authorship, now, involves a consideration of the position of authors within specific histories' (Caughie 1981: 1–2). Thus it is important to recognize the way authorial voice has evolved and been expressed within documentary history. It is possible to trace a route from Griersonian 'exposition', with its heavy reliance on commentary, to Cinema Verité and Direct Cinema's observational techniques, as a reaction to these limitations, through to the interview style that attempted to redress the limitations of Verité, ending up today with the self-reflexive documentary. However, the evolution is not as tidy as this – reflexivity, for instance, began with Vertov in the 1920s, and so cannot be seen simply as a modern-day phenomenon. Likewise, elements of Cinema Verité style were later integrated with other techniques in a 'mix and match' approach (see Chapter 2)

Equally, it is neither possible nor desirable simply to transplant theories of authorship in fictional film to the specific case of documentary, not least because the idea of a single, all-embracing approach has been challenged as scholars recognize the requirement for work on authorship within specific fields (Caughie 1981: 3). Furthermore, there are neglected areas of enquiry that this study seeks to address, such as the place of the author within industrial and cultural institutions and the way that commercial considerations influence the author – especially important for television documentaries. Debates about fictional film have centred on how far the director transforms the film material into an expression of his personality, but documentaries need to be assessed less in terms of what they reveal of the directorial personality and more in terms of how that individuality is expressed in the content. Individuality is not so much a test of cultural value as a means of communicating authorial voice or message.

The exercise of authorial voice by a filmmaker in a television context is usually at its most obvious in a single documentary as opposed to a series, for the latter may be constrained by a format that has to be adhered to. The single documentary's voice can surprise – something that pleases broadcasters (who always want to find new ways of engaging and entertaining audiences). Yet when it comes to marketing and distribution, broadcasters favour returnable formats or long series which can act as building blocks in the schedule – with the result that the authorial voice of a single film can be drowned out by numbers. In this respect, TV can threaten the profile of documentary's authorial voice, whereas it may flourish in the context of cinema and DVD, as witnessed by the success of Al Gore's *An Inconvenient Truth* and by Michael Moore's esoteric brand of authorial voice, in *Roger and Me* for instance. What is surprising in both these cases is that they deal with serious subjects – global warming and the decline of America's traditional manufacturing base, respectively.

Choices about the style and tone of authorial voice are made early on by producers (Chapman 2007: 2–4). Producers of essay, science and history documentaries traditionally choose the more formal, usually linear, and 'objective' third-person voice. But this does not necessarily entail adding a voiceover commentary: a film's authorial power may be plainly observed in the style of editing. Claude Lanzmann's *Shoah*, a film about the survivors of Nazi death camps revisiting the physical and mental locations of their incarceration, contains neither archive footage nor narration, and moves from generalities to specifics, yet it is overtly authorial in its attempt to tell the viewer about the human condition.

Uses of documentary and authorial voice

Nichols interprets voice as a continuation of the rhetorical tradition and the way an orator of old would address issues requiring a social solution (Nichols 2001: xvii). One of the differences is that there are a variety of ways in which voice can emerge, and there are no quick fixes for logical understanding. Although documentary defies scientific analysis, we can associate certain techniques that are used in the service of authorial voice, according to certain functions of documentary, as identified by John Corner (2002: 259–60):

1. Documentaries that form part of the 'project of democratic civics' tend to have extensive and heavy commentary, since they act as a form of promotion or national advertising. In the case of Lorentz's *The River* (1937), 'The Roosevelt administration is described implicitly as a formal mirror of the Mississippi' (Arthur 1993: 116). Arthur demonstrates, in relation to this film and to *The City* (1939), how 'Promotion of New Deal ideology provided a foundation from which to allegorize the role of documentary in a naturalised landscape of cinema.' Corner notes that within this category, 'a directly affective as well as a cognitive impact is often sought, an intention for which the use of music and a range of rhetorical tropes, visual and verbal, gives support' (Corner 2002: 259–60). Certainly the filmmakers involved in New Deal sponsored films had progressive intentions, hoping for a form of production that

'retained the human scaled collaborative ethos of their former radical projects while enhancing the ability to affect public opinion' (Arthur 1993: 117).

The Griersonian tradition was didactic, and the voiceover served to provide authority, even if it appears presumptuous by its domination of the visuals. Griersonian-sponsored films of the 1930s and New Deal documentaries may not build strong individualized characters for audiences to identify with, but structurally they do allow for dramatic expectation and closure, and the message is often communicated in a wonderfully poetic way. In fact, in *Listen to Britain* (1942) the poetics is even stronger because of the complete absence of commentary. Even in the classic *Night Mail* (1936) it is wonderfully poetic, underlining the point that a traditional 'voice of God' narration is designed to operate with the visuals to help us interpret what we are seeing, and to influence what we think about the images that are represented, in the way a novel narrates a commentary. Still used extensively on television in wildlife series and documentary specials such as history series, this mode of address is widely accepted by audiences who recognize the educative role of documentary, even if it has been discredited in art-house circles.

2. With the second category, 'documentary as journalistic enquiry and exposition', frequently used in television current affairs, the 'reportage' involves not so much promotion as the need to examine visual evidence, often through the use of witness.

3. The third category, 'documentary as radical interrogation and alternative perspective' (Corner 2002: 259–60), does not have an authorial voice that claims any 'official' position, or journalistic aim, but rather a critique of the mainstream. When an author comes from the same milieu or culture as the subject, he or she will have a different relationship with the content than a complete outsider. A wide range of techniques are used, sometimes presented in a different format to traditional television journalism. These can include Direct Cinema observation, forms of dramatization, or ways of presenting testimony that involve extended interview. There are plenty of innovative examples that challenge traditional commentary, such as Trinh Minh-ha's questioning in *Naked Spaces* (1985) of normal soundtrack narration that is presented as a means of confusing the issue of authorial voice.

4. In the fifth category, 'documentary as diversion' is a form of factual entertainment, usually for television, in which techniques borrowed from fictional formats are used. These present what Corner calls 'high-intensity incident' (reconstructed accident, police raid), or 'anecdotal knowledge (gossipy first-person accounts) and snoopy sociability as an amused bystander to the mixture of mess and routine in other people's working lives' (Corner 2002: 260). As authorial voice is here overshadowed by the entertainment function, which impacts on representation and viewing relations, this use of documentary style (rather than documentary project) is not our main concern in this chapter. Reality TV may be authentic footage, but it cannot be categorized as 'documentary' because there is no authorial voice. The visual moment is captured in a superficial way as evidence that is not analysed critically using any abstract, symbolic montage or argument.

'New documentary' in the 1980s and 1990s

The problem with applying matching categories to forms of authorial voice is that some films do not fit neatly into one category or another. What has been euphemistically called 'new documentary', from the late 1980s and the 1990s, rejects the boundary distinctions of traditional documentary modes. Some 'new documentaries' reaffirm that documentary is always a complicated form of representation. They also demonstrate that it is possible to combine self-reflexiveness with observational techniques, interviews, voiceover and sometimes the on-screen presence of the filmmaker. The role of the documentarist as an active producer of discourse as well as a witness and participant emerges as distinctly different to the role of a neutral narrator or knowledgeable reporter.

Although the films of Errol Morris, Ross McElwee, Michael Moore and others do not obviously share a political outlook or social ambit, they are all organized around 'a set of strategies in which authority and verisimilitude are rhetorically embedded in a negative register of denial, mockery, and collapse' (Arthur 1993: 127). This definition merits further examination. In Moore's *Roger and Me* and in McElwee's *Sherman's March*, authorial voice centres on what did not happen – the interview with Roger Smith, the account of General Sherman's attack on the Confederacy – so that aesthetics in the service of authorial voice becomes one of failure. On the face of it, our evaluation should be made easier by virtue of the fact that both filmmakers are on screen, and thus central to the recording, but their self-absorbed disconnection (McElwee fails to find love, Moore fails to procure an interview with the boss of General Motors) gives the impression that they are out of control, when in fact their position is a very powerful one. Their presence 'is marked by a studied self-deprecatory distance and a result-ant celebration of formal disjuncture and disorientation' (Arthur 1993: 128). Textual (non-) authority becomes vested in the immediacy of the pro-filmic event, but unlike Direct Cinema, this is embellished by a complex combination of other post-production techniques such as associative or metaphoric editing patterns, discursive sequencing, and analytic commentary. Although technology of recording, as an instrument of cinema, is visible and used reflexively as an inadequate mediator on location, neither Moore nor McElwee examine the post-production editorial conventions through which their authorial voice is enhanced. This limits the distinctiveness of their challenge to the conventional vehicles of authorial voice.

Alternatively, the range of techniques used to critique can involve disruption and distancing, influenced by non-realist cinema, such as Trinh Minh-ha's abandonment of the spoken word in *Reassemblage* (1983). She presents imagery with a non-verbal soundtrack. This film may well come across as a postmodernist critique of anthropological documentary, but it needs to be viewed within the context of post-colonialism and not simply as an example of the capacity of postmodernism to destabilize. There is still an authorial voice, although there is no central thematic focus and the film does not give the viewer any anthropological knowledge about rural Senegal in ways that we are used to. Rather the authorial voice attempts to demonstrate the instability of both the viewer's and the social actor's identity, to underline how this can change. Meaning is left open, uncertainty is emphasized. Commentary by the director tells us that this is a film about Senegal, and then immediately asks, 'but what is Senegal?'

Technically, the director then proceeds to break every rule in the book for traditional film production – which in itself establishes an authorial voice. Jump cuts are used to present different takes exploring the meaning of various camera positions, the voiceover talks tangentially to the pictures and the soundtrack begins and stops abruptly, as if seeking to tell us that the materiality of film involves processes and choices that are not usually discussed. What exactly is the message of this apparently non-authoritarian reflexivity? We are left to ponder. A generous interpretation may well conclude that Trinh Minh-ha is offering 'ways of knowing and experiencing that are more attuned to cultural hybridity, heterogeneity, and contingency' (Stollery in Aitken 2006: 1109). This can still be an uncomfortable message for audiences – which is precisely what is intended.

Role of subject matter

With documentary, we have an additional element to consider: whether authorial voice is connected to aesthetics and approach, or to subject matter, which exists outside the film. In this respect, Corner refers to the 'thick' and the 'thin' text.

> The more a piece of documentary work displays such features as, for instance, a strong narrative and diegetic crafting, the placing of its human subjects as 'characters', a self-conscious styling of its images and sounds, a reflexive play across its own project, the easier it is to approach it as an artefact, the outcome of expressive authorship. The more it adheres to the core conventions of exposition and illustration, the more aesthetically modest it is, the more propositionally and descriptively direct, then the more it is necessary to engage it within the terms of *what it is about*, to take the 'outward' route into the world of the referent and the theme.
> (Corner 2000: 683)

So, with the former, 'thick' text, the substantive topic may only be a 'second-ary' ingredient, whereas with the latter, 'thin' text, such as an investigative film, engagement with the topic is absolutely necessary. Yet predictably there are some documentaries that don't fall easily into either one category or the other, and seem to display elements of both as described above. *An Inconvenient Truth* clearly requires engagement with the topic, but stylistically it also contains production elements of 'thick text'.

Case Study: *An Inconvenient Truth* (2006)

There can be a tension between what Corner calls 'the outcome of expressive authorship' and what a documentary is about. This lies at the heart of the debate about authorial voice as it relates to director David Guggenheim and presenter/author Al Gore's *An Inconvenient Truth*, as an example of a non-linear, activist-inspiring film that uses the Internet to empower viewers.

The film mounts a persuasive case for immediate action against global warming. There is plenty of data and the science is 'deep-layered, vivid, and terrifying' (Denby 2006), but it is also concise and accessible. The authorial voice derives from the subject matter outside the film, but also from Gore's performance as the 'talking head' conduit for information. Although his attempts at humour

Fig. 5.1 Al Gore uses PowerPoint to demonstrate the effect global warming has had on the environment.

tend to fall flat, and the brief personalized sequences showing him on the road assuming the mantle of eco-warrior seem a little contrived, the film is involving and interesting. The overall impact, editorially, is undeniable. Critics usually focused on the substantive topic – that is, what the film is about: the way global warming affects everything on this planet, from oceans to hurricanes, in an interconnected way. The message takes precedence over technical or performative aspects, although most critics noted that Gore's media projection was surprisingly good for someone who had previously been dubbed 'Mr Freeze'.[25] However, once again the saving grace for performance is connected to content, since, as most critics noted, it is Gore's passion for the environment that makes his performance warm, engaging and believable. He openly admits that his motivation in making the documentary is to change the minds of the American public about the urgency of the issue.

The way that Gore presents his argument merits analysis. First he sets the stage by providing a reason for the audience to listen – colourful images of the earth taken from space remind us how beautiful the planet is and how many theories once considered to be fact turned out to be fallacious. Simultaneously he has set the stage, engaged the audience and framed the issue to support his arguments. There are no bullet points or boring presentation of numbers; instead he ensures that we remember the argument. Thus, when Gore wants to emphasize that temperatures rise with increases in carbon dioxide, he shows a climbing graph, but then climbs himself into a mechanical lift that raises him five foot into the air, while continuing to refer to the rising graph: 'When some of these children who are here are my age, here's where it's going to be. You've heard of off the charts? Well here's where we're going to be in less than 50 years.'

Documentary is a personalized medium, and this one is no exception, despite its theme. Gore's own family stories provide further leverage for him to argue against the critics: if we can identify with him, then the chances are that we'll identify with his arguments. In fact, the narrative is driven by the intercutting of

Gore's private and public personas. Referring to his sister Nancy: 'She died of lung cancer. My father had grown tobacco all his life . . . He stopped. It's human nature to take time to connect the dots. I know that. But I also know there can be a day of reckoning when you wish you had connected the dots more quickly.'

The director wanted a personal story, and to this end conducted long audio-only interviews with Gore, in which he pushed the former Vice President to be intimate, in order to provide the film with an emotional drive. Yet Guggenheim has been criticized for failing to reveal much about Gore, while simultaneously lionizing the man more than the cause: 'the film's efforts to humanise Gore are only remotely tied to his passion for the environment . . . the picture's attempt to connect the near-death of Gore's young son with the father's love for the earth is as manipulative as the film's use of Katrina footage . . . The brainwashing style of *An Inconvenient Truth* . . . makes Moore look like a sober, impartial journalist' (Larsen 2006).

One difference, of course, between *Fahrenheit 9/11* and this film is that Moore does not come across as saviour of the world, whereas there is a danger that Gore will fall into that trap, leading critics to the conclusion that '*An Inconvenient Truth* not only makes the wrong argument – that Al Gore can save the universe – but does so poorly' (Larsen 2006). The criticism is repeated in the Australia/New Zealand edition of *Time South Pacific* (6 May 2006), describing the film as 'the tale of a scorned washed-up politician transformed into a laptop-wielding ninja whose Power Point could rescue the planet from the forces of greed and indifference'.

Gore presents a repeatable message and calls for our help. People can reverse the trend: 'The only thing we're lacking is the will to act, but in America that will is a renewable resource.' But is a repeatable message propaganda? The film has been called 'A shamelessly propagandist documentary that has all the artistry and subtlety of a campaign ad . . . [a] dull and didactic presentation'

(Larsen 2006). Despite the hype surrounding the film, the warm reception it received at the 2006 Sundance and Cannes film festivals, and the award of an Oscar for Best Documentary, there have been two main and interconnected criticisms over the way the authorial voice is presented in the film. The first points out that Gore spends too long on the problem and not long enough on the possible solutions, although this is probably due to the fact that climate deniers have in the past had a disproportionate influence in media coverage of global warming, especially in the United States. The second criticism is that the debate would have been sharpened if dissenters had been shown on screen debating with Gore, or at least if interviews with them had been played off his contribution. This would have demonstrated the importance of discourse in raising and validating Gore's role as facilitator of environmental awareness in this respect.

Instead, we are given the presenter in authoritative 'expert' mode – but then perhaps this was what needed at the time. Authorial voice, like all other aspects of documentary, is a reflection of historical context, and in this case the time was right for Al Gore's 'scare-them-green agenda'[26]: 'the film is a computer-enhanced lawyer's brief for global warming alarmism and energy rationing' (Lewis 2007). If the role of documentary is to reflect, or to stimulate, controversy then *An Inconvenient Truth* has certainly done that, but it has also managed to bring the most important technical and scientific problem of our time into the public sphere in an accessible way at a moment when it was needed, as illustrated by the British government's decision to send a copy of Gore's film to every secondary school in the country.

The *New York Times* summed up the role of context and the timeliness of content for documentary in its discussion of the Academy Award nomination:

> For the moment, at least, one of the jobs of non-fiction filmmaking, perhaps its major

responsibility, is to deliver uncomfortable news to a reluctant audience. While other documentary modes continue to flourish and cross-pollinate – biographies of the famous and notorious; wrenching tales of individual misery; uplifting stories of success against the odds; archival excavations of history – the Academy seems at the moment especially focused on larger problems, on public issues that won't go away no matter how fervently we might wish they would.   (Scott 2007)

In the past, the Academy has turned down Moore's films and others as not being 'documentary'. This time, it seems that Gore was able to preach to the converted.

Historical contexts

The correlation between trends in documentary and historical period is not strictly chronological. Cinema Verité was a reaction against the 'voice of God' tradition; the interview film was a reaction against the editorial limitations of observational cinema. The self-reflexive documentary – dating back to Vertov in the 1920s and Rouch in the 1960s – owes much to trends in visual anthropology. It is also a reaction against the limitations of assuming that subjectivity and the positioning of the filmmaker and viewer is not without its own difficulties, giving priority to the process of construction of meaning. If the authorial voice in Direct Cinema derived from the choice of event and individuals to be recorded, and in the 'scientific' nature of so-called objective observation as a claim to the real, then a different claim to the real emerged with the likes of Godard, de Antonio and Rouch. The 1970s political involvement of the filmmaker became more fashionable because it focused on meaning more forcibly at a time when political events such as Vietnam and other 'protest' issues seemed to be polarizing viewpoints worldwide.

Direct Cinema and observational films

Taking Direct Cinema as an example from which to extrapolate authorial voice, 'it is possible to locate in the denial of conventionality a textual crisis of authority, a twinned symptom of fulsome speech and reticence, an ambivalence toward what has been called by Nichols (1985: 261) the "documentary voice"' (Arthur 1993: 118). Faith in the new portable synchronized sound equipment of the early 1960s replaced authorial intention. This resulted in an aesthetic of long, unscripted, hand-held takes that were structured only by the response to pro-filmic 'stimuli'. Narration, musical scoring, analytical editing – all potentially aspects of authorial voice – were sacrificed at the altar of the moment of recording, with the aim of 'showing', not 'telling'. The movement has its own philosophy, but how do we identify its authorial voice?

Contextual influences on the refusal to use commentary were as strong in 1960 as they were during the Depression of the 1930s in relation to sponsored film with its heavy use of commentary and partisan intervention. History is now rejected because the movement confused textual authority with what could be construed as authoritarianism. 'The implied aversion to language in its ordering, or depletion, of sensory impressions is a pervasive – and quite powerful – facet of the anti-authoritarian program of sixties countercultural and political opposition' (Arthur 1993: 119). Direct Cinema filmmakers didn't like preconceived agendas, hence they insisted on decontextualization within the film by expecting the individual spectator to make up their own mind.

Their preference was, instead, for a 'reality' effect which capitalized on immediacy and directness, giving the impression that everyday events were being captured without any intervention, recording dialogues on location synchronously with portable sound recorders and cameras.

> Whereas in an earlier period, argumentative mastery or the ability to coherently assemble fragments of reality signalled an objective reckoning of historical process, here non-closure or simplicity of design are equated with unbiased access . . . In Direct Cinema, social history is transposed into a kind of portraiture; dramatization of social process replaced by dramatization of the camera recording process. (Arthur 1993: 121)

Thus, with Direct Cinema we need to appreciate the political, anti-authoritarian influences of the period, but also that aesthetics is used in the service of authorial voice, measured even in terms of each single camera movement: 'In Wiseman's and Leacock's films, the gesture of zooming from medium shot to close-up serves as formal correlation of the desire to delve into inner, psychological states while clinging to a façade of unguided attention' (Arthur 1993: 123). The argument is that Direct Cinema's own cinematic agenda of transparent observation, capturing people in action, letting the viewer come to their own conclusions about them, unaided by commentary, actually encodes specific political and ideological assumptions symptomatic of the age.

There is a certain political timidity about observational documentary that has its uses in a number of different institutional contexts. The form is considered to be non-interventionist, presenting an unmediated picture of the world, which unfolds as it is recorded, that is, as we see it. Long takes, natural sound and available light often support the unmediated feel, creating the impression that the event would continue even if the camera was not present. We are deliberately diverted away from the idea that a narrative has been constructed (through the choice of when, what and how long to shoot, and through the editing). Instead we are positioned as observers in this constructed narrative. This is different to the expositional style that develops a theme with an authoritative narrator, presenting 'objective' knowledge as evidence through interviewees, often showing both sides of an argument.

During the 1990s when Britain's Channel 4 was threatened with privatization due to its commercial success, programme makers found it convenient to use the more measured social restraint of 'fly-on-the-wall' documentaries rather the more up-front documentary essay form. The advantage of a film that served to narrate army or medical life, for instance, was that a story based on strong real-life characters left viewers to decide for themselves whether individual examples should be generalized into a critique of wider society: broadcasters could not be accused of open didacticism. 'Fly-on-the-wall' has continued as a style into the twenty-first century, proving once again that categories of documentary style cannot necessarily be allocated exclusively to specific historical periods.

Case study: *Être et Avoir* (2002)

The contribution of authorial voice to the triangle of authorial intention and skills, subject matter, and audience interpretation can be achieved in subtle ways. It is possible to argue that every documentary – even Nicholas Philibert's *Être et Avoir*, a fly-on-the-wall study of a rural French primary school – has something to promote. In this case, the combination of the teacher's credibility with the impression of a pre-bureaucratic version of school teaching, add up to a validation of the profession, something that audiences pick up on: 'LOVED IT! Inspiring teacher who never raises his voice – *this* is what teaching is all about. Wonderful rapport with pupils – brings out the best in even the reluctant ones' (quoted in Austin 2005). Some viewers expect authorial voice to emerge from content and informational values, which are 'seen as central to documentary . . . a part of a generic promise which *Être et Avoir* fails to fulfil'. One respondent commented typically: 'I like more information from a documentary. This one washed over me in a pleasant way but I wanted to know more about the children, their backgrounds, the area, their expectations, etc., etc. It was like a magnifying glass over an area

that didn't move – very frustrating after a while' (quoted in Austin 2005).

Être et Avoir doesn't try to explain itself with voiceovers or inter-titles. Although there is occasional talking directly to the camera, the filmmaker adopts a slow pace, in line with his subject matter – the learning of the children. In this case authorial voice emerges in a different way, through the evolution of characters. Production style, with shots held for a long period of time and very relaxed editing gave a feeling of barely mediated authenticity, allowing the quiet charisma of the main social actor – the village school teacher – to emerge. This in itself carries a message, for his on-screen performance gave what one viewer described as 'an image of a kind, dedicated man who would be the backbone of any educational system' (quoted in Austin 2005). Compared to theatrical fiction films, there is less narrative, less forward motion, and few technical devices to engage the cinema audience for which this documentary is intended. Yet with *Être et Avoir* Philibert demonstrates that it is possible to evoke mood and feeling in a nuanced way with the first-person perspective.

Use of interviews

It could well be the limitations of observational cinema which have led to the predominance these days of the interview documentary, in which social actors address us directly, rather than a narrator/presenter who would give an impression of either 'authoritative omniscience or didactic reductionism' (Nichols 1985: 24). Indeed, use of a presenter can personalize an experience, as he or she is able to talk directly to the audience; this can strengthen contact and the involvement of viewers. As presenters tend to evolve their own style, the authorial voice appears to be directly theirs, when in fact the director/producer may still have tremendous influence. For a successful working relationship between director and producer to emerge, their views must be compatible (Chapman 2007: 114, 127).

In retrospect, it has sometimes been claimed that American Direct Cinema, which generally tried to be as unobtrusive as possible, tended to avoid interviews since they represented a way of manipulating reality. In fact, filmmakers routinely conducted (and extensively edited) interviews – the voters on the streets of Wisconsin act as a classic example. As Jeanne Hall has pointed out, the rhetoric of observational documentary has tended to set the agenda for contemporary discussions of that genre (Hall 1991: 28). Nevertheless, it seems that the use of a string of interviews to construct a narrative provides a middle way between the two poles of either letting the event speak for itself (observation) or providing a single authoritative voice (narration).

This form of documentary is founded on participants' stories, and it is the fact that viewers are given access to the real world through the narratives of social actors that makes the authorial voice more the product of a partnership with the filmmaker, although control of the message still ultimately resides with the latter in their selection and arrangement of the actors, what they say, and how long they are given to say it, even if participants are provided with the space to tell their stories at their own pace. A collection of interviews will serve to diffuse authority, so that the filmmaker effectively enters into a discourse which creates a gap between individual interviewees and the overall voice of the documentary. The filmmaker's voice can sometimes appear, as in *Harlan County USA* (1976), to be a sympathetic observer, or even as the voice of a companion to the interviewees who shares their reactions, as in *Not a Love Story* (1981). This will mean authorial voice appears less assertive, although still responsible for the control of the textual system that has been chosen.

There are problems with assigning editorial responsibility to the voices of social actors, especially if their conceptual analysis is limited or inadequate. However, the testimony of an individual is often 'emblematic' in that it stands for a bigger issue and a wider constituency. Even a *Video Nation* BBC programme, where the individual makes their own statement to camera, is likely to be construed by audiences as a personal evidential statement that is part of an argument about society. If views are accepted uncritically, the documentary may amount to little more than a PR vehicle, without any sense of hierarchy between voices.

Thus the filmmaker needs somehow to lead us to question whether an individual social actor is telling the truth. There are ways of constructing a documentary that address this issue, usually in post-production. In *In the Year of the Pig* (1968), de Antonio makes it clear that no single contributor tells all of the truth by retaining the gap between individual interviewees and the overall message. This is achieved without the use of narration or the filmmaker's on-screen presence. The filmmaker's authorial voice is controlling but unspoken, as we are presented with a perspective, historical overview and discourse, achieved by visual representations consisting of an overlay of archive shots and stills with the voiceover of social actors. Interviews are positioned within a hierarchy of levels that reserves ultimate authority to the text itself (for the film has a voice of its own). A pre-title sequence juxtaposes images of American Civil War soldiers with those of Vietnam GIs, offering an interpretation without stating this verbally. The authorial voice is layered, dialectical and complex, for not every interviewee is telling the truth. For Nichols, this is the quintessential self-reflexive strategy: 'Neither omniscient deity nor obedient mouthpiece, de Antonio's rhetorical voice seduces us by embodying those qualities of insight, scepticism, judgment, and independence we would like to appropriate for our own' (Nichols 1985: 27).

Nevertheless, documentary interviews remain problematic. It is a mistake for filmmakers to interview only people with whom they agree, for the dialectical sense is thereby lost, and the resultant message is too flat. Field avoids this in *Rosie the Riveter* by using a compilation of archive footage intercut with inter-views to create a more layered effect. While Field's social actors are given suffi-cient screen time to develop as personalities, this is not always the case (Chapman 2007: 119–21). In some documentaries, interviewees can appear like puppets or stereotypes recruited for the line of the film, while in more complex documenta-ries the filmmaker will establish a voice for the textual system that rises above the voices of individual contributors, that is greater than the sum of its parts. In these situations there are three layers of voice, which can be discerned in a documen-tary like *In the Year of the Pig*: the textual voice of the whole, deriving from the style of the film and its constructed meaning – indicated in the pre-title sequence mentioned earlier; the voice of individual interviewees, who do not all agree and each bring their own perspective; and the surrounding historical context, which remains there, independent of the film – in this case the Vietnam war.

However, witness contribution in the form of memories can be unreliable – people tend to invent and embellish, usually unintentionally. Yet in many docu-mentaries, such contributions are used as the sole authority for the factual claims made. Rosenthal alludes to two separate television series that both deal with the flight of the Arab population from Haifa after 1945. *The Mandate Years* (1978) was made by Thames Television and *Pillar of Fire* (1979) by Israel Television: 'In *The Mandate Years*, the incident is recalled by a former British army commander who is hostile to Israel and very sympathetic to the Arabs and who claims that the Arabs were forced to leave. In *Pillar of Fire*, an Israeli witness, General Yadin, recalls how the Jews begged the Arabs to stay' (Rosenthal 2002: 306).

Films in which witnesses tell their own story have provided the leading model for contemporary documentary. The fact that the documentary approach is grounded in the experiences of social actors, who are frequently the subject of the film, means there is a consideration and respect for what ordinary people have to say as a form of authorial voice: 'In the hierarchy of voices that speak in documentaries, the voices of ordinary persons, speaking as persons, tend to have a privileged status over the voices of experts, officials and commentators' (Scannell et al. 1992: 324). This is not always the case in documentaries about history, science and specialist issues, including current affairs television docu-mentaries, but it is true that not all contributors who speak in documentaries have equal status, irrespective of how much screen time they are allocated. It is precisely this inequality within the authorial voice that feminist documenta-ries have sought to redress, by, for instance, correcting historical inaccuracy or neglect, or by signalling women's hitherto neglected contribution to past events. Women themselves become the central authorial voice in films like *Union Maids* (1976) and *Life and Times of Rosie the Riveter* (1980), serving to register the place of working-class women in history. One criticism here has been that newsreel sources are used uncritically as if 'truth' is accessible and sometimes available within official sources, although this point is unfair in the case of Field's film, which deliberately sets out to challenge the myths presented by contemporary war propaganda about women (Chapman 2007: 119–21).

Documentary's preference for the lives of everyday folk represents in part a reaction against the norms of news coverage: 'If, in news, private life is de-valued, it is re-valued . . . in the strategies and tactics of broadcast documentary whose narratives are designed partly in antithesis to those of news' (Scannell et al. 1992: 344). A case in point is the approach of Paul Hamann towards Sinn Féin leader Martin McGuinness, as depicted in the television documentary series *Real Lives* (see Chapter 3). However, the opinions of members of the public are limited, in that, by comparison with politicians or experts, they have a narrower subjective quality: 'They lack the generalizing power of the opinions of public persons' (Scannell et al. 1992: 344). Yet there are a whole range of styles in which an interview can be presented, and these aesthetic changes represent different forms of authorial voice. In *Capturing the Friedmans* (2003), family members are presented to a sceptical audience, but they are given the space to tell their own version of a sexual abuse scandal, making the structure of visual perception visible, and reminding us that it is constituted by the knowledge that it produces.

Errol Morris adopts idiosyncratic techniques as if in recognition of this limitation, turning it into an advantage. His films contain static monologues, with social actors sitting and talking directly to camera. Morris himself is never seen or heard, there is no explanatory voiceover or inter-titles to guide the audience: 'The words of the filmic subjects, the *mise-en-scène* and visual imagery, and the juxtapositions of his editing are his primary rhetorical tools' (Dorst 1999: 274). Even when Morris resorts to voiceover, as in *A Brief History of Time* (1992), it is not traditional usage – he changes the technical quality to create a 'cyborg' effect which serves to integrate production apparatus with text.

But it is in Morris' *The Thin Blue Line* that the interplay of visual and spoken testimony best demonstrates how authorial voice can emerge from a range of techniques. Witness accounts to camera are alternated with limited dramatizations of the subject that is addressed in these interview segments. The participants seem to be generating their own cinematic text, rather than being guided. This gives the impression that they are integral to the text and to the production device, rather than merely being recorded by it. Morris is aiming for a first-person documentary, and in this film it is one in which the textuality of participants is difficult to separate from their involvement in the production device, enhanced by a visual text. It is often created as a re-enactment of a point referred to by an interviewee and used as a 'cutaway'. Different witnesses provide different versions of the same event, which Morris replays visually in a variety of ways – such as using dramatic editing, slow motion, selective sounds, images of official documents – so that the nuances in different versions are re-played 'to the point of gruesomely comic absurdity' (Dorst 1999: 275).

The absence of the interviewer's voice means that there is none of the hectoring interrogation of some on-screen investigative journalism, and no tangible hierarchy of authority evident with the voice defining or containing the message, which emerges as an uninterrupted (and often unedited) soliloquy. Instead, the audience have to decide on the negotiation of information through these monologues, unaided by fixed framing in which the camera avoids zooms and dollies. Speakers are tightly framed but not named, placed in their real-life environments, but framing, lighting and other visual techniques create the feel of a staged representation. In terms of authorial voice, it seems that Morris refuses to interpret the events he documents, which results in a very postmodern style of indeterminate meaning and relative, oblique truth (see Chapter 1).

Use of voiceover

Voiceover represents a use of the technical apparatus of film to insert an authorial presence on the linguistic side. But voiceover may be that of a commentator or presenter, a reporter, a social actor whose words are continued over different pictures, or off-camera dialogue between social actors, or between a presenter and social actors, with 'cutaway' images. A variety of ways of using sound and images can have a range of different effects. In *The World at War* (1974) series, the reliance on a traditional voiceover commentator (Laurence Olivier) creates an overall sense of neutral omniscience. Yet there is one moment that contrasts and challenges the style, by indicating to the audience how documentary footage can be used at different points in history for ideological ends. The director, Jerry Kuehl, uses some shots, along with their narration and music, from the 1935 *March of Time* series. The contrast with his own assemblage of footage, compiled in the 1970s and used in parts to illustrate the views of a particular revisionist historian reflecting at that time upon the Second World War, is a reminder that authorial voice is a product of its context, as is documentary more generally.

The way that linguistic anchorage through 'voice of God' commentary tends to mask ideological concepts in the traditional travelogue is amply demonstrated by Chris Marker in *Letter from Siberia* (1957). He gives us a sequence of almost identical shots three times over, but each with a different interpretation in narration. One is 'objective', but followed up by a disclaimer stating that it is impossible to be objective; one is pro-communist; another is anti-communist.

Balancing evidence with argument

Do filmmakers get the balance right between evidence and argument – is there even an ideal balance to be had? On the one hand, documentary usually makes statements about life that appear to have a general application, but on the other hand the images and sounds used as illustration will inevitably carry a particular and specific origin. Their function within the text will confer a meaning, but the way this is construed by viewers will depend upon historical time and context. The extent to which underlying assumptions, aims and values associated with the production are evident to audiences will vary: a reflexive approach will provide indicators, but an observational film will leave viewers to make their own judgements, for the priority here is to present a revelation about a moment in history rather than interpretative indicators to help us formulate conclusions about it. This means that there is little sense of constructed meaning, of a textual voice addressing us. Nichols considers that we are 'too easily engulfed by the fascination that allows us to mistake film for reality, the impression of the real for the experience of it' (Nichols 1985: 22).

In Wiseman's observational films about institutions, the sense of context and of meaning as a function of the text is weak. In *Titicut Follies* we are certainly left with an impression that there is a blurring of the boundaries between insanity and sanity. We learn nothing about the policy approach of the managing authorities, the background or 'back story' of the inmates. During the court cases over Wiseman's lack of informed consent for the filming of *Titicut Follies*, witnesses for the prosecution referred to out-takes that would have made it a different sort of film and so provided the audience with different sorts of messages. Expositional footage was not used which could have provided a contextual and educational background, such as an interview with a manager about the programmes and goals of the institution, a speech at the officers' training school, and a guided tour for high school pupils in which funding problems are explained. Alternatively, these could have been intercut with some of the more horrendous scenes involving individual inmates in a way that would have ironically juxtaposed theory and practice.

Additionally, when Dr Ross made his rounds, accompanied by the film crew, he would turn to camera in order to state briefly what the condition of the patient was – material which could have been used in a traditional documentary way or, as has been suggested, 'in a film self-consciously examining documentary conventions and how people imitate media roles when filmed'. Furthermore, an acknowledgment of camera presence could have served to reduce potential audience concern that participants may have been unknowing or unwilling subjects. But Wiseman retained an observational and non-interventionist style. He also rejected footage that could have made the film self-reflexive because participants in certain shots acknowledged the camera, evidenced not only visually, but also by what they said. One guard repeats, 'We have failed, but it's not us in here who have failed, it is you out there' (Anderson and Benson in Gross et al. 1988: 77).

Observational film will not necessarily prompt audiences to challenge existing social preconceptions. Ellis points out that during the 1980s in Thatcherite Britain, observational documentary style was widely used as a means of showing hardship and deprivation as a response to government policy, with the assumption, of course, that the plight of social actors did not require comment – just showing it would be sufficient to move audiences towards a political conclusion. In fact, the effect was often to confirm 'either the hopelessness of the situation, or the feckless nature of the characters'. Technically, the strategy to combat this would have been to provide explanation or comparison within the film. There is a certain logic to the solutions provided by a documentary that combines a number of different techniques. 'By assembling fragments of evidence from the world, from observations of actions to the testimonies of witnesses and the commentaries of experts, the combinatory documentary attempts to organize a coherent explanation or investigative structure' (Ellis 2002: 117).

In the twenty-first century, combinations of techniques for documentary have continued to expand. Inexpensive editing software, increased accessibility via the Internet, and its use to market a film and/or empower the viewer, plus a variety of approaches to telling a story, whether it is a personal account or a debate on a global issue – all have made an impact. One hallmark of the current explosion of documentaries about aspects of the Iraq war is the combination

Fig. 5.2 US Marines hold prisoners at Bagram Airbase in Afghanistan in Alex Gibney's case study film *Taxi to the Dark Side*.

of journalistic enquiry with radical interrogation of the subject, used to amplify political criticism. This has been exemplified by some very effective and powerful expressions of authorial voice in documentary. There have been a variety of films that have each made an impact using different methods. Dealing with the reasons for going to war, Robert Greenwald's *Uncovered: The Whole Truth about the Iraq War* (2003) acted as a landmark documentary to expose the Bush Administration's case for invading Iraq after 9/11. An impressive line-up of statesmen, CIA officials, ambassadors and Washington insiders reveal the government's duplicity about the supposed link between 9/11, Al Qaeda and Iraq, and how truth is distorted in order to 'justify' going to war. As the war progressed, Deborah Scranton's *The War Tapes* (see Chapter 4) allowed viewers to see soldiers' images of war without imposing an ideological voice. Yet only one year later, journalistic enquiry and radical interrogation seem to have intensified, exemplified by two films. Alex Gibney's *Taxi to the Dark Side* tells the appalling story of an Afghani taxi driver who was kidnapped, taken to the US air base at Bagram in Afghanistan, tortured for information and died of his injuries. In the second film, Charles Ferguson uses his expert status to address the policy implications and bigger issues that must inevitably arise from the disturbing investigations of people like Gibney. In *No End in Sight*, Ferguson argues that 'the principal errors of US policy – the use of insufficient troop levels, allowing the looting of Baghdad, the purging of professionals from the Iraqi government, and the disbanding of the Iraqi military – largely created the insurgency and chaos that engulf Iraq today'.

Comparative Case Study: *Taxi to the Dark Side* (2007); *No End in Sight* (2007).

Alex Gibney's *Taxi to the Dark Side* – a 2008 Academy Award winner and Tribeca Film 2007 Festival winner – is a horrifying documentary murder mystery that examines the death of Dilawar, an innocent Afghan taxi driver, from injuries inflicted by young, inexperienced US soldiers in 2002. Gibney's direct style of journalistic documentary concentrates on a single case study that ruthlessly tracks the details and contacts to source. In terms of authorial voice he allows the appalling truth of the abuse to speak for itself in this report on the last days of Dilawar's life.

Using journalistic skills, Gibney interviews Dilawar's family and the soldiers who tortured him, as well as showing coverage of visiting dignitaries and post-mortem reports. The film is a journey that begins at the driver's village in Afghanistan, where Dilawar had picked up three passengers, never to return home. Gibney tracks Dilawar's trail to Bagram air base where he died at the hands of military interrogators. Gibney uses the incident as a framework through which to broaden his enquiry about the treatment of 'enemy' prisoners and proceeds to Guantanamo Bay to document more horror stories of physical and mental torture meted out by CIA agents and sometimes by untrained soldiers. The film shows clips of interviews with soldiers, a released detainee, lawyers, and politicians including US Attorney John Yoo describing horrific practices, combined with sickening images of Dilawar's body beaten almost to a pulp. Using the clips together with photographic evidence of abuse from Bagram as well as news footage, Gibney constructs a series of questions about the reasons why the US government defied the Geneva Conventions and made unprecedented policy changes post-9/11 with regard to these prisoners.

One scene describes the conditions of Bagram air base as a reception centre for prisoners with potential high-value information. The soldiers describe the place itself as having a certain smell, and the detainees as 'very evil people' who 'definitely had violent intentions'. The film then shows a photograph of the young and terrified Dilawar, arrested on 5 December 2002 at the air base. Gibney's voiceover describes the young man as 'designated a "PUC", a person under control, number 421'. Sergeant Anthony Morton recalls that the prisoner was accused of 'something to do with that [*sic*] he was a triggerman for a rocket attack, and that's about all I know'. Dilawar was dead five days later, his death recorded as homicide. The film shows horrific photographs of Dilawar's battered and bloated body, the Army coroner describing 'massive tissue damage in his legs', and later testifying that they had been 'pulpified'.

Gibney further amplifies his sense of cold anger as the film cuts between images of the body, close-ups of post-mortem reports, and voiceovers from soldiers justifying their actions at the time as being condoned by the 'top brass' at Bagram. The film contains coverage of the top brass visiting Bagram, including Defense Secretary Donald Rumsfeld and General Tommy Franks. The soldiers are recorded saying that some senior visitors wanted to see the prisoners in 'hell on earth', and have the torture charts shown and explained to them. Gibney trains his camera on a chart with arrows pointing up and down with numbers attached to them – the soldiers in the film explain to Gibney that the upward ones signify the prisoner must be strung up from the wrists for the recommended number of hours and the downward ones mean the prisoner may sit for a prescribed time.

Gibney's film has a strong narrative but he does not follow a linear format, instead preferring to use the example of a specific case to argue that it is a symptom of larger ills in US political apathy towards the treatment of all its 'War on Terror' prisoners, and an example of unacceptable brutality in the armed forces.

The voice in this instance is that of Gibney's human and political outrage conveyed in an arrangement of clips, photographs and talking heads. Later in the film, Gibney cuts to a clip of George W. Bush criticizing as 'very vague' Common Article 3 of the Geneva Convention which says 'there will be no outrages upon human dignity'. Gibney uses this clip to condemn the unprecedented acts of the Bush Administration with regard to the torture of those 'persons under control'.

In comparison, Charles Ferguson and Audrey Marrs' *No End In Sight*, the Sundance Special Jury Prize Documentary winner in 2007, concentrates on telling a story about the processes behind the Bush Administration's decision to invade Iraq in 2003. The filmmakers use the authorial voice and the position of analyst and scholar Charles Ferguson to present and examine an alarming catalogue of errors made before, during and after the invasion. Ferguson pinpoints errors in judgement within the context of the history of US/Iraq relations, cites evidence of ignored intelligence information, and highlights the lack of any follow-up plan on the part of those in the government who orchestrated the invasion.

In this chronological account of the Iraq fiasco, focusing especially on decisions made in the spring of 2003 immediately following Saddam Hussein's overthrow, Ferguson uses his specialist expertise to analyse and dissect the decision makers' backgrounds and adopts a critical political stance. His authorial style is that of a strategic analyst whose film includes a number of talking heads explaining how there was no proper occupation plan, and how the occupying force was inadequate and the troops ill-prepared. The film also shows three White House edicts from L. Paul Bremer demonstrating that at the time of his appointment as Presidential Envoy to Iraq that year, replacing General Jay Garner, no plans for an interim Iraqi government had been made. Furthermore, no 'de-Ba'athification' was planned, and there was no aim to disband the Iraqi armed services.[27] The interviewees comprise reporters, soldiers, academics, senior military figures and Republican officials who were in Baghdad. One commentator says: 'There wasn't enough time [to make suitable] arrangements, but maybe for the next war.' All the participants support a view of the government's gross manipulation of the truth to achieve their desired effect: to trounce Saddam Hussein.

Ferguson's film embraces a more intellectual approach (than Gibney's) in that it portrays the intrigue and high-level chicanery adopted by the Bush Administration in its efforts to fabricate a reason for invading Iraq. However it is Gibney's film that packs a more visceral punch as a tragic account of unedifying human behaviour, and as a shocking story of the real price of war.

Using authorial voice to extend a film's debate

Digital media and the Internet have allowed easier access to a range of voices, and in some cases this seems to have made the potential impact of authorial voice stronger than ever. There are a myriad of specific topics readily available on the Internet, as well as the potential for online discourse between an author and the target audience that can encourage input and facilitate activism, offering fresh ways of seeing and hearing an issue. *An Inconvenient Truth* demonstrates how a documentary can capture the political mood of the moment when this is combined with specialized knowledge.

In addition, modern high-budget documentary making in the US makes use of increasingly sophisticated marketing methods through Internet communities to promote a big budget product with a global appeal.[28] Viral marketers use a combination of social networking and technological tools to elevate interest in their products. This is done through a contractual marketing strategy whereby, for example, when the user clicks on certain sites or advertisements, they are taken to another website. Another strategy, syndicated blogger feedback, played an important part in taking the promotion of *An Inconvenient Truth* to a wider audience. Technorati, an Internet marketing and blogger site, which labels itself 'the most popular blog in the world', worked with Paramount Classics in marketing the film to 'partners' (Technorati do not use the word 'audience' as they believe in marketing 'conversations' [Searls et al. 2007]).[29] They considered film-buff bloggers to be of real importance in spreading a buzz about the film. This allowed virtual communities to intensify their engagement with the film's premise.

In 2007, Technorati produced a marketing case study charting the unique explosion of interest in *An Inconvenient Truth*. Searls explains Al Gore's problem:

> At a pre-screening of the film *An Inconvenient Truth*, Al Gore was worried there might not be enough word-of-mouth around the movie to ensure a strong opening weekend. At the time, he had no visibility into the fact that there were already tens of thousands of posts about the movie – a force that touched off a tidal wave of attendance not only opening weekend but well beyond. The marketing behind the film, and later the Live Earth concerts, went on to embrace this conversation and make it increasingly visible and potent.   (Searls et al. 2007)

Distributor and marketing agency worked together to create a global presence through a careful strategy of viral marketing that encouraged a general debate about the theme, as well as a more specific online discussion of the film itself.

> Working with Paramount Classics, Technorati syndicated all posts about the film onto a staging system from which Paramount chose the most interesting posts twice daily and published excerpts and links to them on the site. The film gained tremendous word-of-mouth momentum. In March 2006 the number of posts per day with the phrase 'an inconvenient truth' was between zero and 10. In early June, when the syndicated blogs appeared on the film's web site, it shot up to between 600 and 800. In addition to conversation about the film, the site included posts about global warming, creating a 'big tent' for all sides of the global warming controversy. While Paramount edited out posts that were abusive or contained personal attacks or bad language, contrarian views were welcome under the tent, and posts questioning the validity of global warming were among the most visited links. In fact, in the days after the film first came out, one could go to the site and watch how both sides of the issue were framing their arguments and developing their messaging. The site truly showed the live, moving conversation.   (Searls et al. 2007)

Conclusion

The example of what *Titicut Follies* could have been, but was not, demonstrates the range of choices available to the filmmaker when it comes to authorial voice. Just as every documentary is individually crafted, so also every analysis of authorial voice will be different for each documentary. The potential combinations of techniques that can be mixed and matched are extensive. In order to fully appreciate authorial voice, visual and linguistic factors need to be taken into account.

The way these are juxtaposed, interact and are synthesized will influence any assessment of authorial voice.

In fact, elements of authorial voice are everywhere in a documentary, for they constitute an integral part of definition of the genre. No factual film can escape this, even if the filmmaker is consciously trying to subvert conventions. Quite the reverse – this in itself is a statement of message. There are no wrong or right ways to create a voice for a documentary, but there is definitely a skill involved in striking a reasonable balance between evidence and argument and between aesthetic and editorial considerations in both 'thick' and 'thin' texts.

The nature of the expression of authorial voice is influenced by fashion, itself a creature of historical context, institutional cultures and the requirements of each individual project. The dynamism of the campaign connected with *An Inconvenient Truth* has now faded, but there is no doubt that effective and imaginative marketing strategies such as Technorati's viral one helped to promote the film's authorial tone in a unique manner, thus vastly increasing its reach and appeal.

The way the messages are construed by audiences will vary according to the setting in which a film is viewed and the subjective perceptions of individual viewers, as will be examined in Chapter 7. In short, authorial voice is complex and multi-faceted, and in some cases Internet usage can ensure that the message of the film, its authorial voice, becomes integrated into a wider form of informational awareness – as with the Iraq war and the issue of global warming. Like the debates about truth or definitions of documentary, aspects of authorial voice will keep the interpretative community in business for many years to come.

6 Reflexivity
Techniques and Reflection

Summary

This chapter assesses the meanings and manifestations of reflexivity by differentiating between reflexivity as a general process and individual reflexive techniques. The argument presented here is that the latter are now so widely used that standard definitional tools have been rendered inadequate. Instead of trying to force them to fit, or over-defining the multiple aspects of reflexivity by creating an extensive list of categories, we should concentrate on the implications of reflexivity for audience appreciation and awareness. Indeed, changes in reflexive approaches demonstrate the fluidity of the technique and how it can impact upon audience.

The contributions that reflexive filmmakers have made to film theory through their work over the years have been important. Anthropology pioneered debates about reflexivity as a technique in documentary filmmaking, demonstrating that the significance of issues and methods extends beyond the use of certain technical and aesthetic devices. More generally, there tend to be four components to reflexivity, all of which interact with each other as a coherent part of the whole: producer, process, product and audience. In terms of the last component, films with reflexive elements have a distinctive effect on audiences because they draw attention to aspects of production and impinge upon debates concerning truth and reality, challenging the realist Griersonian and Cinema Verité tradition that conceals the apparatus of filmmaking.

The reflexive tradition was pioneered by Vertov, who revealed the process of documentary organization and the interrogation of the material in *Man with a Movie Camera* (1929) (Chapman 2007: 15, 113). A reflexive approach was later espoused by Rouch, but has developed more recently into 'an aesthetics of failure', fetishized, according to one writer, by proponents such as Ross McElwee and Michael Moore (see below). These 'performative' documentaries raise questions about the role of style and subjectivity as elements of reflexivity that are used to interpret reality; more recently some British TV presenters, such as Bruce Parry and Donal MacIntyre, have adopted, and adapted, the mantle as performers in formulaic ethnographic series.

In the past, stylistic reflexive techniques served to break with documentary norms, by introducing unexpected turns that put the spotlight on stylistic aspects, such as in Trinh Minh-ha's *Naked Spaces*, which challenged the normative guidance usually provided by commentary. Cheaper equipment and the Internet have facilitated the making of autobiographical material that often features increasingly inventive performative techniques to convey that which is not easily represented. Reflexive techniques are now so widespread – having been adopted in 'mockumentary' films as well as more mainstream documentaries and personal films – that the boundaries are blurred between the truly reflexive and the mimetic.

Introduction

Self-awareness is commonplace in every form of communication these days, but this has not always been the case. Throughout the nineteenth century, science and the social sciences were dominated by the positivist belief that humankind could discover meaning in the world through empirical research that would objectively unveil true reality and inherent meaning. Viewed historically, reflexivity as an attitude can be seen as a sign of a modernizing society: people begin to open out and reflect upon other cultures and societies. In more highly advanced environments, the position of individuals within society is evaluated both historically and geographically.

Direct Cinema influenced observational styles that became standard on TV during the late 1970s and 1980s as the need for verisimilitude became a requirement of television journalism. The documentary style was adopted for reportage, but since the early 1990s there has been a steady revival of reflexive techniques in television documentaries which have challenged the emerging popularity of these observational techniques. This can be seen as connected to poststructuralist and postmodernist critiques of the potential for neutral, objective knowledge. The techniques of objectivity that reflexivity will challenge include 'the integrity of the filmmaker's refusal to "influence" the pro-filmic event, a film style which minimises manipulation, and the implicit authority of the professional who claims to "stand back and neutrally observe"' (Allen 1977: 39).

Reflexive documentaries refer to some of their own processes in the final product, so that problems attached to filmmaking itself are incorporated into the documentary's text and into its sense-making procedure, along with editorial or production processes that contribute to identity or meaning. This has the effect of questioning conventions, so that we are more aware of the documentary as a construct. 'Documentaries then become structured articulations of the filmmaker and not authentic truthful objective records' (Ruby 1977: 10). By indicating its own processes of production, a film can make audiences aware of the limited extent to which a production team can maintain a neutral stance or document the truth accurately. It is for this reason that self-reflexivity has turned into a reaction against the emphasis in traditional documentary on verisimilitude. The introduction of reflexive elements implies that the documentary maker may act as an interpreter of reality rather than an objective recorder of the real world. This creates a triangulation between audience, representation and represented (Nichols 1991: 232).

Reflexive elements in documentary films can manifest themselves and be construed in different ways and these are likely to challenge conventions. As stated above, objectivity or neutrality will be questioned. Subjective qualities need to be themselves commented on within the main body of the film. Usually it is possible to distinguish between the film text and the prior social reality on which it is based, and within which the apparatus of production is located. Some reflexive approaches, however, are so inherent to the filmmaking process that even this distinction can become blurred. Errol Morris argues that 'part of what makes great documentary is to capture some of that complexity between the person making the movie and the people who are in the movie' (Gourevitch 1992: 47). He invented what he called the 'Interrotron' – with which his own image is projected onto a video screen mounted over the camera lens, allowing him to be removed from the scene of the interview. This has the effect of connecting social actors more closely with the recording apparatus, making the distinction between the two less clear.

First-person or subjective media, sometimes using autobiographical or gender inflected frameworks to produce meaning, can also be reflexive. Even films that do not appear to be overtly reflexive, such as Resnais' *Night and Fog*, can emphasize to the audience that documentary is a personal statement even when it confronts a historical fact, so that once more, objectivity is challenged. It seems that filmmakers have not always examined the implications of inserting reflexive elements, and have sometimes included reflexive elements without intending to do so. Ruby argues that this is the case with the Maysles' *Grey Gardens* (1975), in that 'big' Edie and 'little' Edie Beale would not ignore the presence of the camera, but the filmmakers were forced to include the footage. In this case it meant that the circumstances of the shoot were dictating the form of the film, which happened to reveal the process and producer (Ruby 1977: 9).

Is there such a thing as 'accidental' reflexivity? Ruby points out that 'accidental' reflexiveness is a contradiction in terms, for reflexivity depends on deliberate intent, pointing to a tradition 'in which the producer is publically [*sic*] concerned with the relationship between self, process, and product' (Ruby 1977: 10). At first, Direct Cinema films like *Don't Look Back* (1967) seemed to have lots of microphones in shot, out of focus shots and sound recordists in the frame, to the extent that this became a technique signifying that directors were not in control, which was a way to make audiences believe in their authentic approach. Hand-held camera work, and Cinema Verité style more generally, are not necessarily synonymous with reflexivity, although these may be part of the reflexive filmmaker's palette. Cinema Verité, by employing techniques such as hand-held camera work, reminds us of the limited perspective that the operator of the technology actually has.

Traditionally, audiences are not supposed to see what happens backstage, so the processes of production will be hidden to the viewer because a film will offer a topic as a historic, scientific, or cultural given. On other occasions, the filmmaker will want to demonstrate that documentary is a construct, that there are limitations to his or her ability to achieve verisimilitude, or that there have been difficulties in production. Indeed, he or she may choose to make these very constraints the subject of the film, as Moore did with his pursuit of Roger Smith in *Roger and Me* (see Chapter 8). Such an approach implies self-awareness – but does that necessarily amount to reflexivity? An examination of how reflexivity has evolved, and the accompanying critical analysis of a range of reflexive elements, will demonstrate difficulties in arriving at a definition and the need for the emphasis to move towards assessing the impact of reflexive techniques on audiences.

Reflexivity and anthropological films

Anthropology, as a social science, carries an implication that other kinds of science do not involve: the study of people's behaviour means that they can 'talk back', become actively involved in the project, and thereby influence the results. Nevertheless, anthropologists have, in the past, had a professional perception of themselves as objective social scientists (see the following case study) – a notion that has gradually been challenged by discussions about reflexivity. When a film-maker arrives with camera and recording equipment in the midst of a different community, they themselves become 'positioned subjects' who are operating within a limited 'scopic regime' and the technologies that they apply are culturally moulded (Pauwels 2004: 41). All of these factors are influences which need to be taken into account – and to do so within the film itself is referred to as 'reflexivity'.

A number of factors conspired to make anthropologists more self-conscious in their use of film, including an increased personal involvement with their subjects, the existence of multiple field studies of the same culture, and assertions of independence by native peoples (Ruby 1980: 163). In anthropological and travel films about non-Western cultures, a reflexive strategy can make a gesture towards recognizing the presence of non-Western people in the transaction. 'To be reflexive, in terms of a work of anthropology, is to insist that anthropologists systematically and rigorously reveal their methodology and themselves as the instrument of data generation' (Ruby 1980: 153).

It is debateable how far reflexive themes can truly provide a more democratic element to the film when the power is still with the filmmaker. In specific situations, 'reflexive strategies offer a formal recognition of the rights of indigenous peoples to be heard, even if there is no way for Western filmmakers to escape the fact of their final controlling power over the films they construct' (Nolley 1997: 283). An alternative strategy is to introduce a level of self-conscious confusion – as in Trinh Minh-ha's *Reassemblage*. She challenges realist ethnography by drawing attention to its problems, including the power of the camera to represent and misrepresent, with the filmmaker taking a role within the film as a character as well as maker.

The process of representing the 'other' merits further scrutiny. In *Voices of Orchid Island* (1993), the indigenous culture of aborigines on a small island south-east of Taiwan is represented by an outsider from the socially dominant group outside of the island. Although the film includes critical methodological reflection within the body of the documentary, the anthropologist-filmmaker Tai-li Hu has still been criticized for appearing to give authority to the aboriginal subjects while actually controlling the structure of the film. Inevitably in such projects, choice of interviewees, the direction of interviews, choice of shots and the construction of the themes will all remain in the hands of the director/producer. Tai-li Hu appears to recognize this by using the plural of 'voice' in the title. In other words, there is no claim to speak exclusively on behalf of the aborigines (Tien 1994: 34–5).

Nevertheless, the director's sense of anxiety about filming the cultural 'other', and of being watched suspiciously during the shoot, seems to emerge, for the very presence of the camera runs the risk of angering the subjects who are being filmed.

She is wary because, on a previous visit to the island, she had witnessed an aboriginal youth angrily snatching a camera from a tourist's hand – an incident that acts as a warning to her (Chiu 2005: 99). The audience also have to face this problem: in interviews, several aborigines complain about the intrusiveness of cameras in the past, when they have been unaware that they were being photographed. Ironically, as the interviewees say this, Hu's documentary camera is roaming around, but quickly stops when a child protests, 'Don't shoot'. We, the viewers, are part of the problem. The aborigines remind us of the ethics of documentary – they need to be informed of a shoot first; yet, during one interview, an aboriginal wearing nothing but a traditional thong moves in the background, probably unaware of the filming. The effect is to remind the audience that this is something we should not be seeing: shots consistently question the presence of the camera. 'It is this self-conscious treatment of anxiety and the problematization of the gaze through sophisticated film language that make *Voices of Orchid Island* a distinct documentary in the history of visual anthropology in Taiwan' (Chiu 2005: 102).

Anthropology's 'crisis' since the late 1970s has involved a new interpretative and questioning approach to the colonial underpinnings to representational practices. In turn, this has been prompted by a political context of decolonization, independence struggles and liberation movements. This backdrop opened up the potential for the filmmaker's influence on documentary meaning to become a negotiation between the audience and the medium. The nature of such changes can be contextualized by reference to Stuart Hall's theorization of a 'politics of identity' in relation to ethnicity and cultural diversity, featured in some of his now seminal essays from 1987/88. He considers that the first phase of realism in ethnic filmic representations has been superseded by a 'politics of difference' since the 1980s, a politics that rejects clear-cut binary oppositions of black/white, straight/gay, male/female in favour of a *self-reflexivity* that foregrounds the specificity of the filmmaker's position and the 'constructedness' of identity (Hall 1987: 117).

When the filmmaker involves him or herself in the visual text, it serves to remove the distant, observational gaze, which encourages a 'myth-making process *about* the subject [to turn] into a dialogue *with* the subject'. Hence, alternative forms of representation challenge the ethnographic imagination. In *Soft Fiction* (1979), for instance, Chick Strand describes her exploration of female sexuality and fantasy as an 'ethnography of women' (she began her career as an anthropologist). She avoids the exotic 'other' and the colonial relationship by looking at her own culture of white, middle-class film artists, so that women can tell their own story to their friend in her home, and decide how they will be framed and how they will perform for the camera. But this creates other tensions: is the film merely narcissism masquerading as ethnography? Narcissistic elements within representation raise another question: is the presence of performance inevitable?

> The idea of transforming the ethnographic film from an observational tool, one which records daily life and/or ritual as data, into an expressive, intimate, experimental documentary requires a sense of cinematic address as performative. It also presumes that cultural identities and ideas of the individual subject are constructed as performances – for the self, for others, for the camera – within various cultural arenas.   (Rabinowitz 1994: 166).

Two British documentary television/presenters, Bruce Parry and Donal MacIntyre, each approach ethnographic subjects from different trajectories. Explorer Parry devotes his life to filming remote communities and participating in their daily routine. In *Tribe* (2007) and *Amazon* (2008) he takes part in sometimes risky rituals in order to understand the communities' way of life. Unlike the subjects in *Orchid Island*, *Tribe*'s members are aware of the filming process and encourage Parry to be a witness to their lives on screen, sometimes to his intense discomfort. In some episodes of *Amazon*, other communities had bad experiences with the film crew and ejected them from the village.

Cultural shock is reversed in *Return of the Tribe* (2007), when Donal MacIntyre, best known for his investigative journalism confronting dangerous groups in urban areas, invites Papua New Guinea's Insect Tribe to London as visitors. A series of highly constructed set-ups are designed to find out how the tribe will react to snow, urban wildlife, British communities and London working life.

Comparative case study: *Tribe* (2007); *Amazon* (2008); *Return of the Tribe* (2007)

The anthropological explorer Bruce Parry and the investigative journalist Donal MacIntyre demonstrate two very different aspects of filming themselves interacting with tribes. In his third series of *Tribe* Parry frames his study around six tribes as they carry on their daily lives, but with Parry included in their rituals. Parry acts as an interpreter of common and varying traits between tribal and non-tribal communities. '*Tribe* is about looking at the way other people live and asking questions about the way we live' (Parry 2008).

One episode featuring the Matis tribe in western Brazil shows the presenter having a substance squeezed into his eyes, ostensibly to improve his hunting skills. The Matis themselves, like Parry, find the procedure extremely painful, and they sit for some time rubbing their knees, chanting 'Quick ants crawling, quick ants crawling!' to distract themselves from the discomfort. Immediately before Parry has the treatment he tries to avoid the procedure, nervously talking to camera, but is seen being commandeered by the elders. His hunting skills are not improved but he does outline his admiration for the tribe's experience. Throughout the film he constantly talks to the camera explaining what is happening and at times the film becomes a

feature for documenting Parry's own journey of doubts and achievements. Another episode, in which he visits the Tanzanian Akie tribe, the film features Parry confronting his greatest fear. In the scene, the hunter-gatherer tribesmen tease Parry, encouraging him to overcome his fear and plunge his hand into a bees' nest to harvest wild honey. In this case, the type of reflexivity represents cultural difference and individual enquiry that serves to demonstrate the communication of a sense of self within certain contexts.

In another series, *Amazon*, the presenter explores the juxtaposition of tribal and industrial demands on land surrounding the Amazon, and investigates the impact of logging and drug cartels on remote communities. He adopts his usual interlocutory style to explain his experience living with the tribes and questions the big organizations involved about their priorities. One scene shows Parry harvesting the coca leaf with an Ashaninka community in the lawless Louisiana area of the Peruvian High Andes. He explains that the tribe have only the coca leaf as a source of income and that he and the tribe are taking major risks. Later, his apparatus is a cause for concern when the tribe refuse to let him film a festival – he explains that some tribal members did not want the BBC filming their community. They become openly hostile to Parry and threaten his team, forcing them to leave the locale.

In a reversal of Parry's filming approach that becomes progressively more politicized, Donal MacIntyre's *Return of the Tribe* adopts an apparently more apolitical stance by inviting a tribe to his home in London. (MacIntyre had met and filmed Papua New Guinea's Insect Tribe in his 2006 *Edge of Existence* series where he interacted with the tribe.) In *Return*, Chief Joseph and Sam in particular are shown around the sights, with MacIntyre on voiceover and occasionally appearing on screen to witness the tribe members' reaction to Western culture. MacIntyre is quietly pleased to avenge his discomfiture at the hands of his hosts (saying that it is now payback time!), his mistakes having been the butt of their jokes in Papua New Guinea. He films Joseph's amazement on encountering 'magic' doors and snow, and also the elder's sense of outrage at not being able to meet the Queen when visiting Buckingham Palace. 'Why can I not go in to meet the Queen? I am a chief.' 'Well,' explains MacIntyre, 'we did ask . . . '. However the filmmaker's intention is not simply to scoff at his guests' confusion – he uses the construct of the film to point out the borderlines of understanding where the self is placed within an unfamiliar setting. In setting up certain situations MacIntyre forces some extreme reactions: for example, in one clip Sam will not go out in the snow, others close their eyes at the sight of a bare deciduous tree, and they refuse to let the tribe's women go into 'the big spirit house' of St Paul's cathedral for fear of them being struck down. Other scenes indicate a sense of self-assurance. On spotting a squirrel a young man wants to catch the animal and 'put it on [his] head' and dance, since that is what they do with their catches at home. At the end of the film, as a type of anthropology in reverse, the tribe are ready and more than willing to go home, shocked at the stress of British working life. What we are not made aware of is the potentially destabilizing effect that the episode had on life when they returned home. It is difficult not to conclude that television's entertainment imperative, the drive for different formats and the stamp of the MacIntyre personality have resulted mostly in cheap laughs for the audience.

Nevertheless, Parry and MacIntyre do expose, first, issues of cultural difference, similarity and representation; second, the results of positioning the social self within a community with conflicting values. Where is the reflexivity here? The reflexive approach is inherent in the manipulative positioning of the presenter; the resultant activities being filmed manifest reflective styles that stem from this stance. These become interesting to the viewer when they are subject to unforeseen change as a result of the production process – but at what ethical cost to the social actors?

Vertov and the reflexivity of process

In some films the featuring of the apparatus of production almost becomes the subject of the documentary; Vertov's *Man with a Movie Camera* (1929), for instance, records everyday life in 1920s Russia at the same time as revealing how this process works. Furthermore, cinematic devices such as slow motion, time lapse, frame reversals, non-continuity editing and other techniques are used to integrate the production apparatus within the text of the film. This reflexive experiment with the boundary between cinematic apparatus and documentary text demonstrates that Vertov was well ahead of his time.

Vertov was the first documentary maker to argue that audience consciousness should be raised by the style of the film. Whereas fiction was entertainment fantasy, pictures of the everyday events of ordinary people could be transformed into meaningful Marxist statements by revealing the process (not the producer), in order that audiences might develop a critical attitude. *Man with a Movie Camera* combines a dual role for reflexivity: as a contribution by Vertov towards a larger political struggle and as a techno-ideological tool to enhance audience awareness of specific production skills. An analysis of this two-part role for reflexivity reveals how agit-prop and 'organically' reflexive production techniques can be intertwined, demonstrating the ideological scope for exploiting technology.

Vertov is reflexive about process, not self, because he believed that a visual consciousness would enable people to see the world in a different, more truthful, way. The filmmaker appeared on screen only as a worker who is part of the process. He shows us how the film is constructed, by explaining within the work itself how it operates and is organized. He de-mystifies, shunning the so-called glamour of fiction films. For instance *Man with a Movie Camera* begins with a scene in which the cameraman films people travelling in a horse-drawn carriage from a car that is moving alongside. We are then taken to the cutting room where the editor assembles bits of this film into a sequence: Vertov is showing us not only the effect of editing, he is also deconstructing 'the impression of unimpeded access to reality' (Nichols 2001: 127).

The apparent narrative about a day in the life of a Soviet city seems to act more as a vehicle for the analysis of movement, in that the particular movements of film production – the 'how' elements – come before the 'what' – the content of the film. Thus the opening shot is of a cameraman, the second of what we presume he is shooting – a building with fast-moving clouds in the background. Reflexivity is prioritized over more traditional narrative: the film tells a story about itself, about the activities of the cameraman instead of a central narrative character about a social actor.

The film can be seen as an analysis of visual movement in the service of a political dialectic. We experience the cameraman's movement as he films the movements of a population that get up, go to work, visit the beach, play sport and listen to music. Then we experience the editor's movement while she is cutting and organizing film material; and finally we experience the movement of an audience viewing a film, seeing themselves being filmed and viewing a film.

If Vertov is to use the documentary form to raise consciousness, then production workers must be seen as part of the industrial proletariat: thus visuals of the process of filming take over from shots of productive labour, linking the two. Similarly, Vertov makes a connection in his montage between a sewing factory with machines and the work of editing, which becomes part of cinema's social function as labour. Yet in the editing sequence, we never see the film being joined together, only being cut, studied and classified. There is no single, definitive moment of fusion in this dialectic process. For Vertov, montage is an ongoing construction and de-construction process, from the moment a subject is chosen to the final end product: 'Like other Soviet filmmakers of his time – most notably Eisenstein – Vertov considered montage both the essence of cinematic form and the foundation of cinema as a dialectic medium' (Mayne 1977: 84).

Documentary images are usually assumed to have originated in the historical world and we also often assume that what happened when the camera was present and the historical event being filmed were the same thing: for example, Bob Dylan goes on stage in *Don't Look Back*. In this film we don't see D.A. Pennebaker as filmmaker, but in other films we adjust assumptions when we become aware of how the presence of the camera has had an influence, and conversely we can also reflect on what may have happened before or after the camera was switched on. This process is all part of the documentary mode of engagement – but reflexivity takes us further. Our assumptions of literalness, of a link between the real historical world and the images used in documentary to portray it, can all be challenged by reflexivity. The viewer is less likely to accept the 'reality' presented by the film as the only one available to be shown if the filmmaker introduces a suggestion of the process of selection or production choice. However, there must be a point to the revelation: it should not be accidental or narcissistic. Certainly McElwee's personal revelation in *Sherman's March* was not accidental, but it can be criticized for being narcissistic.

In short, self-referentiality in a documentary can actually result in the perception of realism being reduced, because the mediated nature of the discourse is given priority. Such is the case in Trinh Minh-ha's *Surname Viet, Given Name Nam* (1989), where language itself is the subject – both film language and that of the participants. In this case, the reality of the historical past is marginalized and, in the process, documentary's ability to represent it is challenged. By shifting the emphasis onto process, do reflexive films become too abstract and contrived, thereby reducing the attention given to real world issues? For example, in *The Persecution of the White Car* (2001), Argentine filmmaker Sebastian Diaz Morales uses documentary footage shot in Durban, South Africa to weave an apparently haphazard collage that presents the idea of film as moving thoughts in a dream, using a conversation between a man and a woman who comment on the film as a whole and on each scene. As the film progresses, 'one suggests to the other that something needs to happen in order for the film to remain interesting – an act of self-reflection whereby the work takes shape as a documentary about its own making' (Muir 2003: 81).

Audience reflexivity

Charlotte Govaert (2007) argues that the theoretical standpoints of Weiner (1978), Ruby (1980), Nichols (1991) and Winston (1995; 2008), who maintain that 'reflexivity heightens the viewers' awareness with respect to the problematic relationship between reality and documentary film', are unsubstantiated by empirical research, and are based on unproven assumptions. Such assumptions, she says, centre on the idea that 'audiences read reflexive elements as cues that they are not watching a slice of unmediated reality but instead a construction' (Govaert 2007: 245). Her solution is to propose a more detailed categorization in the form of six modes of reflexivity designed by Babcock as a basic communication model for further analysis (expressive, procedural, referential, poetic, conative [*sic*], and meta-narrational).[30] On Govaert's reflexivity chart, *Man With A Movie Camera* scores 11 out of a possible 18 points, employing five of the six categories, the only exception being the referential (Babcock 1975; 1984: 1–14; Govaert 2007: 260). Such attempts at categorization probably amount to an over-definition of the phenomenon. Furthermore, the model itself is interpretive and based on Govaert's judgement of awarding points for each reflexive aspect spotted, according 0–3 points to each according to weakness or strength of the aspects used. Govaert admits this limitation but hopes that the model can help to explain why and how two different films use the same reflexive aspects in different ways to communicate a message to an audience. In fact her hopes are in vain because the model does not account for the difference in the use of the same reflexive modes in, for example, Morin and Rouch's *Chronicle of a Summer* and Trinh Minh-ha's *Naked Spaces*, both very different films which may well tick the same boxes or accrue the same number of points – each scores two points in the expressive category.

Govaert admits that is it difficult to measure an audience's response. Indeed, the fact that reflexivity is as much about the making of the film as it is about the subject matter, and that it tends to problematize the relationship of the filmmaker to the social actors, means that it is the role of the viewer which is likely to change. At its best, use of reflexivity can serve to strengthen the viewer's consciousness of his or her relationship to the documentary and what this entails. Viewers are encouraged to think for themselves rather than accepting a pre-digested package. Audiences have to re-adjust their assumptions, so that their expectations are different for reflexive films, for they do not simply involve an exposition of a subject, they also bring the documentary back to the question of its own status and that of the genre more generally, by revealing how the text is constructed. Furthermore, the terms and conventions of viewing are questioned:

> The phenomenology of filmic experience, the metaphysics of realism and the photographic image, epistemology, empiricism, the construction of the individual subject, the technologies of knowledge, rhetoric, and the visible-all of that which supports and sustains the documentary tradition is as much the focus for the viewer's consciousness as the world beyond. A thickened, denser sense of the textuality of the viewing experience is in operation.   (Nichols 1994: 62).

There are two ways in which audiences have to work harder, questioning both our political beliefs about the world we think we know and our beliefs about the nature of a film genre that we frequently (like other media) take for granted.

Rouch and his collaborator Morin followed Vertov as pioneers in questioning the nature of documentary through their methods. Rouch was attentive to form and more interested than Vertov in the personal and philosophical problems of doing research. The sociologist Morin once described *Chronicle of a Summer* (1960) as being Cinema Verité in emulation of Vertov's 'Cine Pravda' (Ruby 1980: 168): not so much a documentary as a research exercise that draws on the interaction between author and actors with shared concerns (Ungar 2003: 9). For Rouch, *Chronicle of a Summer* was also an attempt to shape an idea beginning with a basic question: 'are you happy?' Rouch and Morin's study of a film within a film was groundbreaking at the time: 'their images continuously interwoven so that in the end what we have is something "sui generic", something absolutely new' (Hoveyda 1961: 248; Chapman 2007: 16, 65, 97).

By revealing the mechanics of documentary interviewing, the filmmakers introduce a form of interactive reflexivity. The final two sequences are openly reflexive and self-conscious in the way that the film being made is referred to, with a discussion taking place between the group of participants after seeing a rough cut of the film. 'In a sense, the participants are given an opportunity to re-structure the previous reality with a commentary of their own and hence exert a measure of control previously reserved for the filmmaker' (Allen 1977: 39). Unlike most self-effacing anthropological filmmakers at that time, Rouch and Morin acknowledge that they are organizing consciousness in their role, and that this has not been entirely successful. In the final sequence the two filmmakers evaluate their experience, recognizing at least a measure of failure when Morin refers to 'the difficulty of communicating something'. Their experiment had led to complicated disclosures. The ending revokes the initial question around which they had based their research: 'are you happy?' They have not been able to resolve their study about the quality of life measured in terms of personal happiness. Throughout the production there have been tensions over levels of 'staging', the recording of unrehearsed disclosures, and effects such as editing, when more than twenty hours of rushes had to be reduced to a final product of 88 minutes (Ungar 2003: 15; Chapman 2007: 114). The unresolved hypothesis of the film seems to have a wider historical significance, emerging not just from the production itself, but out of the uncertainty of the historical context of France in the 1960s, exemplified by the Algerian war and culminating in the riots of May 1968 and the beginning of the fifth republic. Do reflexive films per se always consist of unresolved hypotheses by definition? The idea deserves attention for its more general application as a definition of reflexivity.

Producers and filmmakers have to give a clear signal of intention to the audience if, for instance, they want to introduce elements of reflexivity. Without any such indication, the audience will be uncertain as to whether they are reading more (or less) into the film than was intended. On the other hand, too much reflexivity can create an impression of overt narcissism, while reducing the amount of knowledge of the subject matter the audience might be able to acquire through the viewing experience – Michael Moore's films have been criticized for falling into this trap.

As already demonstrated, in the performative and reflexive documentary, the filmmaker's presence influences the event as depicted for viewers. Thus, ironically, the documentary form also invites viewers to dispute truth claims and to argue against them, and there are filmmakers who set out deliberately to destabilize the genre. It is difficult not to conclude that some reflexive films appear to place the viewer in a burdensome position, for they have to ascertain what is fictional and what is not, a task which is only exacerbated by the increased potential for technical manipulation of images. In terms of production techniques, audiences have developed different sorts of viewing strategies, and degrees of tolerance, for different types of factual genre. When audiences watch the news, or an investigative documentary, they expect them to be truthful and accurate. Audiences have their own criteria for judging factual television, which allows them to apply 'a fact/ fiction continuum' to it (Roscoe and Hight 2001). So, for instance, audiences will still see theatrical documentary films such as Watt and Wright's *Night Mail* (1936), or Morris' *The Thin Blue Line* (1988) as documentary rather than fiction, despite the films' reconstruction of events using people originally involved.

Nevertheless, the existence of a fact/fiction continuum does not diminish the importance of truth to viewers. In fact, Hill believes that their biggest expectation is one of truth-telling, which is by far the strongest criterion that audiences apply: 'Audiences value the truthfulness of factual programming. The more fictionalised factual programming becomes, the less the viewers value it' (Hill 2005: 175).

Political challenges and the audience

How can reflexivity be political? With politically reflexive documentaries, the audience become the agent of change: we can bridge the gap between the world as it is and the world as it might become. The film is not the agent, we are. First we need to appreciate the processes of the 'agit-prop' function. Take *The Woman's Film* (1971) for example, a film which expects us to question the stereotypical image of women, and the role of advertising, by being introduced to an alternative way of thinking. This is represented by women who have challenged the conventions and have radically different ideas about the nature of the feminine. The challenge is not to our assumptions about form so much as our awareness of social organization and the assumptions attached to it – politically reflexive documentaries present the way things are, but also invite us to imagine how things could change. It can be argued that reflexive documentary during the 1980s was often political and addressed issues of form, seeking to 'de-familiarize', that is, to challenge classical documentary techniques. Political challenges influence the viewer's consciousness, and to this extent, reflexivity can act as a form of 'consciousness-raising'. However, it can also be argued that reflexivity carries the potential for underestimating the critical powers of audiences (Plantinga 1997).

How does political reflexivity differ from the stance taken in more traditional political films? The latter will usually attempt to persuade the viewer to adopt a clearly committed position, whereas reflexive films will challenge the viewer to analyse the complexities of the subject matter, and also acknowledge some of the intricacies involved of making a film about it. In doing so, a documentary can challenge the dominant ideology and encourage a progressive social awareness in the viewer. This does not mean that the viewer will necessarily be motivated to *do* something to try to change society. Television viewing is not particularly conducive to activism. However, most reflexive films are shown within the independent sector rather than within the institutional setting of TV.

Reflexivity with deception

There are other choices: political reflexivity can also use parody, satire, pastiche or irony to broaden the viewer's awareness beyond the text to a wider social agenda. However these too can be problematic from the viewer's point of view. A documentary parody that pretends to be actual footage, when in fact it is staged, scripted or acted, can have the effect of confusing audience assumptions about what is fiction and what is non-fiction, or at least causing them to question these assumptions. Mockumentary entails a reflexive response by the viewer, because it assumes that audiences will recognize and acknowledge the fictional nature of the text, but the extent of this reflexivity will vary from viewer to viewer and from film to film. Although the film cannot strictly be called a mockumentary, when in *Surname Viet, Given Name Nam* Trinh Minh-ha used a range of commentaries without any hierarchical relationship to one another, it still produced a frustration amongst audiences that extended to resentment, for by using actors to perform a script that was originally someone else's book, she had clearly tricked the audience (Chapman 2007: 145).

Viewers are forced to adopt a reflexive interpretation of a film as they uncover the fictional status of a 'hoax'. In the case of *Forgotten Silver* (1995), a film presented as the rediscovery of a forgotten New Zealand filmmaker, the deception that the film was a real documentary was maintained by the broadcasters, which a 'significant proportion of their audiences' found disturbing (Rosenthal and Corner, 2005: 237). The reflexive potential in this case derives from the fakery, supported by the 'extra-textual' status afforded by the broadcasters. The burden of having to discern which parts of the film are fiction is shifted to the audience, in relation to the increasingly reflexive discourse of fact versus fiction. In having to do so, viewers become self-conscious about their own role as the audience, and to this extent reflexivity is present. *Forgotten Silver*, for example, was popular because of its appeal to cultural myths about the early history of cinema, but it provoked a range of audience readings when it was first broadcast on New Zealand television. The hoax was deliberately invented to create audience confusion. The reflexive potential of such 'spoofs' derives from the success of their fakery.

Producer reflexivity

There are several ways that a filmmaker might manipulate the production process for particular expressive ends: by using scripts or actors; by appearing themselves in the scene being recorded; by using camera style and techniques to express their point of view and not simply to record; by using editing to distort or to communicate their point of view. In *Letter from Siberia* (1957), filmmaker Chris Marker adopts self-reflexivity in an essay-critique of the way quasi-anthropological and geographical science documentaries refuse to admit that their perspective is conditioned by ideological and cultural factors. He reveals the 'naturalizing' operations of the genre and the implicit ideological positions the tradition has usually sought to mask. He challenges the way that travelogues have assembled images in relation to soundtrack by positioning his visuals at odds with the soundtrack. This creates a tension between the interplay of the two elements which demonstrates how images are often made to serve a conceptual reality defined by the voiceover. Marker presses the point further by reflexively instructing the audience in voiceover about how film material is manipulated by camera movements and editing. Comments such as 'here's the shot I've been waiting for' indicate how personal the process of choosing shots can be. The narration goes even further in its reflexivity by introducing a note of parody: Marker uses humour to critique the cultural smugness of the travelogue tradition. Thus we are told, with reference to shots demonstrating the contrast between old and new: 'Look closely because I will not show them again.' Yet we are shown them repeatedly.

Whereas Vertov's technique is about defamiliarizing (he never had the advantages of portable synchronous sound and lightweight cameras), Morris' technique has the effect of drawing the audience into the vertical mixing process between apparatus and text. His interviews come across as being 'indigenous creatures of the documentary text' (Dorst 1999: 279). In the process through which truth is manufactured, points of origin and the logic of cause and effect are difficult to locate. Dorst argues that the sort of reflexivity that emerges from *The Thin Blue Line* collapses the boundary betweens the apparatus of production and the text of the film. The distinction between making the film and being in it challenges ideas about reflexivity. Dorst argues that *The Thin Blue Line* is more radical in its reflexivity than *Man with a Movie Camera*. In the latter, the devices of production are bared but the distinction between the text and the apparatus of production remains. Whereas in the former, 'by calling on the viewer to contemplate at each point why this or that film element should be where it is and what relationship it has to other elements, the process of montage construction is constantly in view' (Dorst 1999: 276, 278). Thus the editing process is a central subject of the film rather than merely a reminder that a machinery of production is involved. The way images connect to each other suggests there is no guarantee of the historical authenticity of evidence. This is a postmodernist reflexive move, which, according to Nichols, 'displays an appearance tied less to the historical world than to choices made by the filmmaker' (Nichols 1991: 270).

Subjective reflexivity and personal autobiographical film

Self-reflexivity necessarily involves setting out the specific position from which we speak. However, that position may shift over time as particular issues (be they political, social or personal) arise or fade away. It is possible to create an autobiographical piece that is self-aware, that refers to self and is self-conscious, without necessarily being reflexive. A reflexive documentary takes into account aspects of self that will help the audience understand the process employed and the product that has emerged. Sometimes, a reflexive text will not take its reference from a prior authority or pre-existing agency, but will leave the audience to locate the authority and status of the discourse within the film, through its own, self-referential voice. Reflexive autobiography is a case in point.

However, too much autobiographical content is likely to be at the expense of the wider cultural context being studied, and a reflexive approach that involves the on-screen presence of the filmmaker can look like self-glorification. McElwee is reflexive in *Sherman's March* in a way that Moore is not because as the filmmaker he is not only the subject but also the camera operator/director (and he also edits himself; Chapman 2007: 126). Moore and McElwee typify what theorists (Arthur 1993; Dovey 2000) have described as the erosion of the white male as subject, although like Woody Allen, he remains centre stage, but now troubled and incompetent. Dovey labels the phenomenon 'klutz films' (Dovey 2000: 27–54). Feminists more generally would argue that no such luxury exists for the female, who is still struggling to prove herself within patriarchal society. McElwee offers us his personal failure to find a love match in *Sherman's March*, whereas Moore bumbles through an attempt to expose the leading corporate personality responsible for working-class misery in a world of car industry redundancies in *Roger and Me*, while always remaining firmly in the driving seat. Arthur refers to the phenomenon as the 'aesthetics of failure', a concept not unlike that of Plantinga when he talks of 'epistemic hesitation' (1997: 118). Such uncertainly within documentary reflexivity can be seen as a form of relativism, which is a psychological and sociological phenomenon (Arthur 1993: 16–34).

It is possible to trace a direct line from Rouch and Morin's failed hypothesis to the hesitations and doubts within the postmodernist reflexivity of Arthur's new avant-garde documentary. Doubt becomes the flip side of the longer-term collapse of the certainties of positivism, and there are historical moments that have contributed to uncertainty about epistemological projects, such as the failure of the Left to bring about substantial social change between 1966 and 1972 (MacLennan and Hookham 2001: 9). However, we need to ask why Moore, McElwee and Broomfield fetishize the 'aesthetics of failure'. Is it because the problems they encounter in setting themselves a documentary 'mission impossible' are so great that this is the only form of opposition they can offer in order to undermine the status quo? Or is it because this is the only way they can get a film made. In this scenario, the function of the aesthetics of failure runs the risk of becoming a negative, totalizing end in itself – an attempt to undermine all certainty.

Such films divert our attention away from the referential aspects of documentary. The problem with reducing the referential emphasis is that the film can then appear excessive in its stylistic approach – such a criticism has been levelled at *Sherman's March*, for instance. We gradually lose the reference to General Sherman and the important historical theme of the Civil War, only for them to be replaced by the more mundane question of how Ross McElwee is to find love.

Chris Waitt's 2008 Bafta winner, *A Complete History of My Sexual Failures* (2008), deliberately sets out to make a film on this very theme, but focusing on the question of past success or failure. This time, there is no deviation from the main research question: Waitt asks his ex-girlfriends why they dumped him. He is filmed and films himself with a number of women who excoriate him with varying degrees of disgust and sympathy. Filming equipment becomes alternately an enabling and a disabling part of the process, as Waitt attempts to answer the question 'will I ever learn?'

Case study: *A Complete History of My Sexual Failures* (2008)

Chris Waitt embarks on a journey of self-discovery over a couple of months, visiting twelve of his ex-girlfriends and asking them why he was such a bad partner. He begins the film, looking into camera, explaining that he has been dumped by 'pretty much every girl I have ever met'. A montage shows the variety of ways the women ended the relationship – by answerphone, email, text. One woman dedicated a book to him 'in which the boyfriend character bled to death after having a garden fork stuck in his throat'. He films himself telephoning and interviewing several women (the majority refuse him – one says she feels physically sick) and reacting to their negative responses. His mission-list whiteboard changes at each jump-cut. The names in his book are crossed out. Waitt sinks lower and lower into his seat.

Filming paraphernalia is always a part of the documentary. The extremely scruffy Waitt, armed with sound equipment, doorsteps his

Fig. 6.5 Chris Waitts' film *A Complete History of My Sexual Failures* features filming equipment as a reflexive tool to explore the nature of his doomed relationships.

most recent ex, Alice, only to have the door slammed in his face. His attempts to contact others are shown, including a scene where he is thrown out of an office in Glasgow with the camera still rolling and the manager shouting at him. Other women are filmed talking frankly with him – the majority say he is lazy and inconsiderate, having never returned calls or letters, and in one case (Vicky) never following up on a promise of engagement even though he had bought a ring.

His indolence and solipsism are causes of concern not only in his attitude towards women. The film company's owner, Mark Herbert, rings him up to upbraid him for adopting an unprofessional attitude. He tells Waitt that by not giving the women the common courtesy of formal meetings, he is 'freaking them out' and so not obtaining valuable material – in Herbert's view this is not acceptable for a proper feature documentary. 'This is not some half-hour shit you can put on YouTube.' Herbert, when asked why he thinks Waitt is unsuccessful with women, replies: 'Maybe you're gay', and says that he will have to re-evaluate the film's trajectory. Waitt's reaction is one of stunned silence as his personal and professional identities are bluntly questioned.

His methods criticized, he visits his mother who shows him a box of letters from disappointed girlfriends, castigates him for his callousness, and arranges to set up a meeting with a local ex-girlfriend, Julia. She and other women ask about the process, shots of clapperboards with their names feature in the film, and they appeal to Waitt to give them time to recover. The filming process is as important as Waitt's self-discovery. He makes mistakes with his filming methods that reflect his personal approaches to relationships. The film process gives Waitt access to participants but disables his sense of self-worth. Women turn the camera on him in public and in private and tell him exactly what his problems are. At one point he is described as impotent. His reaction to this news is to film his visit to a consultant who tells him he may have to take medication or inject his penis. After tests he is told that there is nothing wrong with him physically and is recommended to undergo eighteen months' psychological treatment. Waitt's reaction is to visit a dominatrix to see if she can 'cure' him more cheaply. He is filmed being whipped, chained to a wall and abused – an excruciating scene. Later, Waitt says he feels he is going in the wrong direction as he sits with a bag of frozen peas over his zipper.

Eventually he contacts his ex-fiancée, Vicky, for the second time, having failed to turn up a month before, and he realizes he still loves her. But he is too late – she has a partner and is pregnant. One moving scene features Vicky asking for some time to recover from his question about recollecting any good parts of the relationship. Waitt asks also what she thinks is wrong with him. She tells him that he is just too late. Waitt's reaction to rejection is to take seven Viagra pills. The film then follows him running around the streets for the next eight hours in priapic agonies, desperately begging women to have sex with him. He is eventually arrested and spends the night in a cell. One of the women he approached calls him back after the event and doesn't seem at all shocked or appalled by his previous attitude to relationships, and Waitt is suitably enamoured of her interest and feelings.

The performative element of this film is somewhat forced as the protagonist throws himself to the wolves and this process is sometimes unbearably painful to watch. The crucial element to observe is how his planned journey is documented in film, showing how his personal and professional identities effect positive and negative reactions to his presence from participants.

Bruzzi believes that filmmakers such as Michael Moore and Nick Broomfield draw attention to the inherent performance and artifice in any documentary. Performative documentary blurs the boundaries between fact and fiction, for it is a mode 'which emphasises – and indeed constructs a film around – the often hidden aspects of performance, whether on the part of the documentary subjects or the filmmakers'. All documentary is performative because 'it is given meaning by the interaction between performance and reality' (Bruzzi 2000: 154).

This may well be the case. The subjective or personal qualities that emerge when an interviewee fulfils a narrative function can also imply a certain reflexivity, but this can reveal itself with far more subtlety than Michael Moore will ever be able to achieve. In *Shoah*, for instance, contributors act as witnesses, but in the process give us insights into their own personal complexity. A classic example is the Israeli barber (see Chapter 2), who had shaved the heads of those about to die in the gas chambers, as he tries to delay and deflect Lanzmann's questioning away from his memories of working in a concentration camp.

Reflexive documentaries draw our attention to the subjectivities involved in a film in a number of ways. Sometimes interactive techniques are aimed at stressing the emotional and subjective experience of the filmmaker, as with Waitt's experiences. However, being reflexive and being self-conscious are not synonymous. Ruby differentiates them as follows: the former requires the filmmaker

> to be sufficiently self-conscious to know what aspects of self it is necessary to reveal to an audience so that they are able to understand the process employed, as well as the resultant product, and to know that the revelation itself is purposive, intentional, and not merely narcissistic or accidentally revealing. Self-reference, on the other hand, is not autobiographical or reflexive. It is the allegorical or metaphorical use of self. (Ruby 1980: 156)

Self-reference does not necessarily lead to reflexivity. Nevertheless there are some films in which autobiographical elements are intrinsically linked with reflexive elements so that the personal and the reflexive become organically connected. Such is the case with Agnès Varda's most recent work, which shows elements of poetic and creative autobiographical reflexivity. Her 2008 film *Les Plages d'Agnès* is a nostalgic reconstruction of Varda's life and work in which a beach she used to visit as a child is used as a mnemonic spring-board to reexamine her experiences of life.

Case study: *Les Plages d'Agnès* (2008)

Agnès Varda's *Les Plages d'Agnès* is an autobiographical documentary in which the filmmaker returns to the beaches of her youth and explores her experiences in connection with beaches. When she revisits Sète beach in France she recalls all the other beaches she visited at different times in her filmmaking life and weaves the memories sprung from those times and places into her film. Varda edits photographs, vintage footage, scenes from her previous films (dated from the 1950s) and present-day sequences into a journey through her life, during which she examines the joy of creation and the pain of personal loss, death and aging.

Although having spent a lifetime making documentaries, *Les Plages d'Agnès* is the first time Varda has taken such a presence in front of the camera, and her appearance seems constantly to remind the audience that this is a personal point of view of her life. The film starts with Varda saying: *'Si on ouvrait les gens, on trouverait des paysages. Moi, si on m'ouvrait, on trouverait des plages.'* (If people were opened up, landscapes would be found. If one opened me up, one would find beaches.) The film starts with a sequence of mirrors showing her, other people and the film crew operating around her. Her use of mirrors underlines the fact that though this is an autobiographical documentary, there are others involved in informing and shaping her life.

There are also plenty of references to frames and framing as elements of poetic reflexivity in her documentary film; for example she acknowledges the professional framing of her oeuvre by influential people, some of them artists like Braque and Magritte. She also credits documentary filmmakers, for instance Alain Resnais, who edited her first films. Shot in Super8, 16 mm film, digital material and HD format the film is a complex blend of diverse technical views of filmmaking that help to piece together Varda's concept of memory. Though the film is primarily characterized by poetic reflexive techniques, other elements of reflexive documentary operate within the film to give it its unique feel. Varda makes a visual and technical reference to Chris Marker, who 'appears' in disguise, hidden behind a cat portrait, his voice digitally altered when he pretends to interview Varda. Her film is interspersed with whimsical dreamlike sequences of acrobats and circus performers set to music, framing references to her memory of connections to the people she met and places she visited during her life. The autobiographical nature of the work uses expressive and procedural techniques to draw in and enchant the viewer with a vision of the filmmaker's world.

Conclusion

Reflexivity has a wide range of manifestations, and this makes any generalizations, or indeed conclusions, more difficult. We should not confuse discussion of reflexivity more generally with particular reflexive techniques (MacLennan and Hookham 2001: 4). Indeed, the recent BBC phenomenon of the TV presenter (MacIntyre, Parry, but also Theroux, Merton, Palin) who adopts reflexive techniques to hook an audience with his (not yet her) experiences and reactions to strange and unfamiliar situations does not amount to reflexivity in general. Rather the use of reflexive techniques in the television format amounts to an attempt by executive producers to use the specific personality of the presenter to good effect, not to demonstrate the documentary process reflexively, for experimental or philosophical purposes, but to appropriate certain techniques in order to enthral the viewers.

Nevertheless, it demonstrates how profoundly reflexive influences have permeated the production landscape. In his over-enthusiasm for the mode, Nichols notes: 'Reflexive texts are self-conscious not only about form and style, as poetic ones are, but also about strategy, structure, conventions, expectations, and effects' (Nichols 1994: 57) – an acknowledgement of the potential for further analysis of the genre. However, further categorization can be problematic. Thus, according to Babcock's system of analysis, *Tribe* contains elements of expressive, procedural, referential and meta-narrational modes of reflexivity. Parry's narration and on-screen presence relate to the expressive and referential functions of reflexivity, as he is both the driving force behind the filmmaking process and reveals his relationship to the subjects of the film and their world. Babcock's system may offer a useful set of definitions, but its application is limited by the fact that some films could fit in everywhere or in several places.

Stepping beyond the strict confines of descriptive categorizations, reflexive films aim to engage with the audience rather than the historical world: 'Questions of authority may diminish in favour of questions of tone, style and voice' (Nichols 1994: 95). Interpretative work that concentrates on definitions often does so at the expense of other important issues such as the effect on audience, and ethics.

The views of near or distant ethnographic communities (whether in the Amazon, Paris, or elsewhere), cannot always be represented fairly. Films like *Chronicle of a Summer* make us reflect on the ethics and politics of representing others in a documentary that was not made by the participants. The presenter or filmmaker may not want to go too far down the reflexive road; rather he or she may see their role as 'translating' or explaining unfamiliar material for a Western audience, or as providing a Western reaction to the locals, as in *Tribe*, for example.

An excess of reflexivity may mean that the film then becomes a 'meta-discourse' on filmmaking. There is a fine balance to be struck between the amount of knowledge the subject matter and of the production process that is to be revealed. The world needs to be understood if it is to be changed, and indeterminacy by itself will not help to achieve this. As Plantinga has pointed out, there is also a revival of documentaries with a 'formal voice' in that they attempt to explain reality (Plantinga 1997). Even Ruby, a pioneer defender of reflexivity in anthropological film, admits that it is difficult to know how much knowledge of the subject matter and which aspects of the production process should be given attention in the final product, and when, conversely, an imbalance can adversely affect the end result (Ruby 2000: 155). Hence, 'there are no quick or simple procedures for a reflexive approach' (Pauwels 2004: 57), but what matters in reflexive documentary is the way in which this self-consciousness and self-criticism is accomplished, morally, intellectually and aesthetically.

It is certainly clear that reflexivity of process has a larger importance than may at first sight appear from individual gestures on screen. This can be revealed when, for instance, participants ask for the camera to be turned off, or when they look directly into the camera lens, or when they contribute towards or collaborate with the production process. The structure of visual perception is made visible. This brings the truth of the production enterprise into sharper focus, enabling audiences to appreciate that truth in documentary is a matter of perspective. 'Because the only truth of a given scene is the visual mode of address, all a documentary can be evaluated for is whether or not this truth was brought into view' (Butchart 2006: 443).

The reflexive aspects of many 'new documentaries' have challenged the previous truth claims made by the techniques of verity. As Williams puts it: 'It has become an axiom of the new documentary that films cannot reveal the truth of events, but only the ideologies and consciousness that construct competing truths' (Williams 1993: 9–21). Yet it is important to retain on the agenda the need for documentary's quest for some sort of truth, even if that quest seems to be receding. The way the use of reflexive techniques impinges on the truth debate demonstrates that its implications go beyond simply the study of reflexivity.

Reflexivity enables the filmmaker to inform the audience about the process of making a documentary statement. But audiences still perceive the need for certain conventions – over-indulgent reflexivity challenges this, even subverts audience expectation. On the other hand, if a film contains few reflexive elements, audiences may wonder whether they are reading more into it than was intended. In much of the writing on reflexivity, the needs, potential perceptions and expectations of the audience have been overlooked. It is therefore to these that we must turn in the next chapter.

7 Audience
A World View or Viewing the World?

Summary

Can the meaning of a documentary be seen as a dialectical interplay between the text and audience? If so, what is the difference between a film that invites an audience to be pro-active as a social agent for change and a film that leaves them confused, or engenders a feeling of deception? Is it an awareness of the responsibility that the filmmaker has to the audience, and if so, what does this mean for people at the receiving end? Is every viewing experience influenced by existing assumptions, knowledge and expectations?

Scholars have pointed to the need for an unspoken moral contract between producer, participant and viewer, with each party expecting a true and honest version of places, people and events that are to be filmed. If 'faked' material is presented, for instance, this would break the contract. Assumptions by the audience certainly frame the way they receive documentary. Audiences watch, knowing how such films are made, and with expectations that real events will be depicted accurately and truthfully. However, expectations and the positions that documentary viewers adopt are complex and more research is needed to enhance our understanding of this. The democratization of content that has occurred as a result of the extension of video production and the Internet to people usually at the receiving end of media, plus documentary's explorations of race, ethnicity, gender, popular and historical memory, have all served to challenge the role of 'spectator' and 'location', influencing the changing relationship between creators and consumers of documentaries. New technologies, cheap software and the Internet have enabled a crossover of roles and locations between viewer, editor and producer.

Although this chapter addresses all of the questions posed above, most of the answers are not definitive, because the available evidence is frequently ill-defined, unclear or incomplete. There are a number of reasons why our knowledge of audience behaviour is imperfect. First and foremost there is the imprecision of the subject, for the relationship between media and audience is characterized by what Thompson has called an 'orientation towards an indefinite range of potential recipients' (1995: 85). Audience research is useful for examining the complex relationship between documentary text, audience and wider political contexts. However, it is conducted under a range of different circumstances, so there is not necessarily any consistency. A person's reading can have gaps and inconsistencies, while on other occasions patterns may be discernable. Attitudes change over time, according to social and political context, but there is a thread of continuity in the long-term existence of 'documentary desire', which is a desire to know.

Introduction

The potency of media is undeniable. Thompson calls it a 'symbolic power', defining it as 'the capacity to intervene in the course of events, to influence the actions of others and indeed to create events, by means of the production and transmission of symbolic forms' (Thompson 1995: 17). This chapter examines the implications of this power for audiences. Yet understanding the role of audiences is a difficult issue that needs to be appreciated at both micro and macro levels: 'embedded both in the macro-environment of political economy and in the micro-world of domestic and daily existence' (Silverstone 1990: 174).

The idea of Cinema Verité is to establish trustworthiness by giving the appearance of non-mediated reality. I say 'give the appearance of' as this is precisely what Cinema Verité attempted: it presented evidence and allowed audiences to make up their own minds about it. Truth-telling as defined by observational film is impossible – an insight is more realistic. But audiences need to apply and sustain an informed scepticism, and cannot be protected from their own failure to do so.

A lot of things can happen during the viewing process, emotional and intellectual – shock, boredom, pleasure, interest, being informed. These are all *active* responses which can challenge assumptions about the form, or add to our knowledge of the world, or both. The response can also depend on the setting for viewing – a classroom will be different from a home, and a festival screening different from that of an activist group like a trade union, for instance. At such screenings, directors may introduce some input to the viewing situation by handing out notes, or conducting a discussion afterwards, or by inviting a specifically targeted audience. The institutional context of a documentary's production and reception will influence the way audiences 'read' a film.

The case studies of *The Family* (1974; 2008) and *Battle for Haditha* (2007) show in different ways how a real story is presented to the audience as a document – but is it documentary? In longitudinal and observational documentaries, participatory or non-participatory, we see the audience perspective as an identifying factor: the viewer discerns national, local and class-bound distinctions, and creates a narrative. The lack of a narrative script and investigative question can be as much of a problem in defining what documentary is, as it can if it is over-narrativized, as in docu-dramas such as *Battle for Haditha*. Audiences can become confused about the truthfulness of the filmmaker's work.

Although media institutions have the potential to shape knowledge and influence values, the way that this relates to audiences is complex and changing, for the mass communications process is full of uncertainties, witnessed by the fact that audiences interpret messages in their own way, or ignore them. Every viewing experience is accompanied by previous baggage, and is therefore subject to the attitudes, assumptions, knowledge (such as recognition of the face of a famous person on screen) and expectation that audiences bring to the process of viewing.

Audience researcher Thomas Austin asks the following question about the audience's position in relation to television and screen film contexts: 'If documentary is about gaining mediated access to "the world", where exactly is this world in relation to the audience?' (Austin 2007: 2–3). In his set of case studies gauging audience responses to certain documentaries he also analyses the manipulation of films in terms of scheduling, format, distribution and advertising. In discussing certain films (*Être et Avoir, Touching the Void, Capturing the Friedmans*, as well as wildlife documentaries and films about class identity), he assesses the viewers' reactions and conflicts with televisual and filmic formats. He uses the Internet to set up a series of questionnaires recording responses to films (2007: 84–6), and explores how online sales that boosted DVD viewing figures were a factor driving the boom in documentary making, especially in the US (2007: 16, 20). He notes that the majority of documentary filmmakers increasingly appeal to a 'niche taste' in television, on account of the increasingly segmented audience who have a need to be surprised by the truth. This segmentation, he observes, is viewed by scholars and filmmakers as either opening up opportunities or as potentially corralling 'a mainstream audience . . . into ghettoes' (2007: 23). In noting 'a key change . . . in the continuing proliferation of, and growing audience shares won by, cable and satellite channels beyond the major networks', Austin points out television schedulers' tendency to commodify their product into a 'portfolio' (2007: 21, 23), variously packaged to appeal to certain predetermined demographics at different times of day. He outlines as slightly outmoded the notion that in Britain television is the main platform for documentary, despite current publicity about the dominance of US films in cinemas influencing the UK's changing mode of delivery to the big screen.

Austin reminds us that a documentary's purpose is to re-present the world to the audience, as a form of 'mobilising practices of distinction, disgust or denial' (2007: 178), thereby enlightening them. Some examples will demonstrate the potential range of audience reaction. Such practices have caused viewers to position themselves differently when watching a documentary and they have felt betrayed by films such as Mitchell Block's *No Lies* (1974). This film, like Michelle Citron's *Daughter Rite* (1980), uses Verité techniques to give the impression that real people and not actors are involved. In her film, Citron tries to bridge the gap between earlier Verité-realist films and the newer anti-illusionist ones (Kaplan 1982–3: 64), but the anger of realization indicates that a different audience identification takes place for documentary than for fiction. Citron has studied the way audiences react to her films, and points out that audiences feel safe if what they see matches what they're told they're seeing, for they have a psychological investment in the aesthetic codes and contracts that make up a film's reliability (Waldman and Walker 1999: 284). Her film *Daughter Rite* 'violates this safety', thereby breaking the codes. Citron recounts how during a discussion after a screening one woman said she felt angry because she had empathized with a character whom she believed to have been real, only to feel betrayed when she discovered that the character (who had been raped by her stepfather) was fictional and portrayed by an actress.

By contrast, audiences seemed to feel less cheated by another of Citron's films, *What You Take For Granted* (1984). The emotional stakes in this more 'sociological' film were not so high, although according to the filmmaker it was more manipulative. Audiences have come up with a variety of readings about which elements in the film are documentary and which fiction – in fact, all the characters and the entire film, except for a top and tailing montage of documentary footage, are fictional. Yet the 'conscious way in which they engage in figuring out the aesthetic puzzle of the film allows them to feel more active as viewers and thus less manipulated' (Waldman and Walker 1999: 285). The filmmaker concludes that this film is an ethical success, but that this is only achieved by a more subdued emotional tone, which she considers a high price to pay for an autobiographical work. Nevertheless, both of these films created a self-consciousness on the part of the audience.

The meaning of a documentary can be viewed as an interplay between the text and audience – a process which requires viewers to be active, using their own experiences and identity in the way they sort the meaning. The audience must make a comparison between their existing understanding and what is represented on the screen, which they may either accept or reject. A variety of interpretations of any given text are likely, for sense-making involves a negotiation between a viewer's perspective in a particular situation and what the text brings to them. Influences may include their job, class, gender, life experiences and viewing environment. A builder, for example, may engage with a DIY documentary on television in a different way to a viewer with no specialist knowledge in the area – or the builder may decide to switch channels because he has no sympathy with the advice given in the programme. Likewise, the reaction of a group of people viewing a film together may be different to that of a lone individual. Traditionally a one-way street of disseminating information or opinion to the viewer, documentary's emergence on the Internet has altered the dynamics of that relationship. The nature of audience involvement through the Internet changes the dynamic of their understanding and interaction with documentaries, particularly if viewers are invited to become politically involved in open-ended debate on open-source platforms, thus blurring the lines of the traditional positioning between editor, audience and producer.

Research

The complexity of the issue clearly calls for more research, but the question of audience is a neglected area in the case of documentary. It is reasonable to assume that the media institutions who make or show documentaries would know what audiences think. After all, such organizations are in an ideal position to find out by collating information, but in fact there is a certain distance between producers and audiences, with the former often unsure about what the latter think and how programmes are being received. However, the process of quantifying such information can also serve to package viewers and turn them into a commodity, which is arguably a form of exploitation, since media institutions have power over audiences deriving from the economic control that large corporations have over their markets. Documentary is not immune to the process of consumerism, of treating the audience as a commodity to be bought and sold, as changeable as the media itself.

When researchers attempt to reconstruct the way audiences interpret media products, they do so within a conceptual framework provided by theory; but different theories of audience behaviour are based on different models of communication. Using these, researchers are not interrogating a body of objective, scientific knowledge – rather a complicated and changing set of practices and influences that extend beyond the practice of viewing. Studies of the relationship between media and audiences demonstrate how variable and unpredictable responses are across time and space. Ang for instance, has demonstrated how research – which represents a form of surveillance – has failed to understand television audiences (Ang 1991: 80–3). Since the inception of the Internet, audiences have become even more difficult to define and measure. Nevertheless, in the commercial sector of cinema, Hollywood surveys the audience across a range of media products, formats and tie-ins, and the influence of marketing people has redoubled through the integration of marketing and audience research. This sort of corporate power means that individual creative workers and audiences have less power and ability to influence the nature of their relationship. An individual documentary, made outside of any controlling institutional frameworks, may escape this fate, but if it appears on the Internet, the likelihood is that it will be subjected to 'counting'.

Counting values on the Net

Viewing and comment figures on the Internet's larger sites such as Google and YouTube have yet to be analysed in any meaningful way as indicators of an audience's relationship with documentaries. When they are collected it remains to be asked what such figures mean. At its simplest level a viewing figure of 1,606,610 (as at 12 April 2007) viewings for Dylan Avery's *Loose Change* (see Chapter 1, and later in this chapter) on YouTube is just that, a record of the size of the audience. At a more complex level, questions could be asked about why so many chose to look at this site – is it sensational? (yes); is it provocative? (yes); is it a good well-made documentary they could trust? (no). The notion of audience demographics is more problematic as the film is projected right to the computer owner and at their convenience: we simply have no way of knowing about his or her views or environment unless we ask. Security and data-protection issues on the larger websites forbid general access to the member viewer's details – but since his or her contact details are present in the commentary box, a researcher could feasibly approach a finite group in this manner.

Perceptions of responsibility

Perceptions of responsibility will depend on our understanding of how audiences react. Although this is a field of study in its own right, most of the research addresses the effects of television more generally, rather than documentary specifically. Nevertheless, an appreciation of media theories provides a wider context. The models for further research have become well-established over the years but have tended to concentrate either on the effects of media products or on uses and what is called 'gratification'. This involves analysis of how media is received. Influences on research methods are various and diverse, having stemmed from literary criticism and reception aesthetics, cultural studies, critical communications and social science methodology, including feminist theory and interpretative micro-sociology. Yet they all theorize around three aspects of communication – audience, message and social system – which influence processes and outcomes. These are also referred to within the humanities as text/discourse, recipient and context.

Since 1980, when David Morley's work introduced a breakthrough (see Morley 1980), much research has examined how far audiences resist constructions of reality that the mainstream media offer. The trend has been to view audiences as increasingly active and also selective in the way they use and interpret media messages, while social context is viewed as more and more influential in the formation of audiences, genres and institutions and also in the interaction between the media and recipients. As processes and attitudes evolve, 'audiences, rather than "reading out" messages from media, are seen to "read in" quite *diverse* meanings into mass-mediated texts' (Jensen and Rosengren 1990: 218). Thus audience de-codings are plural, the context matters, and viewers do not always agree with textual analysis. In short, 'the audience has become *visible*, theoretically, empirically and politically, having previously been marginalised and devalued within media theory' (Livingstone 1998: 4).

By being part of an interpretative community audiences contribute towards the production of social meaning and cultural patterns. Themes and genres will be assimilated by specific audiences in varying ways. There are, however, limitations to audience research; it has often been concerned with macro-discourses rather than local producers and recipients, but when research into the latter is undertaken, results cannot be generalized. Research into effects and uses and gratification aims, like most research, for replicable studies of representative samples from well-defined populations, although reception theory, cultural studies and literary criticism research aims for qualitative, empirical case studies. These are the kind of examples presented in this chapter – but they are specific and should not be used to generalize. Each documentary or documentary series will be different, and may be viewed in a variety of circumstances, according to historical period and environment. The audience reading of a film is never permanently fixed, but constantly being reconstructed, with a range of interpretations.

In addition, there is always the problem for researchers of non-audiences, that is, of how to find audiences who do not care about a film. This accounts for why so many audience studies have concentrated on fans, who obviously prove easier to research because of their commitment (Austin 2005). However, those who do not vote, or tick boxes entitled 'no comment' or 'not applicable' are still part of the population, although they tend to be written off in surveys as 'non-people'. This is not just a trend that researchers need to measure, but also a source of counter-examples that go against the grain; for a documentary maker with intent to influence, this is particularly important, although we cannot jump to conclusions:

> The counter-examples are of considerable theoretical interest, because they are central to our understanding of what the media mean to (all) people and why they engage with media in the diverse ways that they do . . . But this claim should not be confused with the claim that such cases are quantitatively representative of audiences. In other words, possibility is distinct from probability.
> (Livingstone 1998: 15)

One group of researchers has distinguished viewer response to television programmes into three types – active, social and critical – a distinction which can be applied more specifically to documentary. 'Active' response centres on how a viewer's interpretation of the text engages him or her, according to prior frames of reference which help to formulate an interpretation. People who view a documentary will not do so completely passively: they approach it with a variety of different sorts of prior social and political knowledge. Equally, they will come from a range of social backgrounds, according to class, ethnicity and gender, which will determine the cultural context within which they operate. Gender, class and age will introduce discursive factors that shape social interactions around the viewing experience. This background influence will be shaped by forms of subjectivity, individuality and membership of different social groupings. 'Social' refers to the viewing experience, contextualized by factors such as how the film is transmitted – on video/DVD, on broadcast television, with or without advertising, whether the viewer is alone or part of a group, how much conversation is taking place, and so on. 'Critical' refers to the process of negotiation with a text, as viewers either accept, reject, or criticize the information given. Audience members can be 'reflexive' in that they are able to refer to wider social, political and/or economic debates about any given events or issues. This will help them to understand specific documentaries, especially those dealing with issues of 'experiencing' survival in extreme or unfamiliar worlds. As Austin says about *Touching the Void*: it 'was marketed to deliver just such an experience, via investments in character, story and setting' (2007: 80).

Stuart Hall also identifies three basic ways in which audiences can react to a text, although he concentrates on processes of 'encoding' and 'decoding' rather than on the sender and the receiver (Hall 1986). This is a semiotic way of viewing content in which 'the range of meaning depends very much on the nature of the language and on the significance attached to the patterned arrangement of given signs and symbols within a culture shared by sender ("encoder") and receiver ("decoder") alike' (McQuail and Windahl 1993: 146). But Hall recognizes that this is not always the case, hence there are three options for the audience when the culture of the sender and the receiver differ. Audiences can accept the message without question, which would mean accepting a 'dominant' reading (as communications are subject to the media's hegemonic code). Or they can decide not to question the existing political-economic system, but still challenge aspects of a situation with which they disagree – these contradictory dominant and contrary elements then represent a 'negotiated' reading. Or, finally, the viewer can adopt an 'oppositional' reading, hostile to versions offered by the dominant media.

There is a complex interaction between the fields of discourse accessed by the audience, the constraints imposed by the viewing context, and the narrative structures of the text. A documentary text is therefore likely to be open to interpretation, with a meaning that is both negotiable and polysemic.

Changing viewing environments

Historically, documentary has served a useful purpose as a 'duty genre' in the broadcasting schedules, that is, as a mark of public service commitment

(Winston 2000: 40; 2008). When documentaries on social issues first revealed the extent of poverty, bad housing and unemployment, it was the first time that visual recording had become available to ordinary people to describe what their lives were like. *Housing Problems* was the first documentary to record working-class people on location. For audiences, this was a big step forward. 'Giving them a voice by obtaining location sound with the bulky studio optical recording systems of the day was an exercise in technological audacity as great as any in the history of the cinema' (Winston in Gross, Katz and Ruby 1988: 39). Of course there were limitations in the way this was done,[31] but at least cinema audiences and later broadcasters were acknowledging the rights of such people to address an audience.

The introduction of lightweight, synchronous sound portable packs during the 1950s enabled the documentary maker to be much more mobile, and to develop a more fluid style. This in turn was enabling both for participants in a film, and for audiences. The emergence of the Sony 3400 Portapak in the early 1970s empowered communities and facilitated the impact that groups like Top Value Television had on television. Their influence implied that documentary did not have to be professional: amateur use of camcorders now became valid, and was even legitimized by the introduction in the 1990s of the BBC's long-running and pioneering series *Video Nation*, for instance. From the 1960s through to the present, we can trace three parallel trends:

- The availability of increasingly more portable and cheaper forms of technology has led to an enlarged community of filmmakers. Audiences are able to become filmmakers, and the crossover between these two positions is more fluid.
- Contexts for viewing and reception have become more diverse.
- Documentaries have been offering participants a greater role in relation to the shape of the film and its content.

The Internet has played just such a role enabling the audience to become involved making films, particularly conspiracy documentaries. 'Fledgling directors equipped with cheap editing programs such as iMovie have found a new outlet on the Internet, and an audience of millions who just can't get enough' (Stevens 2007).[32] Films such as Dylan Avery's *Loose Change* (now on its third and supposedly final cut), challenging the official version of 9/11 and claiming that it was a 'carefully planned, controlled demolition' orchestrated by the US government, garnered over 1.6 million viewers on YouTube. *Loose Change* encourages the audience to participate in two ways: with the intent both to influence and to encourage, the filmmaker exhorts his viewers to participate in protests and in cheap filmmaking. First, through effective editing and cutting, the audience is led to believe the film's critical premise that 'the United States Government was . . . criminally negligent in allowing the 9/11 attacks to occur'; second, the filmmaker seeks to influence his viewers to protest, to become activists through his website and, though the use of cheap editing software, perhaps make films themselves and upload them to the Web. *Screw Loose Change*'s Mark Iradian saw Avery's film and was inspired to use similar editing software and to post his riposte on Google video as an empowered viewer.

Obviously in a pioneering age, reactions would have been different to that of today's audience. The public life of documentary began in cinemas, and it is important to bear in mind that viewing a film in an auditorium is a different experience to viewing it in one's home. In the former, audiences are captive, they pay attention, in a state of expectation and perhaps wonder. They will wonder at *March of the Penguins*, they will all laugh together at Michael Moore's egotistical satire. The impact, en masse, is more formidable. But when people pay, they also expect more: documentary in the cinema needs to be bigger and better in terms of its impact. Viewing positions vary and are constantly being modified according to the style of documentary as well as context and historic period. The influence of television has brought a greater entertainment bias, with bizarre or exotic topics presented in a more relaxed and colloquial way, seeking to divert rather than to inform or challenge the audience. Audiences watch TV under mundane conditions, not as a memorable evening out. In a multi-channel environment, viewing consists of glances: television programming is designed for channel zappers, for audiences who patch in and out, half-watching. This makes the task of exposition in documentary more challenging. Television is more intimate but ephemeral or transient: it represents the accessible, the familiar, the shareable for a whole population (Scannell et al. 1992: 334).

However, audiences are discerning. According to Ellis, factual genres have communities of viewers who understand the 'protocols and ideas of appropriate behaviour which are sustained by concrete institutions and common practices' (Ellis 2002: 206). Thus, it is easy to recognize a BBC wildlife film. Viewers of a documentary approach the activity with a basic understanding and acceptance of conventions and techniques, such as an appreciation that gaps in time can be linked by voiceover commentary and montage, because the film is pursuing an argument. Similarly they will recognize that, particularly in a current affairs documentary, once a problem has been posed, the film will start to hypothesize possible solutions. The viewer has been conditioned to expect certain characteristics of the genre, thus cues from the text and experience of previous documentaries will prompt them to start, almost automatically and subconsciously, to formulate their own hypotheses. These will either be confirmed or rejected as the film unfolds.

In an observational documentary the social actors play themselves, and it is their very imperfections and human weaknesses that allow audiences to speculate about the characters' motives within the evolution of the storyline, and within the carefully defined situation which the event or organization will provide. Institutions like a hospital or school will provide a context within which audiences can apply their own analytical tools. However, the conclusions that individual viewers are likely to reach will vary: different people in different circumstances at different times can draw a variety of conclusions.

Case study: Paul Watson's *The Family* (1974) and Jonathan Smith's *The Family* (2008).

Paul Watson's 'fly-on-the-wall' reality series *The Family*, the first in Britain, documented the working-class Wilkins family's fortunes in a cramped flat over a Reading greengrocer's shop. The film is intrusive; it documents an intimate and sometimes painful slice of life as

Margaret rules the roost over her husband Terry and their four children. Her head perhaps turned by the camera's presence, she spills the beans about one of her offspring's parentage as the result of an affair. Her nine-year-old son is reduced to tears; the film's forensic gaze implicates the viewer in witnessing his distress.

Audiences were fascinated by the twelve-part series: around 10 million tuned in to watch this real-life soap, some becoming so engrossed that when Margaret's eldest daughter married her fiancé in church, around 20,000 people descended on the streets outside.[33] The large viewing figures and attendant visitation by enthralled viewers is not only indicative of the power of a real-life film to affect an audience, but is also a reflection of the then dominance of three television channels in the UK as conveyors of others' lives to the nation. Margaret Wilkins alluded to the power of imagination when she remarked in 2003 on the exploitative nature of such films' warts-and-all coverage:

> When you see your life through other people's eyes, it does change things. The only advice I would give to anyone tempted to take part in a reality show is to think twice. The film-makers are going to exploit you – they are not your friends. It's hard, though, because you relax when the cameras are with you 24 hours a day.
>
> (Kendall 2008)

Conversely, in 2008, Jonathan Smith's *The Family* demonstrated a wariness about how the effect of filming the Hughes family life 24/7 will be received by the audience and how they might react. The series, in choosing to document every aspect of a 'normal' middle-class family, whose children attend grammar school, seems to buck the trend of Channel 4's

recent sensationalist brief for real-life coverage. On the Channel 4 website Smith explains his reason for choosing such a normal family:

> We met families who were desperate to be on television – everything from the family with psychic kids to the wannabe Partridge Family. Our search became less about what we didn't want – people who just wanted to be on television, families so extreme the audience would not recognize any of their own lives.
>
> (Smith 2008)

Unfortunately the majority of the programmes focused on the family's rows with the nineteen-year-old daughter Emily about coming home late – not exactly a major attraction for audiences. However, the family do reconcile their feelings and re-establish calm and order at the end of the series. After thirty-four years, and countless real-life series and reality shows spread over the television networks and the Internet, both social actors and viewers are wiser to the siren call of fame.

It is fair to say that if the after-life of such documentaries has a deleterious effect on some participants, others suffer from withdrawal symptoms and may act up to regain attention – several *Big Brother* contestants being a case in point. However, no one has yet measured the effect of the viewer's withdrawal symptoms on the cessation of a series. Simon Hughes is sanguine about the potential interest in his family as subjects: 'There are hundreds of reality shows on TV. There will be people who recognise us for a short time and then there will be another programme. Our lives will change for a little while and then be back to normal' (Kendall 2008).

The viewer's role of sympathizer and emotional participant in social documentary is linked to the compulsion to witness individual participants going through stresses and crises in life; the style raises the enchanting prospect of psychological and possible physical involvement with the social actors in the series. The anticipation of progress is an obvious draw for the viewer as they wait to see if a subject will be transformed by their experience and/or simply forget to mind their manners or observe social mores, which is what the producers and audience hope for in their search for entertainment.

The 'contract' with audience

Documentary makers produce cultural works in which responsibility to the audience entails an obligation towards truthfully conveying the kind of representations that are offered, and there is clearly a lot at stake. Just as audience reaction is a function of the age, so our perception of responsibility changes. It relies on an understanding of what audiences expect to see and receive when they watch a documentary. There are a number of different hurdles that stand in the way of maintaining a responsibility to the audience. Content-wise, sponsorship of a documentary can lead to a film that appears to be partisan because financed by an organization with a particular viewpoint that comes across in the film. The promoter as corporate sponsor has been ever present since Revillon Frères financed *Nanook of the North*. As corporate sponsorship grows, so does the potential for compromise by the documentary maker.

Recently, responsibility to the audience and respecting their 'right to know' has also become an issue for new hybrid forms such as mockumentary and Reality TV, with implications for the relationship between audiences and the documentary genre. Audiences tend to see documentary as more accurate than, for instance, dramatized reconstructions of real people's stories in television reality programmes (Hill 2005: 61). The expectation is that events would have happened as they did happen even if the filmmaker had not been present. That said, audiences do accept a certain amount of staging, but they also expect clear signals for this – such as a caption to introduce a dramatized scene.

In a 2003 survey in the UK, almost 80 per cent of those questioned claimed to be interested in watching documentaries on TV, and nearly 60 per cent believed that documentary provided accurate information, as opposed to only 42 per cent who believed docu-soaps were accurate, although infotainment shows scored 68 per cent for accuracy (ITC/BSC 2003: 60). The documentary maker has the capacity to inform and empower, and the potential to challenge power, so responsibility towards the audience is important. In the Gramscian approach, media are seen as sites of struggle over meaning and power.

> Audiences may use the media in empowering ways to contest, resist and negotiate dominant meanings, beliefs or values around, for example, consumerism, femininity, national identity or religious nationalism. But, depending on their circumstances and the contexts in which they consume and discuss media, they may absorb and accept dominant media representations of social realities that serve to reinforce inequalities.   (Gillespie 2005: 226)

Viewers can be managed and regulated: debates about censorship and 'dumbing down' demonstrate how controversial and how important audiences are to the equation. The advent of Reality TV and docu-soaps has made audiences themselves now more aware than ever of representational fraud.

What does responsibility to the audience involve? Traditionally, public service broadcasters have believed that such responsibility was more important than, for instance, responsibility to shareholders for commercial profit. Of course, the commercial reasons for wanting to learn about audience reaction are very different to the civic, democracy-supporting rationale of public service broadcasting that seeks to address viewers as citizens, not consumers. Documentary writers talk of an unwritten 'contract' between the producer and audience, but in the context of production ethics, the contract is more properly seen as a three-way one between director, social actors (participants) and audience. As documentary's ability to represent real life accurately is limited, this contract may be based on the false premise that a documentary can tell the truth in the first place. Direct Cinema is characterized by an approach which seems to encourage charges of duplicity and voyeurism that disturb the balance in the relationship between participant, filmmaker and audience, at the expense of the participant. However, audiences in the twenty-first century are used to a variety of non-fictional presentations, and can usually recognize manipulation when it appears in the finished product. The contract never promises to avoid manipulation altogether; people make varying interpretations of what they see in a documentary.

Audiences need to be able to tell what kind of programme it is they are watching and to understand the compromises involved – which is one reason why public service broadcasters and regulators have devised guidelines and codes of practice in order to protect the audience. However, so-called protection of audience interests can run dangerously close to a form of proscription whereby broadcasters and regulators decide what audiences should or should not see, and that amounts to censorship.

Genres, activism and engagement

Problems arise when a film contains a mixture of fictional and non-fictional elements, which can lead to audience confusion. Reality TV may digress from the standard documentary norms, but truth-telling remains the criteria which allows audiences to judge 'good' and 'bad' programmes. Viewers seem to have reservations about the contrived format and overt elements of performance in some Reality TV series, when participants act up for the cameras. In contrast, audiences trust wildlife documentaries, along with the news, as being truthful.[34] Reality TV shows that depend on surveillance footage have obtained high ratings,[35] presumably because their 'rawness' becomes equated with reality, and hence with truth.

Spoof documentaries, or mockumentaries, tend to use recognized documentary techniques to gain the trust of viewers, only to undercut this in order to amuse the audience and also often to bring a critical pressure to bear on a topic and on the documentary form itself. This has the effect of challenging the contract between producer and audience. There are a complex range of interpretations open to audiences when it comes to the parody, potential for critique, and deconstruction of the genre that mockumentaries tend to present. This can amount to a challenge to the connection between filmed images and unmediated reality, and to the idea that the filmmaker should be objective and maintain an ethical relationship with the participants. *Man Bites Dog* (1992), for instance, challenges the value system constructed by audience expectations of the ethical and political stance of the documentarist.

It seems, therefore, that audiences should expect to have to work when they watch a film, but the documentary maker must make demands on them with integrity, since that is part of the contract. Words written by James Agee, in relation to how he expected readers to respond to America's most famous work of photographic reportage ever, *Let Us Now Praise Famous Men*, epitomize this thinking: 'For I must say to you, this is not a work of art or entertainment, but it is a human effort which must require human co-operation' (Agee and Evans 1960: 111). Continuing this way of thinking, filmmaker Ross Spears made a documentary equivalent entitled *To Render a Life* (1992), which, by its reflexivity, asks the audience to question the moral implications of the medium while comparing the circumstances of several poor Southern families to the three families featured fifty years earlier by Evans and Agee. The opening segments of Spears' documentary juxtapose wealth and poverty in a traditional way with a facile irony which, arguably, invites audiences to take a patronizing attitude of superiority over the apparent 'victims' of the social system. In fact, because this technique is not used again, the invitation to the audience is to critique the norm of social documentaries that appear to patronize their subjects in such a way, as social actor Alice waves at the filmmakers from the porch of her home, reminding us of the collaboration between filmmaker and participant in this construction. Audiences are made to recognize their position as voyeurs when Spears films a Harvard lecture on the Agee and Evans book, reminding us that social documentary tends to involve affluent people intruding into the privacy of poor people, in order to create a product that becomes commodified. This point is illustrated by shots of the book being printed, taken off a conveyor belt and packed by a female worker: a hint at how a process that starts with creativity, ends up by implicating the audience in exploitation.

Spears makes a conscious decision also about what *not* to do: there is no examination of the political and institutional role of the welfare system as it may relate to the social actors. This, according to one reading of the film, is because a 'too-searching scrutiny of the failures of government would shift the audience's attention to institutions and away from a recognition of how, in spite of their hardships, the families portrayed lead emotionally abundant, richly textured, and even deeply satisfying lives' (Raeburn 1996: 200). In other words, 'victim' status has been avoided, but at the expense of facilitating more overt audience consideration of political change. One responsibility towards the audience has been acknowledged, another – for some documentarists at least – has been avoided. Audiences can feel outrage at the problem – the way that society abandons needy people – but they cannot use the film to consider the solutions.

Case study: Nick Broomfield's *Battle for Haditha* (2007)

Though it is clearly based on actual events and available information, we cannot call this film a documentary since it uses heavy narrativization in its plot sequence and use of shots. It is rather a docu-drama, in which the filmmaker seeks to manipulate the audience to think about decision-making and responsibility.

A consideration of the role and location of the audience in the context of a film whose tagline is 'There are many ways to see the same story' is problematic. Broomfield investigates the killing in Haditha of twenty-

Fig. 7.1 An audience eye view: an Iraqi family hide behind a sofa while missiles rip into their living room in Nick Broomfield's *Battle for Haditha*.

four Iraqis (men, women and children) by four US Marines set on avenging the death of a colleague on 19 November 2005. The docudrama is a re-enactment of the alleged events, casting local Iraqis in the roles of civilians and insurgents,[36] with Marine vets reprising the military roles. The film is shown from those three viewpoints with digital screen splits to show concurrent events. The juxtaposed scenes allow the audience to witness the causes, processes and results of actions leading to the deaths of civilians and insurgents.

Three axes concern the audience, according to Douglas Pye, who labels the film 'interpretive journalism' (Pye 2008). These are: the temporal juxtaposition of scenarios; the spatial displacement from the real world; and the implication of the audience. The temporal axis roots the audience in a linear cause and effect situation where the events are understood as a result of the stresses of war. The spatial element of using actors displaces the viewer from the 'truth', especially when Broomfield shows insurgents briefing a young Iraqi girl to say that a Marine beat her. The

implication of the audience in procedures concerning the execution of death warrants meted out to the Iraqis is unavoidable. The audience may now know that war is not fought man to man but man to screen, and the connection of soldiers to the assassinations is therefore remote.

Two scenes in *Haditha* are of particular interest as examples of audience implication. In the Shovel scene an old Iraqi man is filmed walking down a road from a party with a shovel on his shoulder: he is going to plant a tree. A screen shows a Marine operations room deciding that this man is an insurgent and must be neutralized; the order is given, and the following scene shows the man caught in the crosshairs of gun sight from a military aircraft. A bomb is dropped and the man is killed. In the Spyhole scene an Iraqi man waits in a room for some sign or a visitor. The operations room scene briefs us to the fact he is thought to be an insurgent and the order is given to kill him; we then see a Marine go up to the door of the Iraqi's room. The camera shifts to the Iraqi's point of view as the knock at the door draws him to look through the spyhole – straight down the barrel of the Marine's gun. At that second, the audience apprehends that the Iraqi knows of his imminent death, and thus the viewer is involved in experiencing a mixture of fear and revulsion.

Haditha refuses to align itself with any particular viewpoint for a sustained period. In its triangulation of ideologies covering three strands of war (civilian, marine, insurgent) we are forced as viewers to extemporize. We share an overview with Broomfield, in predicting the shovel man's death, in being included in the executive procedure of the operations room, and in being forced to share the spyhole man's terrified realization that he is going to die. The film is powerful in the way in which it paralyses us with a horrified fascination. It is ultimately a manipulative piece, transforming the viewer's relationship with documentary from a traditional passive role to a more active one in a docu-drama, with the introduction of local actors for added 'authenticity' and the use of digital manipulation resulting in a position of implied responsibility.

The evidence so far raises the question: how should audiences be expected to engage with a documentary or docu-drama? The *Outfoxed* (see Chapter 4) website allows you to 'make your own movie' through its creative commons licence, which allows a user to sample clips freely in their own creation, even using some Fox News clips.[37] The ability to access and use such material further blurs the traditional boundary between manufacturer and receiver, though there is no record of how visitors to the *Outfoxed* website use the licence, so it is not possible to gauge the effectiveness in any meaningful way. However, 'pseudo-geekery' offering participatory devices that allow users to become quasi producers does not necessarily ensure civic or community engagement in the real world when the home PC is turned off. It is precisely because documentary aims to encourage awareness and activity within the public sphere that most examples of documentary audience research – which are admittedly still few and far between – have concentrated on the intellectual and social processes of negotiating meaning.

Jane Roscoe (1999) made a study of a series entitled *An Immigrant Nation* (1997), shown on New Zealand TV. When interviewing focus groups who had seen the programmes, she found that they adopted the 'burden of representation' in that they felt obliged to comment on any representations of their communities that they considered to be inaccurate portrayals. They thus assumed a role as spokespeople for their communities, and were critical of stereotypes and of the way small groups appeared to represent an entire people. They were critical of aspects of the production, especially the choice of interviewees and the length of interviews, and they had expectations about how documentaries should be made, in particular anticipating a long research period, which was not feasible within the limitations of the budget.

Documentaries in the series were made with the aim of giving communities the opportunity to tell their own story. The programmes shaped the way in which the people interviewed later talked about their immigrant identity, but their response and criticisms also indicated that the nature of representation in the documentaries was limited. So, for instance, audiences who were interviewed also had expectations about fairness and 'truth' – particularly that representatives of the communities in the films should accurately reflect social reality. Roscoe concludes that 'these documentaries open up a space to talk about issues concerning national identity, immigration and narratives of New Zealand's past'. Hence the concept of the 'citizen viewer' – whereby 'viewership' is considered as potential citizenship (Dahlgren 1995) – is important, for it allows the audience to engage critically as part of the process of democratic political involvement: 'the concept of the citizen viewer furthers our understanding of audiences as active, social and critical' (Roscoe 1999: 147).

In another study, examining a television series entitled *New Zealand Wars* (1998), Jane Gaines demonstrates in addition that a 'visceral' dimension can be included in assessments of audience engagement. This is an argument concerning how radical filmmaking politicizes viewers by aiming to inspire 'political mimicry' of the on-screen activism. It is worth considering what this actually involves in terms of how viewer response is conditioned by documentary structure and historical consciousness. The series presented a revisionist history of local struggles against British colonial occupation which caused a vigorous public debate during and after its prime-time screening on TVNZ, and provoked an emotional response when shown to focus groups of indigenous origin. The series illustrated the potential of TV to 'undermine popular preconception of history and promote the process of decolonisation' (Gaines and Renov 1999: 77). The aim of historian presenter James Belich was to empower Maori views with his reinterpretation of the causes, course and consequences of the colonial wars, in order to bring discussion of race and culture, previously marginalized by historians, into the public sphere. Familiar present-day locations were combined with performative sequences and a haunting soundtrack to establish a connection between past injustices and turbulent contemporary cultural relations. Rhythmic editing, painterly images and the soundtrack produced a 'visceral' dimension capable of prompting strong emotional responses (Perrott 2002: 70). Factors such as age, ethnicity and gender certainly influence individual responses, but the visceral dimension of emotional response comes from instrumental sounds having culturally specific meanings, such as the singing of Waikato's famous 'ngeri'. Traditional ballads expressing solidarity inspire action, according to Gaines (Gaines and Renov 1999: 92). The people interviewed said they felt like being sick, or wanted to burn the British flag, overcome with feelings of disgust, pride, resentment, anger. But Gaines has also suggested that documentary audience engagement does not necessarily translate into political activism. In this case, the viewers who had the most highly charged reactions could be divided into two categories: those who wanted to reinforce the status quo, and those who were too marginalized to be able to effect change through their opposition, because they lacked the ability to create 'the infrastructure required for mass dissemination and organisation' (Gaines and Renov 1999: 76).

Thus, although political documentaries may want audiences to contribute to the particular struggle represented, measuring whether such films have actually moved audiences to do something about the situation portrayed is difficult. It is one thing to identify the appeal of political films through the senses, as did Eisenstein when he talked of the 'emotive vibration' in montage (1949: 80). It is another to make the leap towards claiming that audiences may be stirred into action, for this introduces questions of how to identify the sort of activity provoked by the film, and what outside influences come into play. However, although particular communities can respond emotionally to didactic film structures such as those discussed above, not enough is known about the effect a political documentary might have on an audience not directly involved in the struggle the film represents.

In short, in order to assess the effect of a film on an audience, we need to know more about the political conditions in that audience's world. The Rodney King footage offers a prime example of a 'documentary effect' linked to an actual event, for while appeared that the video of police brutally beating a black person provoked the riots and looting, in fact it was the context of the '*world* of the footage – the world within which police conduct humiliating strip searches on young black men – that *made* people riot' (Gaines and Renov 1999: 96). Images of struggle such as scenes of rioting, people clashing and moving en masse, backed by rhythmically edited popular music, are often used by filmmakers because they want audiences to carry on the same struggle. Examples include *In the Year of the Pig* (1968) (see Chapman 2007: 13, 26, 54, 115, 149), *Word is Out* (1977), *The Battle of Chile* (1979), *Berkeley in the Sixties* (1990), *Handsworth Songs* (1987) and *Union Maids* (1976). In the latter for instance, Woody Guthrie sings traditional solidarity ballads in order to 'reach audiences at the juncture of the physiological and the psychological and to use musical associations to "produce" . . . not just affiliation but action' (Gaines and Renov 1999: 92). The creative mimesis can be celebratory, as in the case of George Stoney's *Uprising of '34* (1995), about a failed strike among Southern cotton workers during the Depression in the United States, with the potential for audiences to 'respond to and engage in sensuous struggle, in the visceral pleasure of political mimesis' (Gaines and Renov 1999: 100).

Documentaries that deal with the politics of gender and sexuality have an important role outside of the circles within which they are viewed. The plural, diverse nature of public groups actually has the effect of challenging traditional, homogeneous concepts of the public sphere, as first outlined by Habermas (1989). As Livingstone points out, 'the links between the personal and the political make it obvious that identity and solidarity mediate access and participation within the public sphere'. The result is a public sphere 'in which the concept of rationality is itself up for negotiation rather than a consensual given' (Livingstone 1998: 10).

Documentary activists tend to believe that the purpose of their films is to convert the audience to a particular perspective. So, for instance, feminist documentary endeavours to inculcate the audience, whether male or female and regardless of individual subjectivities, into a feminist perspective. Feminist filmmakers were able to reach new audiences though the creation of their own alternative distribution outlets during the 1970s, especially in Canada, the UK and the US. Cambridge Documentary Films, for example, received a lot of feedback from their film *Taking Our Bodies Back: The Women's Health Movement* (1974), which was shown in schools and colleges, health-care institutions, women's groups and libraries. The film's content – dealing with pharmaceutical advertising in medical journals and how the marketing of antidepressants targeted women patients – led audiences to draw wider conclusions about the nature of female representation in the media. Their next film, *Rape Culture*, looked at cultural messages that perpetuated and reinforced rapist behaviour. The producers expanded their audience to include rape crisis centres – a relatively new phenomenon at the time – and also women's centres and colleges that were introducing feminist theory. The audience was active in responding – women nationwide sent in letters expressing their 'outrage at the politics and violence encoded in these images' (Lazarus 2001: 247).

There are some directors, such as Emile de Antonio for instance, who by their own admission want to challenge the audience by presenting a viewing experience that will make the viewer think (Chapman 2007: 149). This is one approach, but requiring an intellectual response is very different to a requirement to make leaps of faith, as the audience are expected to do in *Who Killed Vincent Chin?* (1987). Here, we are taken on a journey through a highly charged political situation, and are faced with conjecture at almost every turn. At the end of this ride, we are invited to continue the journey elsewhere, as social agents and social actors, to achieve a resolution to the incomplete story. When a documentary like this requires an audience to interact by completing the story itself, it actually reproduces the very dilemma that history itself presents: the picture is never final or complete. It is constantly changing, and we, the audience, must actively contribute to the filling of the inevitable gaps. It seems that some films, particularly when viewed by sub-cultural groups, can encourage a resistant reading, although any claims that this is the case have to be qualified by a reminder that we always tend to know more about the producers and the production than we do about the audience itself.

Participants in a documentary are least able to check what the audience reaction has been to their involvement in the film. The aims of the filmmaker have traditionally taken precedence. Thus, Michael Moore's aim in *Bowling for Columbine* was to leave audiences angry. Certainly his indictment of the American 'society of fear' had an impact, backed up as it was by Moore's own publicity stunt at the Oscars, a Cannes Film Festival award, and by much discussion of the film's formidable box-office success: in 2002–3 it became the biggest selling documentary in history.

The jury is still out on the effects Moore's documentary approach has on audiences, in the face of some well-documented views on his production ethics. The charges against *Bowling for Columbine* are essentially the same as for *Roger and Me*: factual errors and inaccuracies, exacerbated by manipulative editing using cut and paste for satirical purposes, at the expense of serious exposition of content and substantial, fair, political argument (Chapman 2007: 124). We have to ask here, for instance, what message audiences are likely to take about Moore's implied depiction of Charlton Heston as a racist, since the latter, despite his support of the US gun lobby, also has a history of civil rights activism, and marched with Martin Luther King in the famous 1963 demonstration in Washington, DC – ignored by Moore.[38] In terms of correcting impressions, a few seconds of commentary to this effect would have sufficed, but would it have diminished the satirical impact for the audience? And is Moore's satire really concerned with fairness in the light of his stated mission that audiences should leave the cinema angry?

Although scholars argue that the effect social documentaries have is by and large minimal, there may well be indirect effects, whereby documentaries contribute to a slow and unobservable change in public perception over a period of time. The effect may be cumulative, involving other media and public organs. Al Gore's *An Inconvenient Truth* was a surprise hit that was not predicted – probably because of its uncomfortable message. The detail it gives on rising temperatures, increasing sea levels and threats to wildlife, together with a message that there are actions – including support for the Kyoto agreement – that can be taken, had a clear effect on audiences. As *America* magazine put it: 'There is little chance that one can emerge from the theatre doubting the reality of the environmental threat' (17–24 July 2006). *The New Yorker* went even further: 'If even half of what Gore says is true, this may be the most galvanising documentary you will ever see in your lifetime' (26 June 2006). *Variety* had predicted that the 'pic may prove an awkward fit for theatrical distribution. Exposure through academic/activist channels and perhaps self-distributed, one-night-stand bookings . . . could work best' (6–12 March 2006). How wrong they were.

In fact, this stunning lesson in political communication has a structure that is carefully pieced together to create mood by playing off an idyll – the summer time dream of enjoying nature by a river – that is threatened by a series of environmental nightmares and dangers. Audience reaction is anecdotal, nevertheless, comments such as these by Jonathan Freedland restore our faith in documentary's power:

> I am ashamed to say it took a movie to make me realise what, above all others, is surely the greatest political question of our time . . . Sure, I had heard the warnings and read the reports: for two decades environmental activists have been sounding the alarm. But, I confess, none of it had really sunk in the way it did after seeing *An Inconvenient Truth*. I can think of few films of greater political power . . . The range of emotions this prompts begins with shock, then anger . . . But soon anger gives way to determination to act . . . It worked on me. Four months after I saw the film, I find myself looking at the world through its lens.
> (Freedland 2006)

Audience reaction to a documentary may not be confined to the subject matter – a fact that close readings sometimes ignore. When talking about the film's effect on him, Freedland comments: 'The film leaves a more direct political thought. You watch and you curse the single vote on the US supreme court that denied this man –passionate, well-informed and right – the presidency of the United States in favour of George W. Bush' (Freedland 2006).

When it comes to 'new media', audiences don't just sit, watch and listen in the way they do in a cinema. Their ways of engaging are more active, involving searching, downloading, chatting, surfing; yet they are also more casual, even if omnipresent (in that an Internet connection is always on). Some see this as a gradual democratization of media usage, in that the balance between user and maker, and the relationship between the two, has changed dramatically.

Television meanwhile has become more narrowcast and diversified. Globalization, the Internet and fragmentation all means that the producer must choose a specific audience rather than assuming a more broadly defined set of viewers, although the relationship between documentary maker and audience should still be one between citizens in a democracy, 'rather than consumers in a giant content-candy store' (Singer 2006: 12). The interest in open-source technology (see Chapter 3, on Brett Gaylor), documentary and the audience lies in the flexibility of assumed roles and localities adopted by the viewer. The crossover of editorial, production and onlooker roles shift as the once passive recipient of information transforms into an active contributor. Ironically, the so-called independent platform of the Internet has become an institution in itself (Chapman 2009). Thus the hoped-for democratizing effect of the Web has not really allowed an independence from structure but merely an enhanced sense of accessibility to viewers, as the Internet is increasingly appropriated by huge conglomerates.

Audience identification

How then do audiences identify with a documentary? Vivian Sobchack calls upon Belgian psychologist Jean-Pierre Meunier, who sees documentary engagement as an intermediate form sandwiched between the two poles of home movie on the one hand and fiction film on the other. *Triumph of the Will* (1935) provides an example: we do not use the images of Nuremberg to evoke larger personal memories, as with home movies. Although we already have prior knowledge of what Hitler looked like and what he did, we pay more attention to the screen images than we would with our own movies. We learn about Hitler while watching the film – a process that adds a real charge to our knowledge about the historical figure in the viewing experience. 'It affirms what we know in experience: that not all images are taken up as imaginary or phantasmatic and that the spectator is an active agent in constituting what counts as memory, fiction, or document' (Sobchack in Gaines and Renov 1999: 253).

Audiences also identify with knowledge: watching a documentary affirms the viewer as part of a knowledge culture. Experts know, and they know for the viewer, which produces a 'pleasure of the recognition that the other knows and thus I can know' (Cowie in Gaines and Renov 1999: 29). Another aspect of identification in some documentaries comes when audiences take the position of the camera, especially that of the roving, hand-held camera in direct or observational films, so that there are 'scopophilic pleasures' (Cowie in Gaines and Renov 1999: 29). The familiar, recognizable trait of verisimilitude depends, of course, on audiences believing what they see. Identification can also involve the viewer having empathy with the social actors and being moved by their stories as if they were their own, or in contrast to their own. If the world depicted is not believable, audiences will not be able to sustain belief in the verisimilitude of the film.

The pleasure of learning that motivates viewers of a documentary is a process that takes place while we watch the film, although the specific knowledge gained builds on a cultural understanding we already have. There is a dual process of appreciation that takes place which involves a positioning within our minds of the specific in relation to the general:

> However much our cultural knowledge informs us that who and what we see on the screen are partial aspects of a 'real' and more general existential ensemble, in so far as we do not *ourselves* have existential experience of the persons or

events we see on the screen, our *specific* knowledge of these persons and events is contemporaneous with our viewing of the film.

(Sobchack in Gaines and Renov 1999: 249)

This specific knowledge will be added to our general knowledge on the subject, or else rejected (after attention has been devoted to it, if only momentarily) as not being relevant, interesting or useful. Sobchack has signalled the importance of the viewer identification process: 'As much as documentary space points off-screen to the viewer's world, it is a space also "pointed to" by the viewer who recognizes and grasps that space as, in some way, contiguous with his or her own' (Sobchack 1984: 294). It is fashionable to criticize the representation of 'victims' in social documentary (Winston in Rosenthal 1988: 30), but part of the pleasure that accompanies such documentary viewing involves a feel-good factor when we see people who are less fortunate than ourselves: we demonstrate (at least to our inner selves) that we are sympathetic to human suffering, which makes us good people. (Donation to charity probably results in a similar feeling.) But, for this to work, the demands the less fortunate make on us must keep us properly distanced from them, and they must not articulate those demands with too sophisticated an analysis, 'or else they will rival the spectator as knowing subject' (Cowie in Gaines and Renov 1999: 32).

Conclusion

While Austin's work is to be praised for its attempt to redress the paucity of audience research in relation to institutions, he does not address the impact of the newest and most powerful institution of them all: the Internet, how it enables and affects or limits the viewer, and indeed where the location of the audience is in the 'view' he posits. He asserts that as documentary represents a 'world view' (Austin 2007: 178), as a perspective expressing value-judgements on any given topic, any sense of impartiality is lost in the very act of making the films. The audience in Austin's view remains affected by the *experience* of the characters and story. The 'power of documentary enlarge[s] the viewer's capacity for "generous imaginings" of others, for confronting, re-imagining, and grappling with a new, less complacent sense of self' (Austin 2007: 181). However, by concentrating on the interface between textual mechanisms, promotional tactics and the audience's viewing strategies, Austin ignores the issue of audiences being motivated to take an active part in television or film documentaries; nor does he attempt to reposition the audience.

Some argue that documentary makers have a responsibility to educate their audience to recognize documentary for what it is – subjective – so that their expectations of a documentary film will change (Winston 1995: 254; 2008). Of course, objectivity involves encouraging the viewer to make up their own mind about the facts or the situation, which should have been fairly presented. This is not to say that the audience should not be presented with a principal argument, but only that an alternative point of view should also be broached. If no alternative is presented, the film may come close to propaganda – aiming at the propagation of a single perspective.

However, it is clear that audiences often relish the didactic: the popularity of Al

Gore's *An Inconvenient Truth* (see Chapter 5) among certain cinema audiences seems to have resided in the comfort factor of receiving recognizable messages. One reviewer writes of sporadic clapping by movie-goers in Manhattan's East Village, their rapt attention and mutterings of approval, capped by sustained applause over the final credits: 'Only rarely do you witness this kind of interaction between the audience and a film. A cinema is not a theatre' (Usborne 2006).

In a global future, influenced by deregulation, technological convergence and audience fragmentation, protective responsibility to the audience will become more and more difficult, but, some say, more important than ever because of the lack of regulation. A re-think concerning the audience is already happening, but more research is needed as this evolves. Diversification and commercial pressures have caused public service broadcasters to rethink their relationship with audiences. The audience is no longer seen as a unified group but as a collection of diverse groups.

The fragmentation of audiences in a multi-channel environment means that audience ratings are down – a much criticized measure that is imperfect, and that provides questionable data for analysing minority broadcasting (Ang 1991; Austin 2007). The ways that broadcasters and audiences relate is also problematic: 'The informal and, in Britain at least, generally secret way in which audiences relate to broadcasters is through ad hoc, programme-based, qualitative research and other audience feedback arrangements (letters, phone-ins, etc.) that are largely unaccountable and offer little of public or lasting value' (Livingstone 1998: 11).

Indigenous audiences may have another agenda for viewing: viewers can become filmmakers who are, or can become, activists. Here documentary is central to the maintenance and strengthening of world view and identity. For Aboriginal producers and audiences, for instance, creating and enjoying their own films about their own lives facilitates discussion and awareness of cultural practices, histories and political issues. Furthermore, audience awareness of documentary form here is obvious: both makers and viewers are conscious of the identification that is intended to be achieved between participant, maker and subject, and viewer-reception is specific to their political agenda.

How many hurdles should the documentary maker set up for the audience in their interactive role? To engage in the deception of a hoax is questionable. There is an argument that filmmakers should be educating the audience to be better readers of the media, because any communication is bound to be interpretative, and usually influenced by the narrative approach. Yet no matter how sceptical audiences become about what they see, if a filmmaker sets out to deceive them, or at least to confuse them by challenging conventions, the likelihood is that they will succeed. Not all of the responsibility for interpretation can be off-loaded onto the audience.

Equally, a film can provoke a variety of opposing reactions: passivity or resistance, anger or resignation. The effect will depend on context, period, gender, class and race, and existing audience 'baggage'. A documentary may support the status quo, or an alternative vision, and viewers may read the message differently according to circumstances. Either way, the filmmaker has an obligation to the audience that encompasses an ethical responsibility.

8 Ethics
Shifting Boundaries

Summary

Most documentary makers are, to a large extent, unconstrained. As discussed in Chapters 1 and 2, there is often a conflict in documentary between creative output and reality; in exploring this liminal space issues about the shifting boundaries of power, privacy and the public interest arise. Ethics only enters the equation when the right of the filmmaker to artistic expression begins to conflict with the rights of others – with people's rights to, for example, privacy, information or freedom from slander.

Discussion about ethics in relation to film falls into two categories. On the one hand there are the production procedures and process – in particular how should documentary makers treat social actors and secure the 'consent' of participants? Fiction film studies have usually focused on a semiotic approach, but this neglects the central influence of participants in a documentary, who are usually integral to the subject matter. Is the filmmaker compromised when he or she turns the camera onto members of their own community? Is there is an added complication of an unequal balance of power between maker and participant?

On the other hand there are the form and effects of the finished product. Is there a conflict between the public's 'right to know' and the way this clashes with privacy? Technological advances and the advent of the digital age may mean that access to people's lives is easier, but boundaries are shifting; filmmaker intervention and representation can present challenges to public and private senses of propriety. In a digital era when perceptions of public reputations and private rights are at odds with each other (see the later case study *A Jihad for Love* [2007]), and in situations involving excessive intrusion into people's privacy, libel and slander cannot be adequately analysed as a semiotic phenomenon (Nichols 1991: 271). How does the potential of digital imaging challenge or threaten so-called objectivity?

The potential for unethical behaviour in television is exacerbated by market forces that encourage excessive career rivalry, and competition for audiences and ratings. At the same time, the producer has an obligation to satisfy the requirements of commissioners, while also maintaining industry standards. Obligations to the audience and to what has been called 'the contract' between producer, participants and audience are also examined in Chapter 7.

The idea that the camera does not lie is in conflict with realization that, when it does lie, the audience has a right to know that the truth has been concealed or distorted, or that there is fakery. Fresh styles of presentation in linear and non-linear forms are constantly emerging, some of which raise questions of accuracy

therefore no potential action for libel. Furthermore, they agreed to participate, and this consent is crucial.

Robert Flaherty paid participants in *Man of Aran* £5 to risk their lives by taking a canoe out in heavy sea and later said: 'I should have been shot for what I asked these superb people to do for the film, the enormous risks I exposed them to, and all for the sake of a keg of porter and £5 a piece' (quoted in Rotha 1983: 113). For example, islanders were in danger from their proximity to enormous waves. In the film, one participant, Tiger, has to grab the hair of another, Maggie, while filming, to save her from falling into the treacherous waters.

When filmmaker George Stoney went back to Aran in 1976 to follow up he discovered a host of ethical issues, thus his film *How the Myth Was Made* was seen as an exposé of Flaherty's malpractice. In fact, Stoney actually supported the importance of the original film as an historical document of the outlook of the people of Aran. Stoney was concerned for the participants with whom he was making the film: he believed in collaboration, even in post-production when he forfeited much of his own power as director, which is rare. He spent a lifetime asserting that the people about whom he was making documentaries should have been doing it themselves (Winston 1999: 84; 2008). Stoney's experiences seem to support Clifford Geertz's view that, 'If the relation between observer and observed (rapport) can be managed, the relation between author and text (signature) will follow – it is thought – of itself' (quoted in Roseman 1991: 505).

Trust

Given the generally held, even if erroneous, belief in the authenticity of the documentary image, trust inevitably becomes part of the ethical agenda. In practical terms, the issue of how to 'manage' participants in a documentary has to be faced by the production team in every project. A documentary maker needs to gain the trust of social actors before filming can start, but also to maintain a respectful distance.

Is the filmmaker compromised when he or she turns the camera onto members of their own community? While the objective approach to documentary tends to bring a feeling of distance, subjectivity often involves intimacy. The fashion for personal documentaries where the makers use their family or certain family members as the subjects simply complicates relationships between producer and participants, because exploitation is easier, and more likely. This affects relationships after the end of filming, and may remain an issue as long as the film is in an archive and can still be viewed. Participants should be able to retain their own personality, and should not be made to appear differently for the purposes of the film.

By interviewing her family for *The Devil Never Sleeps* (1994), as part of her investigation into the death of an uncle, Lourdes Portillo seemed already to have a head start in terms of gaining trust and access. However, she ended up crossing the line from private into public, and by exposing certain intimacies, exploited the access that would probably not have been granted to an outsider. This actually placed her in a difficult position. In the film she reveals her will-ingness to betray the family for the sake of the film. Her aunt, the wife of the deceased, actually suggests on screen to the filmmaker, 'you make me say things that I shouldn't'. Mexican audiences sensed this to be the case, and did not feel comfortable with the broaching of the public/private divide (Iglesias-Prieto 2001: 144). Our awareness of betrayals at the expense of the aunt is consolidated by the end titles of the documentary which reveal that what we thought was her voice is actually that of the associate producer, playing the widow Ofelia. The sense of betrayal has been rounded off, even if the story has not.

Balance of power

Documentaries are often about the powerless in society. Since the days of Grierson, housing, health, welfare, education and nutrition have provided an almost limitless source of documentary material. But do the victims of society necessarily have to be portrayed as the media's victims as well? The maker too often simply arrives on the scene with a camera, and offers potential social actors little choice, although not all films about working-class and socially deprived people depict them as victims. *Être et Avoir* is about working-class children in a remote rural society that is relatively deprived, but it is a 'feel good' film which was praised in both Britain and France for its 'positive, life affirming experience' (Crick 2004: 24).

Despite positive representation, there is usually still an imbalance in the relative power between the filmmaker and the people being filmed because the former retains control over the production of the images whereas the latter tend to be dependent on the goodwill of the production crew in the hope that they will not be misrepresented. This unequal relationship can be exacerbated if the agenda in terms of the desired messages the film is to communicate and likely outcomes of the project are not the same for the producer/director as they are for the social actors. This tendency is almost inherent in the nature of documentary production (Chapman 2007: 107–9), but there is a counter-balance. Much of the work by women, 'ethnic' and 'minority' writers, artists and Third World communities has developed as a reaction to those with political and economic power.

Documentaries and television interviews from the early days often demonstrate a certain discomfort and awkwardness in performative style that exemplifies the imbalance in power between interviewer and social actor. These days the introduction of reflexivity in filmmaking, a more relaxed and informal approach, and the democratization of documentary have all contributed to the imbalance appearing less obvious on screen – but it is still there. The very existence of a debate, by definition, tends to pose issues in terms of 'them' and 'us'. Ironically, the polarization that we are urged by theorists to avoid is sometimes typified by their own unintentionally patronizing tone: 'There is a *noblesse oblige* that attends power and which suggests the need for all concerned to pause and contemplate the moral implications of the images they produce and distribute' (Gross, Katz and Ruby 1988: 32).

When a documentary is viewed as a text, some power struggles are still discernible, but others that formed part of the production process are left behind. Michael Moore's on-screen confrontations illustrate that power relations between filmmaker and participants can never be equal, they can only be relative. In *Roger and Me*, GM boss Roger Smith exerts his power over Michael Moore by refusing to cooperate with filming. In this situation, Moore has no power; but when his film reaches audiences, he is supreme.

As Margaret Mead once said: 'The more powerless the subject is, *per se*, the more the question of ethics – and power – is raised' (quoted in Pryluck 1976: 25).[39] In *American Dream* (1990), Barbara Kopple used the empowerment of her camera to observe the powerless, in order to communicate information about them to the more powerful. She clearly wanted to show the emotional traumas of the striking workers, in order to elicit our sympathy, but this was achieved only at the expense of their privacy. In a sequence that was cut out for reasons of length, one worker whose job was threatened was feeling confident that he would be able to move to another branch of the meat packaging company in question, and start a new life. Suddenly, the telephone rang, and after taking the call off camera, he then returned and said 'Cut'. Kopple ignored the request and kept rolling while he told his wife that he'd just heard the other plant was going to be sold. Both he and his wife burst into tears. All hope of a future had disappeared. He looked at his wife and said, 'What am I going to do? Meatpacking is all I know' (Crowdus and Porton 1991: 38). Kopple refers to this footage as 'incredible', but does not question the ethical implications.

Since the time of Kopple's film, the impact of documentaries on people in precarious positions of existence has not changed; if anything, ethical issues concerning filming have increased. Advanced digital technology allows greater access, but at a price, especially when filming struggles that involve a clash between notions of state and personal freedoms. Sometimes interviewees are at risk when they agree to be filmed. Such ethical dilemmas for the filmmaker are doubled when the content of the documentary itself also revolves around ideas about ethics. This 'double whammy' is what makes Parvez Sharma's *A Jihad For Love* (2007) both important for this chapter and unusual as a film. The documentary explores ideas of power and powerlessness. Lesbian, gay, bisexual and transgender people around the globe try to find and to hide their love in a Muslim world fraught with danger, since homosexuality can result in capital punishment in Sharia courts of law. The knowledge that the interviewees could have been stoned to death for participating in the film is a sobering thought for the target non-Muslim audience – and this could still be an issue if and when, as the filmmaker proposes, the work is shown in fundamentalist countries. It is interesting to consider, in contexts such as these, what sort of care towards participants the filmmaker needs to exercise.

Case study: *A Jihad For Love* (2007)

Parvez Sharma goes to some lengths to show the risks run by those who dare to find love with someone of their own sex. The film shows how Muslim law and society deal with the issue of same-sex relationships; homosexuality is not tolerated and is considered a crime against religion, which in some countries is punishable by death. In filming his story, Sharma covers three types of power in conflict: the religious, the secular and the personal struggle for freedom of expression.

Sharma, a gay Indian Muslim, first encountered the repressed world of gay

Muslim love on a visit to the United States and decided to explore the topic in twelve different countries. As well as visiting the so-called more tolerant Muslim communities in Turkey, France, India, South Africa, the UK and the US, Sharma uncovered clandestine lives subject to severe oppression in Saudi Arabia, Iran, Iraq, Pakistan, Egypt and Bangladesh, often without government permission. He used inventive tactics to obtain access to his subject matter in risky areas, often working undercover as an aid-worker or a tourist to tell the story of forbidden homosexual love. He taped tourist material at the beginning and end of his tapes and embedded his documentary footage in the middle; he also worked without a tripod so as not to draw attention to himself. Sharma writes on his webpage about the difficulties Muslims in this predicament face:

> . . . many gay and lesbian Muslims end up renouncing their religion completely. But the real-life characters of A Jihad for Love aren't willing to abandon a faith they cherish and that sustains them. Instead, they struggle to reconcile their ardent belief with the innate reality of their being. The international chorus of gay and lesbian Muslims brought together by A Jihad for Love doesn't seek to vilify or reject Islam, but rather negotiate a new relationship to it.   (Sharma 2008)

As we follow Sharma's wide geographic arc, we encounter different Muslim trajectories on homosexuality in each region, as certain groups negotiate their sexuality within hostile cultures. By comparing the types of silence surrounding the issue, alternately discreet or terrified, he was impressed that homosexual or 'deviant' love managed to exist in the face of strict Islamic law. Some interviewees are rigorously orthodox, including an imam who preaches that homosexuality is a crime and is 'obscene and lewd'.

Some gay interviewees lead secular lifestyles while remaining devout in prayer; others leave Islam altogether. Unusually the film is made with a Muslim voice which challenges simplistic Westernized preconceptions of Islamic sexuality. The participants talk of their ethical dilemma in that they are caught between their duty to be a good citizen and their wish to be a good partner, and face persecution in their society. One scene shows a Muslim man and his two daughters enjoying a car ride in South Africa. The father, Mushin Hendricks, is a former imam who was expelled by his community when he declared his homosexuality. When Hendricks asks them what they would do if he were arrested, the elder girl, combining filial love with Islamic education, says she would ask the officials to spare him a protracted death by stoning, and to kill him with the first rock. A different imam points out to Sharma that the only disagreement among jurors trying such cases concerns not whether the defendant is to be killed, but 'how he is to be killed'.

There is a dilemma for the filmmaker in making a documentary on notions of power and powerlessness coupled with the likely impact of the film. His duty to tell the participants' stories is overshadowed by the threat of death, so they have to be filmed in secret. In public, subjects are filmed briefly touching hands, back to camera, walking to prayers; others are veiled, or filmed out-of-focus or in partial shot. In private, some hug each other and dance in full view or speak directly to camera. 'Each of the characters you see on the screen had to negotiate that relationship [homosexuality] with the camera', Sharma says. 'It has taken me years to get to know them and earn their trust' (quoted in Kay 2007). One scene shows a back-to-camera shot of a young Egyptian man, Mazan, watching his own recorded televised trial of homosexuals, and the film then cuts to a profile of his face. Mazan had spent a year in prison where he was tortured and allegedly raped by the Egyptian police. Sharma is intensely aware of placing Mazan at risk but at the same time is compelled to tell the young man's story.

According to Sharma, Islam is the fastest growing faith in the world; he intimates that if it is to grow in numbers it might also grow to embrace more relaxed laws on homosexuality.[40] Sharma's point is that he approaches the topic as a Muslim and that the problem is not merely one of location. Simply moving from a country whose society practises extreme measures against homosexuals, including entrapment, torture and death, will not solve the problem of the clash between ethical and social dilemmas: Islam is worldwide. As a global intersection of Islam with homosexuality, Sharma's film demonstrates that each individual has his or her own struggle with family, friends and society in their own 'jihad' – a term which the filmmaker describes as meaning 'an inner struggle', rather than the Westernized interpretation of 'holy war'.

The film was first screened in September 2007 in Toronto and, as it was screened in other Western countries, quickly gained praise and opprobrium in equal measure from film critics and Islamic communities respectively.[41] The filmmaker plans to screen *A Jihad For Love* worldwide. 'September 2007 is when I started (with a finished film, my first) and now some twenty-five countries and 700,000 people later, the whole world is talking. The movement around this work has begun worldwide. We will be screening next year around the world and yes in Muslim countries as well' (Sharma 2008). It is an uncomfortable prospect to consider the film's after-life: will its subjects be identified, stigmatized, expelled from their communities, tortured or killed?

Away from the threat to filmmaker freedom of expression from repressive regimes, there are many documentaries that are made on a premise of potential equality and collaboration. This tends to be more likely if participants and filmmakers come from the same milieu and see the film as an opportunity to jointly communicate a shared perspective on an aspect of life. The National Film Board of Canada, for instance, experimented with a redefinition of the producer/participant relationship in a series of films about an island off Newfoundland, called Fogo. This happened after a family who had featured in an earlier documentary, entitled *Things I Cannot Change* (1966), were ostracized by the community for revealing the extent of their poverty. At the time the local Fogo community were threatened by enforced depopulation because of the loss of their only industry and source of income – fishing. Rather than targeting a general documentary audience, the films aimed to enable the islanders to communicate specifically with their provincial government: an empowering approach. This was followed in 1969 by a project to train Native American filmmakers, that resulted in a groundbreaking record of the tribal point of view entitled *You Are on Indian Land*.

Similarly in Australia, ethnographers became enablers for the Aborigine viewpoint on land, and with the advent of the new Portapak reel-to-reel video tape recorders, ethnic communities were provided with the technical facilities to make their own films. Campaigning, political or community films, made to encourage consciousness raising, tend to be products of a collaborative effort with the people they are about. In Britain, the BBC Community Programmes Unit pioneered the long-running series *Video Nation* (1993–), again in a democratizing spirit. Collaboration does not solve all ethical problems, but it can help to retain trust and correct imbalances in power. Participants then have the ability to give their interpretation of shots before it is too late – that is before form, structure and pattern are finally decided upon.

Of course, there have been participants who have emerged with benefits from the process of filming and from the exposure that sometimes follows. Oumarou Ganda, who featured in Rouch's ethnographic film *Moi, un noir* (1957) went on to become an important film director in West Africa, while another of Rouch's participants – Marceline Loridan in *Chronicle of a Summer* – became a sound recordist and married the great documentary maker Joris Ivens.

'Informed consent'

The ability to secure cooperation for participation is part of professional competence. The relationship between filmmaker and participant is formalized by 'informed consent'. This takes the form of a piece of paper signed by the participant as a legal release agreeing to the filming, constituting a professional 'consent defence', and providing evidence that people do know what they're involved in. The more private the location and the person to be filmed, the more the need for informed consent.

As a way of correcting the imbalance in power relations, an ethically aware filmmaker will look for ways to protect the rights of social actors. The debate about how to achieve this usually focuses on how much should be disclosed about the filmmaker's intention and aims. Should the producer always tell the whole truth in order to gain consent and maintain cooperation with filming? Should documentary makers explain their own views on an issue to an interviewee before filming takes place? The concept of informed consent is an ethical one, for it retrospectively justifies the conduct of filmmakers who bargain over the participation that is to follow. This is a process which can include white lies, understatement and omission in terms of what is said about the nature of planned filming.

Social actors should retain respect, dignity and pride; they should not be exploited for the advantages of the film. Participants should be fully aware in advance of what is involved in the filming, but the filmmaker will have to guess what the potential effects of a film are likely to be. If 'informed consent' acts as the filmmaker's moral defence, how informed does it have to be before the bargain between participant and filmmaker becomes a constraint on the 'artistic freedom' of the latter?

Sometimes people have unrealistic expectations about the consequences of making a media appearance – instant fame and fortune, for instance – when in fact there may be no obvious benefit at all, or quite the reverse: they could be in danger as a result of it. Facts that may influence the decision to grant permission to film are left out. Often participants are not informed in advance of particular hazards that could arise. In the Rouch documentary, *Chronicle of a Summer*, one of the characters, Angelo the car worker, lost his job because of the filming – which is recorded on screen. The fact that footage will exist, even if it is left dormant in an archive, can make participants vulnerable.

How is it possible to assess whether a participant is truly 'informed'? It can be difficult to know what exactly has been agreed to. Filming can start with goodwill and cooperation, but descend into bad feeling because of misunderstandings and recriminations. Even the most detailed contract can't include everything, and usually filmmakers can't know in advance what the finished film is going to end up like, for this depends on the material gathered and the evolution of ideas during the shoot and in post-production. It is not always possible to predict the impact of the scenes in which participants appear. This can have the effect of changing lives, either for better or worse.

'Privacy' and institutions

Difficulties are made worse when dealing with large organizations where the chain of command may be complicated. Compromises have to be made after negotiation, usually with different people from those being filmed. Organizations and individuals tend to cooperate if they think there is something in it for them, and decisions taken will usually follow a logic of compromise, according to the politics of an organization. Sometimes people agree at the time, but they can become critical after the event when they face the response of others to the film.

A problem can arise when participants are not able to give consent because of institutionalization – in the case of mental patients or prisoners, for instance. These ethical dilemmas of access versus privacy underpinned the legal difficulties experienced by Frederick Wiseman with *Titicut Follies*. Wiseman told a story that people prefer to forget, painfully revealing the horrendous conditions at the Massachusetts State Prison for the Criminally Insane at Bridgewater.

Case study: *Titicut Follies* (1967) and informed consent

The title refers to an annual stage review performed by the inmates of Massachusetts State Prison for the Criminally Insane at Bridgewater, which tops and tails an in-depth recording of activities at this stark, cruel institution. It was unavailable for general viewing for twenty-five years until 1993, and was banned in Massachusetts. The details of what happened raise issues relating to the nature of oral contracts and bureaucratic procedure in situations where the people who grant permission are not those who are the subject of the film. It took a year for Wiseman to negotiate permission to film, obtaining a signature from the authorities to a letter in which he summarized his plans, including procedures, suggestions about the sort of events to be filmed, length of filming and editing (with his editorial control spelt out).

The normal conditions for signing consent forms – freedom from coercion, full knowledge of procedures and anticipated effects, and individual competence to sign – were all in question (Anderson and Benson 1991: 59). It was the first time that an injunction to prevent screening had been obtained outside of advertising on the grounds of failure to obtain consent. The film was so controversial that in legal actions over the case ('Commonwealth of Massachusetts v. Wiseman') it was ruled that the film was obscene and exploitive and had invaded inmate privacy. There were 106 release forms signed, but mostly from staff: out of sixty-two patients who were in the film, most were not competent to sign for themselves and only twelve forms were completed (Anderson and Benson 1991: 73). Wiseman was deemed to have breached an oral contract giving certain senior administrators final approval over the film, and that the privacy of one of the patients, Jim, was breeched. The questions of fairness that remain as a result of Wiseman's legal wrangles, which centre on informed consent, remain unanswered. The people affected are forever commemorated in celluloid.

Studies of the trial records have revealed that consent procedures during filming were vague, and conditions involving releases were also vague. Either before, or more usually just after a sequence had been shot, Wiseman recorded on audio tape an explanation that he was making a film for public TV and theatrical release, and that he would not use all the film that had been taken. He offered to answer questions, and recorded the name, address, telephone number of people who agreed. Rarely did people object, although in most cases, prison officers made the decision on behalf of the inmates. Participants were expected to agree, and if they remained silent, this was construed as agreement. There was no attempt to establish which inmates were competent to agree and which not: Wiseman said in court that he assumed they all were, unless told otherwise.

Later, an officer claimed that Wiseman had been asked to film men who were nude only from the waist up, but he denied this, and his camera operator claimed that the request was misunderstood. The crew did not use hidden cameras, but the telephoto lens used made it possible for them sometimes to go unnoticed, and the directional microphone operated by Wiseman himself was capable of picking up sounds that the naked ear would miss. In one scene, where guards taunt a distraught man, the accompanying correction officer later became a plaintiff in the Commonwealth's legal action: Wiseman claimed that he had asked him if it was all right to film, and that the man had said yes.

The problems of intervention and privacy

Although the litigation surrounding *Titicut Follies* prompted a debate about freedom of speech, and access to information versus privacy, this did not help to solve the issues.[42] The question remains: did the people's right to know what happens inside publicly funded institutions outweigh privacy issues?

There are situations in real life when a documentarist or journalist is observing suffering or misery, and the dilemma arises as to whether they should stop shooting, and/or intervene. Should a camera operator choose to stop shooting and save lives? A news story of people about to commit suicide may provide a 'photo opportunity', but is it ethical for camera persons to stand by and let it happen? Should they intervene at the scene of a disaster or accident, in order to save lives, or are the pictures more important? If filmmakers do intervene, what are the implications for the truth of the situation, the filmmaker involvement and for his or her relationship with the social actor/s? The following situation is often quoted as an example:

> At the conclusion of the Bangladesh war, photographers in Dacca were invited to a 'photo opportunity' in a polo field. It turned out to be the bayoneting of Biharis who were alleged to have collaborated with the Pakistani army . . . People were to be murdered for the camera; and some photographers and a television camera crew departed without taking a picture in the hope that in the absence of cameramen the acts might not be committed. Others felt that the mob was beyond the appeal to mercy. They stayed and won Pulitzer prizes. Were they right?
>
> (Evans quoted in Gross, Katz and Ruby 1988: 17)

Dennis O'Rourke tried to reduce the risks involved in the work of one of his subjects when, in order to make the film *The Good Woman of Bangkok* (1991), he procured his content by becoming the client of a Thai prostitute. The charge for her services was $20, but he ended up buying her a rice farm (as revealed in the documentary), hoping this would allow her to escape the sex trade. It didn't work. The prostitute, called Aoi, kept the farm but refused to give up her trade, on the grounds that in the future there may well be other rich Westerners who could give her material assets.

In fact, O'Rourke had purchased the rice farm *before* the filming started, which means that the way his intervention is portrayed in the film as an event that happened during production, is not entirely accurate. O'Rourke is able to excuse his adaptation of the truth by calling his work 'documentary fiction' (Williams 1999: 183), but as Winston says: 'All films about deviant activities place the film-makers in, at best, quasi-accessory positions' (in Gross, Katz and Ruby 1988: 45). In the film the prostitute makes very clear her disdain for men, and we are left to puzzle about the manipulation of filmmaking, and the ethics of both parties. By participating in the exploitation which is the subject of the film, O'Rourke raises a number of questions: is such a strategy necessary, desirable or even ethically feasible? Should he have intervened in the situation by buying her the rice farm, and what about the un-truthful portrayal of this strategy of intervention? Neither O'Rourke's participation nor his intervention revealed the complete truth. O'Rourke can be criticized for his complicity, and the unequal balance of power is not removed by virtue of the fact that the filmmaker flags it up. A feminist interpretation may be that Aoi's resistance to the moves made by O'Rourke 'grant her more integrity and autonomy as a man-hating, self-supporting whore than she would have had as a "saved" good woman' (Williams 1999: 185).

In *Roger and Me* Michael Moore's on-screen performance is a double-edged sword, for while his comic persona makes the film so creatively successful, it is also ethically problematic. Moore belittles ordinary people on screen for the purposes of his own humour. This raises the question of whether it is ethical to set up social actors for ridicule during the filming process when the participants are unaware of the intention to do so. There is a certain irony in the situation: Moore is using satire to reveal the ethical failures of the powerful, exemplified by the lack of obligation that GM demonstrates towards the town and people of Flint. But does this larger message override the ethical failures of rearranging the order of facts (Chapman 2007: 72) and ridicule of participants?

Voyeurism

There are always moments during a shoot when social actors would prefer that the camera was not turned on, moments that should not necessarily be made public. What's more, the presence of the camera should not determine the course of events. Interviews and portraits aside, documentary ethics centres on the capturing of events and circumstances that would happen anyway, without the camera presence. The filmmaker's voyeurism and the participants' exhibitionism both allow us access to the intimate details of the lives of participants, but at what cost? Is there any less of an obligation to respect privacy where the documentary maker's friends are involved?

The issue of privacy is a complex one for documentary as the medium thrives on a certain feeling of intimacy, personalization and concern about the people upon whose lives the documentaries are based. This is particularly true of Direct Cinema as it benefited from the introduction of portable synchronous-sound cameras that permitted a degree of intrusion into the private lives of members of the public that had never been possible to such a degree before. Previously, filmmakers had to rely on reconstructions and other forms of intervention. These technological breakthroughs and the subsequent increase in the influence of Direct Cinema techniques meant that aspects of the world previously not revealed on film were becoming more commonplace.

Audiences continue to pick up on ethical points involved in Cinema Verité technique. In a viewer survey of *Être et Avoir*, one respondent expressed concern about 'the ethics of using children's vulnerability as the basis of so much of it', while another commented, 'some of the "rawness" made me feel a bit voyeuristic'. When asked what they least liked about the film, one viewer remarked on the fact that the camera kept rolling during a scene when the social actors 'seemed uncomfortable', while another stated, 'I found some of the scenes slightly intrusive' (Austin 2005).

Of course, intrusive cameras are not exclusively the preserve of Verité. Filmmaker Ross McElwee is fully aware of the criticisms he invited in *Sherman's March*:

> The old question of exploitation has never gone away. It's always the queasy center of my anxiety in non-fiction film, this delicate line that you have to tread between filming subjects in such an interesting way that it is not merely a puff piece about their lives, but also respecting their rights and trying to be true to some version of their lives that you as filmmaker and they as the subjects will honor.   (Quoted in Jeffries and Idlett 1997: 21)

On a number of occasions, McElwee continued shooting against the wishes of several individual women who are featured in the film. 'Stop filming, that's cruel', pleads Karen; 'Turn it off. This is important. This is not art, this is life', states Charleen. Calvin Pryluck sums up the essence of ethics on this issue: 'The right to privacy is the right to decide how much, to whom, and when disclosures about one's self are to be made' (Pryluck 1976: 24).

A right to know?

Society may have a right to know about the subject treated in a particular documentary – this is referred to as the public interest – but individual participants also have a right to not feel indignity, shame or humiliation as a result of that treatment. There is a balance to be achieved between these two fundamental rights. We need to distinguish between public and private personae, and to offer protection to the public in semi-public and public areas. In the case of celebrities, intrusion is considered acceptable in many situations: appearances and staged performances are not a threat to privacy, but the use of a hidden camera can be challenged. When cases come to court, media frequently claim that the intrusion of privacy has been in the 'public interest'. There is an historic point here: in the past, media have been considered not just as representatives of the general public, but as the general public itself.

Is it acceptable to invade the privacy of people living in poor housing, for instance, in order to effect a change, and to provide the wider public with information they have a right to know? Ever since *Housing Problems*, the public's right to know has provided an excuse for bad ethical behaviour by filmmakers. Having noble motives and the desire to correct social wrongs does not necessarily justify intrusion into the lives of the poor and weak. Sometimes the filmmaker seems to benefit more from the intrusion than the participants, although in the longer term, there may be social change as a result of the debate that the film has either started or contributed to.

Any damage resulting from invasion of privacy is not normally considered actionable if arising out of the exercise of press freedom; and even if a case is determined legally, this does not let the filmmaker off the hook ethically. In the US, artistic freedom and freedom of expression are still protected by the First Amendment. Legislation such as the European Human Rights Act, policed by the European Court of Human Rights, stipulates that every person has the right to respect for his private and family life, his home and his correspondence. In the US, the First Amendment ensures a constitutional right to freedom of expression, but there may well be moral issues involved in the way a film was made, or what it depicts, or how this is done. So, for instance, the fact that it may be legal to shoot in a public place does not make it necessarily ethically acceptable. A classic intrusion case often quoted is that of the Santo Domingo Pueblo in New Mexico, who sued over the aerial photography of tribal dances when there was a ban on any recording or picture taking of the dances.[43]

When images are made public, the trouble can start: embarrassing facts may be revealed. The effect of exposure through publication of otherwise permissible actions needs to be considered by filmmakers. After the docu-soap series *An American Family* was transmitted by PBS, the Loud family complained that they were portrayed in a false light, creating a wrong impression of their intentions, character and actions. But their right to object was weakened because they had agreed in advance to the filming by signing a release form.

Sometimes a documentary, by revealing everything, can appropriate an aspect of identity which is usually the source of livelihood for the person who objects. A classic example is the successful legal action of Hugo Zacchini, the 'Human Cannonball', whose entire fifteen-second act, which audiences normally pay to see, was filmed and shown on a news programme (see Gross, Katz and Ruby 1988: 13).

Fakery and digital images

It is not sufficient merely to claim that the camera does not lie – there are complexities and contradictions entailed in the act of representation. The fact is, examples of fakery abound, and there are contextual reasons for them. Within the world of television production, budgets are squeezed so that there is less research, directors shoot less and therefore cannot wait for the crucial event to take place, they have less editing time, so the temptation is to set up and construct instead of recording. Wildlife films, where a camera person sometimes waits for a long time to capture the one shot that really matters, have suffered. Chris Palmer's IMAX film *Wolves* (1999) used captive wolves as a stand in for wild ones. The end credits stated this, although the shot itself did not. He defends the use of a white lie in support of a bigger truth: 'I think a film crosses the line in deceiving the audience when it causes them to just completely get the wrong idea about nature' (quoted in Getty 2006).

Can a small lie be justified if it serves to support a larger truth – such as Buñuel's famous *Land Without Bread* (1933) staging of the goat that does not really miss its footing, but whose death is suggested on screen? The underlying intention here is clearly a valid documentary aim – to expose the cruel poverty of the area and its people. Furthermore, it is possible to construe Buñuel's faked elements as a satirical attack on the pretensions of realism. The ethical question is whether the end justifies the means.

Forgotten Silver (1995), with its fictional provenance, provoked a reaction amongst its public service broadcasting audiences: it had the effect of drawing attention to the New Zealand public's naïve nationalistic pretensions and also their lack of historical knowledge. When it was transmitted in New Zealand, viewers believed the filmmakers were offering them a new national hero by reviving cultural myths associated with the history of film. It was, in fact, a 'mockumentary', and the story of an early film pioneer was an invention. According to one reviewer, the film has a significant message: 'The dazzling bricolage that is *Forgotten Silver* implicitly laments the loss of an era in which one could actually make history and not merely rewrite it or artfully deploy its remains' (Sadashige 1997: 938). If this is the case, then maybe the need to unravel issues of subjectivity and objectivity in documentary is part of the condition of the age, part of the act of interpreting history and recreating a version of reality rather than creating it. Nevertheless, for a filmmaker to pretend that a fiction is real amounts to fraud. The film was entirely faked from start to finish, as were *David Holtzman's Diary* (1968) and *This is Spinal Tap* (1983).

Mitchell Block's *No Lies* (1974) is supposed to be a conversation between a rape victim and an increasingly aggressive interlocutor. He tries to suggest that she was party to the act. The credits reveal the entire production to be a fiction, involving actors, a script and rehearsal time. The point is that the images only concur with the narrative for as long as we falsely believe in them. Audiences also have to adopt a certain trust in the veracity of the image. 'Photographical images cannot account for their own production process very eloquently; they cannot tell us where, when and how they are taken . . . In order to work, visual evidence is reliant upon more or less explicit verbal descriptions and personal/institutional warrant that the descriptions are true' (Fetveit 1999: 794). When parts of a documentary are misleading, it is usually because what the narrative suggests about the images is wrong; but it becomes what we may call 'fake' when the images themselves are out of place. Fake material can mislead.

However, there is a difference between fake material and what one writer calls 'material presented in a qualitatively misleading way' (Currie 1999: 292). This is about not so much techniques as their results. Visual metonymy – when one image is used to represent a related idea, image, or experience – is a case in point. An aerial shot of the Eiffel Tower may be used to represent the arrival on screen of Paris as a new location within the narrative. This example would be acceptable to viewers because in such a linking shot the distinction between representation and reality is clear; the trouble arises when we think we are seeing something else. In *Mighty Times* (2004), archive footage of the 1965 Watts riots was used to represent a riot in another city. Audiences were misled about what they were actually seeing – but this civil rights documentary won an Oscar. Just because not everybody has noticed an ethical infringement, does not excuse it. Audience acceptance should not be the only criteria for ethics, for this would mean that the end justifies the means. It would render other ethical considerations, such as how people are treated during filming, unimportant or irrelevant.

Some documentaries contain small parts – a scene or a sequence – that are not entirely truthful. Basil Wright's *Night Mail* (1936) contains shots that were recorded in a studio but that claimed to be of postal workers sorting mail in the train carriage. This film is still preponderantly documentary style, as it consists of a majority of scenes which are 'true', and only one scene that could be construed as fake. In fact, fakery was prevalent in films throughout the 1930s. In *Drifters* (1929), Grierson had a trawler cabin built on the dockside to obtain interior shots. At the time, the technical limitations of lighting instruments, synchronized equipment and film sensitivity all combined to justify sincere re-constructions such as these.

Nevertheless, the filmmaker is still shaping the subject to fit the story that he or she wants, instead of shaping the story to fit the subjects being filmed. Almost every scene in *Nanook of the North* was staged or scripted in some way. Flaherty made a telling statement at the time: 'One often has to distort a thing to catch its true spirit' (quoted in Rony 1996: 116). The most important theme in the film is 'man as hunter'; related to this is the issue of survival and subsistence in a harsh environment. The film was sponsored by the fur company Revillon Frères.

These days Flaherty's great film is an historical document in its own right, as is *Man of Aran* and others. It would be wrong of us to judge him for something that he never intended to do, and to do so in the light of our present trend to defend and define documentary in terms of our presently constructed ideas of 'truth'. We now realize that all forms of experimentation in ethnographic film entail varying levels of authenticity and mediation. The fact is, Flaherty immersed himself in Inuit culture over a period of ten years, and took on a considerable physical challenge – not only because of the nature of climatic conditions, but also because of the heavy, cumbersome and basic nature of his equipment. Flaherty's achievement was obviously successful and impressive.

The premise of documentary has always been that there is some form of bond or connection between what is filmed and the end product, therefore there is an imperative to retain some legitimate referential importance for the documentary image. The ethical implications of the digital manipulation of images raise issues of reliability, realism and simulation, which have stimulated a debate over whether documentary should abandon its claim on the real in the face of the digitalization of images. Digital equipment, and the Internet as a platform, permit ever more wild transgressions in so-called truth-telling in the documentary format. A good example is the film *Zeitgeist* (2007). Filmmaker Peter Joseph seems to be motivated by a desire to advance his activist credentials using techniques comparable to those adopted by Avery in *Loose Change* (see Chapter 1). Joseph's film was first screened on general release, but is now available on the Internet in its entirety. It provides a highly charged selection of anecdotal material, film clips, voiceovers, quotes and book citations, unreferenced and undated, but edited together for effect. Ironically, in his attempts to expose deceit, Joseph has used implicit deception in its creation. He combines three denouncements of deceit and power exercised by the elite, centred on organized religion, 9/11 as an 'inside job', and a supposed plan to create a world government to destabilize the US constitution and dollar.

Case study: *Zeitgeist* (2007)

Peter Joseph's *Zeitgeist* is an example of a non-linear digital format conspiracy documentary compiled with mash-up style (see Chapter 3) overlapping images cut with sound to affect a dissonant story. As a documentary the film corrupts its own power, for it is tainted with simplistic and pernicious memes that have the effect of undermining the serious claims that are made in the content. Ethical issues are raised in terms of the originality of its sourcing and the film's indiscriminate attribution.

The introduction – a musically synchronized sequence over eight minutes long – begins with a quotation, followed by thumping music to illustrate the horrors of war and violence. The music changes to a quiet melody as the Earth comes into view: the scene shifts to the stars, fades to a seascape, and then merges into an image of microbial life. The sequence charts man's evolution. First there is primordial ooze, then a developmental stage of consciousness represented by an image of a hand writing a simple sum. The next step is one that organizes ideologies – here the hand is brushed away and replaced with the Bible and the American flag. This is followed by man as an architect of destruction, symbolized by music changes to an aggressive thumping and by film of the planes crashing into the World Trade Center, followed by more war clips. Images of the victims of war, 9/11 people jumping, and mourners fill the screen. At eight minutes and forty-five seconds the film's title finally appears.

Two main quotations highlight the direction of the film's enquiry about man's ability to create institutions (religious groups, governments, bank cartels) that destroy spirituality. A four-minute Chogyam Trungpa quotation on spirituality at the start of the section is undermined at its end with a quote from Jordan Maxwell's *Inner World of the Occult* criticizing those organizations that for their own profit seek to ruin a simple search for truth. '[These institutions] have misled [the people] away from the true and divine presence in the universe.' The effect is quite comic, though perhaps this is not Joseph's intention. The brain-battering introduction is presumably designed to prime the viewer to accept the filmmaker's version of power-grabbing tactics in the United States. Joseph clearly wishes to state his position that while man is capable of operating in society he is also responsible for creating power-groups in what the filmmaker sees as a conspiracy to maintain global hegemonic rule.

Zeitgeist explores abuses of power in three parts. Part 1, 'The Greatest Story Ever Told', denounces the originality of many religions and states that historicized versions of myths have been used to exert power over the masses. The film asserts that Christianity, 'along with all other theistic belief systems, . . . empowers those who know the truth, but use the myth to manipulate and control societies. The religious myth is the most powerful device ever created, and serves as the psychological soil upon which other myths can flourish.' He visits a Christian religious convention, filming among thousands of ecstatic attendees singing, crying, and praying with arms held aloft. This is a rather weak premise on which to advance the next stage of Joseph's argument on the abuses of power.

Part 2, 'All The World's A Stage', claims that 9/11 was orchestrated as an inside job to generate a collective fear in order to activate and justify the 'War on Terror', to remove public civil liberties, and to promote economic gain for those in power. Clips are immediately juxtaposed with comments to support Joseph's claims that, for example, the Bush Administration knew about the impending attacks on the twin towers; that the military chiefs did not stop the aeroplanes crashing into the buildings; and that the collapse of the World Trade Center was in fact the result of a controlled demolition. Joseph also offers 'evidence' (from, he says, 'notable and credible media') that some of the hijackers are still alive and that one of them, Hani Hanjour, could not have piloted Flight 77 into the Pentagon.

In Part 3, 'Don't Mind the Men Behind the Curtain', in typical conspiracy movie manner, Joseph again twists the 'evidence' to fit his viewpoint: namely, that the protagonists of four twentieth-century wars in which the United States was involved – the two World Wars, Vietnam and Iraq – were engaged in the interest of gaining global economic supremacy. An elite group of bankers are accused of creating unstable financial markets and causing stock-market crashes in order to corner the global financial market for themselves. They are also accused of masterminding the drive to go to war, as banks are forced to push up interest rates in times of combat. Joseph highlights a 2005 proposal to create a North American Union, effectively the US, Mexico and Canada, without borders and with a currency, 'the Amero', that will destabilize the dollar and put the elite in charge. Joseph says the 'investment class' creating the North American Union are the ones behind the European Union, the African Union, and the proposed Asian Union (all four unions are shown on screen) to form 'a One World Government'.

By labelling the so-called power-grabbers as 'the elite', *Zeitgeist* sidesteps the issue of who exactly these people are supposed to be. Furthermore, the ideas are not new – instead the film functions as a fast-paced assemblage of agit-prop, advancing its findings as given knowledge. The film bombards the viewer with two hours of propagandic images, music and voiceover intended to pass off ideas as fact. Several times the film uses television network clips with voiceovers from unidentified people – the effect is to confer the authority of news channels onto the words these strangers utter.

The media are also implicated in the film's assertions that there is a cover-up of the plan for world domination. There are sometimes attributions to sources but it is impossible to tell whether they are used properly or in context. For example, near the end there is a quote attributed to Nicholas Rockefeller that, were it ever to be verified, amounts in effect to a confession of complicity in mass murder. The quote is, however, undated and anecdotal. A conversation is reported in part between filmmaker and political activist Aaron Russo and Rockefeller, which makes the claim that the latter knew eleven months before 9/11 that 'there would be an event', and that after it 'we are going into Afghanistan so we can run pipelines to the Caspian Sea; and we are going to go into Iraq to take the oil and establish a base in the Middle East; and we are going to go into Venezuela and try and get rid of Chavez'.[44] Rockefeller is also cited as saying that people will be 'looking in caves for people they're never going to find', and is described as laughing about the 'War on Terror' becoming an eternal force for maintaining the status quo. People, he claims, would be convinced by the media that it was real, and this would provide a justification for the invasion of Iran.

This argument is furthered by an unethical use of content and of records, as Jordyn Marcellus of *The Gauntlet* comments: 'It's infuriating and prevents any kind of real discussion about the credibility of the original source material' (Marcellus 2008).[45] Marcellus criticizes the film for its duplicity:

> For instance, video footage from the Madrid bombings of 2004 is used during a discussion of the London bombings of 2005, the implication being that the footage is from the actual bombings in London. It is deceptive filmmaking pure and simple and no manner of self-righteous explanation can disregard the simple fact: it's an out and out *lie*, 'creative example' be damned. For a film that rails against deception, there's a lot of deception implicit in its creation.
>
> (Marcellus 2008)

Thus legitimate questions about what happened on 9/11, and about corruption in financial and religious organizations, are all undermined by the film's determined effort to maximize an emotional response at the expense of reasoned argument.

Digitally recorded and edited images can originate from any shot irrespective of whether the recording taken from the real world. Since documentary is supposed to be rooted in the real world, this has the potential to undermine the entire basis of the medium. Even when the starting point is an authentic shot, it can be changed so dramatically that it may no longer bear any relation to the original, and the modifications made to the image may not be detectable. In fact, the concept of an originating 'master', as opposed to a copy, is no longer relevant. However, the power of technology to change what we see on the screen challenges the imperative that documentary should represent the real world. Audiences are left wondering about the extent of manipulation, and exactly how 'real' certain scenes or shots are, in other words, they may feel they are losing touch with reality. 'If the aesthetic nature of visuals leads to a lack of meaning and goes beyond a certain point to the extent that form is privileged over content, this can lead to a "charge of impropriety"' (Corner 1996: 29).

The answer is to distinguish more clearly between institutional uses rather than focusing on common techniques that are shared between commercials, fiction and news/documentary. So, for instance, television news and documentaries are constrained by a sense of responsibility towards the audience for a factual discourse, whereas people working on commercials or fiction films would not feel the same constraints. However, changes in one discourse may affect norms in another area, and our trust more generally. Ethical codes, however imperfect, aim to maintain industry integrity and the public's trust.

Codes and limitations on journalistic values

Documentaries can be both journalistic and artistic. This creates ethical problems because the idea of the 'creative treatment of reality' means in practice that ethical journalistic considerations such as objectivity, the quest for truth and social responsibility can become mixed up with aesthetic considerations prompted by the creative urge. The problem arises in drawing the line between the two. Truth-telling may have been influenced by Direct Cinema, but there is a conflict between truth-telling and other creative influences on the production process.

Documentary can be a form of journalism, but it is not limited to that, although journalism and documentary both communicate something about reality and both try to tell the truth. Neither are totally free practices in that they work within institutional constraints imposed by funding, commissioning editors and boards. Both are influenced by the way that entertainment styles and considerations are used to attract and maintain the attention of their respective consumers. Professional journalism codes, as they relate to the social responsibility of the press for instance, are not dissimilar to Grierson's aims for public education,[46] and to this extent the latter can be seen as a precursor to some of the values of today's civic journalism.

Documentary allows for a greater depth of personal expression and the filmmaker becomes more closely involved with participants in the making of the story. Documentary can be observational and therefore attempt objectivity, but documentaries do not have to be journalistic and may not claim that the public has a right to know. Stylistically they may be closer to opinion pieces, editorials, columns, essays, agit-prop or polemic, autobiography or poetry. In short, documentary's artistic claims make ethical systems more difficult for documentary than for journalism.

A documentary presents a story that the filmmaker wants to tell us, even though it is based on reality. So, there is also the application of a narrative construction within the conventions of dramatic realism. Yet most regulatory codes do not pay sufficient attention to an aspect of this – namely, reconstruction. Variations and degrees of re-enactment connected to previously witnessed events are all considered legitimate for documentary practice. Nevertheless, these sort of devices need to be signalled as a departure from the recording of events as they actually happened. Thankfully, some professional codes, such as the BBC's *Producer Guidelines*, specify that reconstructions of previously witnessed scenes should be captioned as such, and made in a way that adheres to the facts.

Professional codes that seek to govern industry-wide practices and behaviour are common for areas such as medicine, accountancy, and so on. These should be distinguished from national regulatory codes that are often administered by semi-autonomous government-supported organizations such as the FCC or Ofcom, which regulates broadcasting in Britain. Historically, such bodies have emerged from the PSB ethic, but their existence arguably poses a threat to artistic freedom. Traditionally, regulators have expected documentary makers to be socially responsible, because of the audience's 'right to know', but this greater good can mean that the end justifies the means. There are examples where investigations into corruption or criminality have meant that informed consent cannot be sought or obtained – in which case the breach of privacy is justified only by the public's right to know, for the overriding public interest may call for subterfuge and justify any misrepresentation or absence of consent.

The authorities' perceptions of the nature of the content that audiences can be served up varies according to historical context and political circumstances, as was examined in Chapter 4. Regulation from above should be understood in its historical context as a cultural manifestation of the previously paternalistic idea of education. Viewed historically, codes have been imperfect, but should be appreciated in relation to the contexts within which they were developed. They can outlive their usefulness unless they are amended and updated to take into account changed thinking and new circumstances – in the way the BBC's *Producer Guidelines* is revised annually and made available to the public.

The experience of journalism is that voluntary codes provide only a fig leaf. According to Winston, the industry 'ought not to hide behind the shibboleth of a public right to know or the myth of informed consent' (Winston 2000: 162; 2008). Market forces influence outcomes in a neo-liberal world, particularly within the worlds of cinema and television. In the free market context of a casualized film and TV industry, dog-eats-dog because of the economics of survival and excessive competition. Meanwhile television broadcasters do not want to lose advertisers or sectors of the audience by giving offence.

Of course, different delivery systems and forms of exhibition have different audience effects. This impinges upon the relevance of ethical issues. The court case to restrict viewing of *Titicut Follies* (Massachusetts v. Wiseman) recognized this to be so when they limited screening to professional audiences only. 'It is reasonable to suggest that social value could accrue from a film or tape in specialised circumstances whereas social damage would result in other more general situations' (Winston in Gross, Katz and Ruby 1988: 54).

Conclusion

Although ethical standards are never permanently fixed and there is a shifting emphasis in notions of access to participants' very private lives and the associated personal issues, one of the problems for documentary is that it has a longer shelf life for public display than some other media forms. Thus one of the participants of *Titicut Follies* had to endure a screening of the film during a university class he was attending after he was rehabilitated and released, and he stated in court that he lost work because of his appearance in the film (Anderson and Benson 1989: 112–3). In the twenty-first century, participants are still vulnerable, as *A Jihad for Love* surely demonstrates. The content of this film also underlines the fact that ethical judgements are dependent on cultural and historical contexts: one country or person's artistic licence can be another person's ethical breach. Ethical judgements must take varying practices and conventions into account.

Since the advent of computer database records, the convergence of the media, and new surveillance technology, the issue of the abuse of privacy has become more urgent. The documentary maker's duty of care when it comes to protection of privacy needs to be weighed up against the public right to know and the rights of the media to publish. The clash between these rights has not yet been resolved. Digital technology and the Internet seem to permit the elimination of formal boundaries not only for publicizing personal stories but also for the content itself.

As seen in *Zeitgeist*, some documentary makers play fast and loose with the format and content, abusing ethical codes of attribution in the telling of a tale. On the Internet, at least at present, this is impossible to regulate. However, advanced technology also opens up fresh forums of discussion about the simultaneous clash of conflicting ethical codes, whether they are institutional, secular, religious or personal. Documentary is important enough as a medium for all involved – viewers, makers and other interested parties – to address ethical problems more directly in an open discourse about, for instance, the viability of professional codes for documentary makers and whether these can, or should, survive into the twenty-first century.

There are still continuing and difficult issues to face about the truthfulness of screen narrative as a form, the balance of power between maker and participant, and the circumstances surrounding informed consent. Ethics will not go away because too many issues remain unsolved. For instance, can one be unethical in order to achieve the end product, which itself takes what one sees as an ethical stance? There is an assumption that there may be some sort of agenda behind a filmmaker's intentions which needs to be explained to participants, so that they are not manipulated or deceived. However, there is a difference between site specific truths and the underlying truth of a film. If we accept that the underlying truth of any documentary lies within the 'perceptual structure of the visual mode of address' (Butchart 2006: 427), then this ethic is not based in journalistic codes, opinion or universal moral consensus. Instead it consists of a decision as to whether or not to disclose the role of visual perception in the construction of documentary images, and as such, individual truths are specific to a given context: in short, 'truth in documentary is always a matter of perspective' (Butchart 2006: 428).

There is evidence that documentary makers increasingly acknowledge the interpretative nature of their undertaking. As this filters through to audiences, the problem of participant consent should gradually become more manageable because the only truth to reveal is the presence of the camera, and criticisms of misrepresentation will be less likely. It is interesting to speculate whether this perspective could have resulted in a different outcome for *Titicut Follies* for instance – but then it would also have required a more reflexive and self-conscious form of filmmaking. Furthermore the interpretative community, and the institutions involved, would still have had to consider the effect of disturbing content in various viewing situations. Only more detailed research on audience understanding would allow us to analyse whether this approach is compatible with perceptions of documentary, and the expectations and judgements that viewers make.

Conclusion

Documentary is alive and well, diverse and multi-faceted, despite the fact that it has always been a medium based on shaky epistemological foundations. Perhaps it is this aspect of the genre that accounts for the various discursive tensions flowing through the pages of every chapter in this study. By and large, these remain unresolved due to the fact that they are inherent in the nature of documentary. The more fluid the genre becomes, the more the tensions tend to surface. In assessing continuity and change, a constant dichotomy has emerged within documentary as a form of factual representation that respects authenticity and yet simultaneously recognizes the impossibility of aiming for 'truth' in the presentation of 'reality'. Documentary amounts to a negotiation between image and reality, subjectivity and objectivity, interpretation and bias, in which we need to look at the balance of emphasis, but also at factors of scale. There is an unprecedented increase in scale on the World Wide Web – of information, images, communication, entertainment, persuasion, interactivity and participation. This in itself requires further critical reflection beyond the scope of this study.

The main argument of Chapter 2 was that the types of representation identified there reflect notions of connection with society, in personal, group and public terms. According to Stuart Hall there is a further tension between two faces of representation of the multicultural (truthful depiction of behaviour and conduit of a group voice) (Hall 1988: 441). This tension raises an unresolved, contradictory question, calling for and 'inevitable process of cultural translation' (Hall 2000: 6). The same could be said for documentary representation more generally. One tension is the burden on producers to depict participants positively but also to use representation as a form of delegation (speaking for the rest of the community). There is a further tension in relation to the history of minorities and of women as communicated in documentary, for it has become a history recorded through gaps and silences.

As with all forms of representation, political connotations arise when the identities of minority cultures have an oppositional role to the mainstream. Gwen Haworth's *She's a Boy I Knew* is an example of personalization translated into ideas of connection with society. Haworth uses her personal crisis and family reaction to it to raise questions relating to difficulties for the individual in conforming to society's expectations. In many films, representation of disempowered members of society is presented as the triumph of hope over adversity. The music competition in *Autism: The Musical* is a metaphor of hope that does not seek to present autism as a subject but to show children and parents as people involved in a task where autism is an 'obstacle'. Thus, the representation of trauma can be oblique – its understatement does not necessarily diminish its potency.

For trade unions, however, the triumph of hope over adversity has become less achievable since the advent of Reaganomics and neo-liberal individualism. Audiences for labour history films are positioned at a point within the past, the treatment of which becomes a function of political context. Thus representational strategies for depicting striking workers change according to the political climate, as examined in Chapter 2 with the contrast that emerges between *Harlan County USA* and *American Dream*.

Although there is now a wide acceptance – by filmmakers, the interpretative community, and even institutional sponsors – of subjectivity as a creative approach for documentary communication, a tension still emerges, for both subjectivity and objectivity can effectively coexist in the same film. Furthermore, the lack of accountability and the anonymity of online contributors has led to concerns about verification and accuracy, and these very concerns have been expressed online, using the documentary form as a communication vehicle, by people such as Mark Iradian in *Screw Loose Change*. Mash-up documentary makers, such as Brett Gaylor, can use the Internet as a powerful tool to project a mix of image, music and message to a curious and increasingly activist audience. The problem here is a possible lack of definition about what a documentary is in this context – Gaylor's inclusive 'open' style indicates a lack of focus.

The focus on personal documentary has contributed to definitional fluidity and shifting boundaries, discernible in the way that the personal and reflexive is assimilated and hence neutralized by the mainstream, especially television. The case studies of presenter-led ethnographic TV series offered in Chapter 6 illustrate the increased fascination with personality-driven documentaries. The creative impulse seems to militate against impartiality, for it involves an element of personalization – especially in wholly subjective films like *Tarnation*. Digitalization has been used in a way that indicates not only personalization but also the democratization of democracy: anybody could make a film from the fragments of their lives.

From the discussions in Chapters 3 and 6 it is clear that films with greater reflexivity, subjectivity, and with more prominence given to the author/filmmaker, are not easy to define. The push and pull of subjectivity versus objectivity is demonstrated by activist documentaries – 'engaged' filmmaking that particularly sparks debate about balance and agency. Contextual influences and prevailing political climates have a critical influence on what the public see, and the way that they see it. De-funding for independent documentary has acted as an effective restriction on freedom of expression. Advertisers want programmes on television to attract popular audiences but the range of subjects that sponsors usually find attractive, or at least acceptable, is limited. Forms of indirect censorship are increasingly emerging, with a range of manifestations of potential audience reception and input becoming more apparent. Globalization and neo-liberalism seem to have created an environment in which internalized assumptions tend to feed a form of self-censorship that is sustained by market forces. This is a live issue for war coverage: as the case studies in Chapter 4 indicate, forms of both domination and resistance need to be analysed.

Outfoxed: Rupert Murdoch's War on Journalism was made available directly to consumers via DVDs in order to avoid problems with distribution (Ward 2005:

101). The case study of *Outfoxed* in Chapter 4 demonstrates that the exclusion of other views can be interpreted as a form of censorship. Censored films usually have uncomfortable messages but political sensitivities influencing censorship also need to be understood at the level of individual shots, as in *Memory of the Camps* and *A Painful Reminder*.

The power of documentary resides in the potential challenge that its message or argument may make to accepted views. For instance, the use of authorial voice can reflect changes in attitudes toward cultural institutions as well as indicating transformational delivery modes in documentary filmmaking. In the twenty-first century, 'documentary as radical interrogation and alternative perspective' (Corner 2002: 259–60) has emerged strongly in relation to certain issues such as Iraq and global warming. In some cases Internet usage can ensure that the message of the film becomes integrated into a wider form of informational awareness. Marketing organizations are already influencing this area – a phenomenon that deserves greater academic attention. How the Internet enables, affects or limits the viewer, determines where the audience is positioned, and how audience identity is transformed in the light of its increased participatory role, also requires more academic research. With broadcast documentary, audiences hitherto have had their own expectations and criteria for judging factual television, which allows them to apply 'a fact/fiction continuum' – but this is changing. This too needs further research as television is increasingly viewed online.

The impact of technology seems to make cultural reappraisal more challenging, making the words of Roland Barthes even more prescient: 'this is without doubt an important historical paradox: the more technology develops the diffusion of information (and notably of images), the more it provides the means of masking the constructed meaning under the appearance of a given meaning' (Barthes 1977: 46, translation slightly altered). The use of webcams and digital recording devices, and the expression of audience reactions via blogging, all show that the balance of power between filmmaker and viewer is constantly changing. Meanwhile, documentary is becoming increasingly versatile, and documentary elements can be transmitted or exhibited using a variety of platforms. The explosion of sites (the Internet, museums, cable and satellite TV, big screens in public places, community venues, et al.) and situations in which the influence of documentary can be discerned is evidence of its renewed power. The way it is analysed must be equally diverse, fluid and inventive, taking into account the varying contexts and usages. No one methodological armoury will suffice for this challenge, and no one study will provide all the answers. The documentary tradition needs to be augmented, widened, constantly reviewed and enhanced by the process of renewal and reappraisal, taking place globally.

Documentary can still act as a powerful medium for effecting change. In 2004 the BBC transmitted a documentary entitled *Death on Camera* that had obtained the agreement of the family of a black British paratrooper who died in custody to show CCTV footage of the man dying on the floor of a police cell. The appearance of the documentary gave rise to an official enquiry and generated a national debate. As a BBC executive producer said: 'Single films can also make a channel look alive and responsive to big events.'[47] They can also help create them. It may well be that in the digital age people start sourcing content for themselves, and that global, cross-platform, multi-channel and new media transmission can help to prolong the life of a single documentary – if the content is such that it will travel.

In a global world where audiences are dispersed and fragmented, but media in a variety of forms are all pervasive, documentary's influence has simultaneously spread and been diffused. The result is a more complex, less tangible medium. But the dispersal of documentary style over a larger audio-visual area into other genres reduces our ability to give a strict definition of documentary.

Meanwhile, as the gap between low-budget documentaries and cinema block-busters seems to widen, the challenge for documentary studies is to embrace the old and the new, the traditions and the fresh trends, the filmic expressions of both the developed and of the developing world. With a documentary, there is always more to be said: audiences know that the characters live to see another day, that institutions continue, even if they change, and that issues remain unre-solved. The future calls for a flexible approach to study, but the need for critical appraisal of documentary is greater than ever before.

Notes

1 There are already a number of excellent studies: see, inter alia, Winston (2008); Barnouw (1992); Jacobs (1979).

2 *An Inconvenient Truth* earned $11.5 million in the US, in addition to $2 million in the UK and the same in Australia and Germany.

3 See Chapman (2007) for discussion of other production issues relating to this classic.

4 According to Winston, the Discovery Channel covered only around a million homes at the point at which the major US TV networks were axing their current affairs documentary departments, Winston (2005) also suggests that an extremely successful PBS project such as Ken Burns series on the American Civil War (1990) achieved ratings seven to eight times greater than Discovery's average.

5 See Winston 2008. In an interview with the author (16 January 2008), Winston suggested that with his interpretation: 'The documentarist would become like a journalist but in another sense: nobody supposes that the hand of the journalist is not present and that the texts they produce "cannot tell a lie". Their work is a prism through which the world is perceived, and it is the writer's trustworthiness which is the earnest of the authenticity of what she writes. Trustworthiness is earned by the social context of the communication; it is not supposed, as it were, "to come with the territory". Documentarists unashamedly would then be, to use Henry Breitrose's terminology, not a fly-on-the-wall so much as a fly-in-the soup – which is what they really always are.'

6 *Housing Problems* is also acknowledged for its importance as one of the first films to use synchronous sound on location; it is the composition and impact of the film that has been criticized.

7 Renov points out that the peak moments in American documentary history all share an opposition to Hollywood which 'shapes the very contours of documentary authenticity' (Renov 1993: 4).

8 For more on docu-soap see Dovey (2000). While he acknowledges that 'Spheres of activity once regarded as essential components of a healthy civic society as diverse as libraries, museums, sports and leisure pursuits, and here public service broadcasting, are all brought under the control of "free" market commodity relations', he also would like us to consider 'what such programmes might tell us about ourselves and our common culture' (Dovey 2000: 20), a point that can equally be applied to documentary.

9 MacLennan and Hookham (2001: 10) also point out that Renov has not yet elaborated sufficiently on his concept, whereas the exploration by Nietzsche of the way that rationalism (initiated by Socrates) destroyed Greek tragedy, and his division of the aesthetic into opposing Dionysian and Apollonian elements in *The Birth of Tragedy* (1872), has of course had a classic influence on subsequent cultural and political thought.

10 See, for instance, Carroll (1983).

11 'US government agents say they have thwarted a plan by two conspirators to kill the White House front-runner and shoot or decapitate 102 black people. Daniel Cowart, 20, and Paul Schlesselman, 18, were arrested in Tennessee on Wednesday and charged with possession of firearms, threats against a presidential candidate running and conspiring to rob a gun store, the Department of Justice said. The plot is understood to centre on Tennessee where Martin Luther King was assassinated exactly 40 years ago' (Harnden 2008).

12 The term 'Cinema Verité' is often used interchangeably with the term 'Direct Cinema' in the US context. In fact, early film critics and many contemporary documentary scholars such as

Carroll, Mamber and Nichols use the former for both the French and the North American movements. More latterly a distinction has been made between the reflexive presence of the filmmaker in Cinema Verité films, such as those of Rouch, and the lack of self-reflexive and on-screen presence on the part of the American Direct Cinema filmmakers.

13 The comments of filmmakers such as Rouch, Godard and de Antonio galvanized a critique, maintaining not just that the persistent claim of impartiality was unfounded, but also that Cinema Verité failed to address the need of the times for a more openly political approach to documentary.

14 Clifford and Marcus (1986) and Fischer and Marcus (1986) were foundational texts.

15 In Northern Ireland, local community film and video groups have produced a range of testimony-based personal histories which have usually received a very limited distribution, despite one-off funding during the 1980s and 1990s by UK broadcasting institutions such as Channel 4.

16 Renov is not referring specifically to Australian diasporic documentaries, but there are many good examples from this continent, including *Grandfathers and Revolutions* (1999) by Peter Hegedus; *The Mascot* (2002) by Lina Caneva; *Exile in Sarajevo* (1997) by Ama Sahbaz; *A Wedding in Ramallah* (2002) by Sherine Salama; *Homelands* (1993) by Tom Zubrycki; *From Here to Ithaca* (2001) by Fionn Skiotis; and *Maria* (1992) by Barbara Chobocky.

17 See his manifesto, from which there is a link to his WikiFilm with a page of contents (Gaylor 2007b).

18 www.dochouse.org (accessed 25 May 2006).

19 For an introduction to McCarthyism and the effects of the Cold War on the media, see Chapman (2005).

20 Murdoch's conglomerate NewsCorp has swallowed up more and more media outlets and in doing so has created a culture of politicized newscasts and comment. The portfolio includes many UK national and local press publications, Sky satellite programming with a 20 per cent share in the huge Asian TATA Sky market, a slew of US and Australasian press including the *Wall Street Journal*, the US Fox Company including Fox News, and more recently Internet news platforms and networking media including MySpace.

21 *Alternet's* website also announces that 'Robert Greenwald is a board member of the Independent Media Institute, the parent organization of AlterNet.' http://www.alternet. org/mediaculture/21463/?page=2

22 There is a substantial literature on postmodernism and history. For history as a grounding for narrative and documentary, see Jameson (1981) and (1984).

23 The role of film during the Nazi occupation of France and its aftermath has been the subject of much scholarship. See, for instance, Bowles (2006), Butler (2000), Langlois (2001), Lindeperg (1997).

24 See www.freedomfilmsindia.org

25 Gore used to joke that the way he could be picked out in a room full of secret service agents was that he was the stiff one.

26 A phrase attributed to Marlo Lewis, Jr. The conservative CEI journal also stated after the release of the film: 'carbon dioxide – they call it pollution, we call it life' (Lewis 2007).

27 In 2003, Bremer also held the title of 'Senior Adviser, Americans for Victory over Terrorism': http://rightweb.irc-online.org/profile/1053.html (accessed 12 July 2008).

28 Gore's organization, Alliance for Climate Change, received in August 2006 a donation of 5 per cent of all box office receipts for the month from Paramount Classics, distributor of *An Inconvenient Truth*, thus garnering over $1 million for the charity (www.wecansolveit. org). Paramount Classics' President John Lesher said: 'It has been thrilling to watch this important movie become a grassroots phenomenon. People are buying group tickets to see the film and having discussion groups afterwards to talk about the lessons learned from the movie. Audiences who love the film are purchasing tickets for those who are still skeptical about the issue. And major corporations have bought tickets for their employees; it is pretty incredible' (Lesher and Skoll 2006). The way in which audiences participate is of particular interest. Jeff Skoll, Chairman and CEO of Participant Productions, added: 'Equally important has been the incredible response to the film's social action campaign, which has inspired people across the country to take individual action and make a difference in their own communities' (Lesher and Skoll 2006).

29 Technorati's interpretation of partners runs as follows: 'The purpose of conversation is to create and improve understanding, not for one party to "deliver messages" to the other. That would be rude. There is no "audience" in a conversation. If we must label others in conversation, let's call them partners' (Searls et al. 2007).

30 Barbara Babcock (1975: 22) bases her definitions on the structuralist Roman Jakobson's (1960: 350–77) communication theory of language (that language must be examined in the variety of its functions). The six categories are as follows:

1. The expressive function focuses on two aspects of filmic presence, showing the film-maker in frame as the driving-force behind the process and revealing their relationship to the subject matter (topic or persons), for example the TV series *Tribe*.
2. The procedural function involves the presence of the equipment in shot – this indicates a formal consideration of content, showing the interviewer in context. It may also act as an indicator of the evidentiary status of the camera where observation is under scrutiny – for example in *Chronicle of a Summer*.
3. The referential function concerns the problematizing of the relationship between a film and reality, exemplified by *Far From Poland*, for instance. Other films may reject the notion of one-dimensionality and present several views of the 'truth', such as *Naked Spaces*.
4. The poetic function is embodied in those films that show elements of formalism; they address issues of structure, both in production and post-production, as 'a unique self-contained object' (Babcock 1975: 49), as in *Les Plages d'Agnès* or *Man with a Movie Camera*.
5. The conative function in documentary entails a direct address to the audience by the filmmaker, either in voiceover or straight to camera, guiding the viewer as to how to understand the film. McElwee, for instance, dresses up as Sherman in *Sherman's March* to demonstrate to the viewer his passionate interest in the general's life.
6. The meta-narrational function concerns the filmmaker's self-reflexive consideration of their own work as a comment on the film's message and the filmmaking process itself. This is exemplified in *Chronicle of a Summer*.

31 The limitations, as judged by later thinking, would include a lack of explanation about the structural causes of social deprivation that lay behind the testimonials. In the absence of such explanation, social actors can appear to audiences as victims.

32 The article also shows how anyone can make a cheap digital home video and upload it to the Internet: http://www.telegraph.co.uk/connected/main.jhtml?xml=/connected/2007/04/14/nosplit/dldoc14.xml

33 See also Martin Jackson's (1974) article, containing a report from the 'wedding' episode of *The Family*, which provides both audience comments and viewing figures.

34 Eighty-nine per cent of people in a 2003 ITC/BSC survey in the UK thought wildlife programming was as accurate as the news.

35 Five million in the UK for a one-off documentary entitled *The Secret Policeman* that won an RTS award for its undercover investigation into racism in the British police force (Hill 2005: 38).

36 Nick Broomfield used Iraqi non-actors in the film. One woman, 'Shukrieh Hameed, says she had seen her own son shot dead by insurgents in front of her home in Baghdad two years earlier. An hour later [on set] I am standing with her and Broomfield on the roof of her home as she watches the Marines shoot the students. Two of them, in this recreation, are her sons. She screams as her husband runs into the room to get an AK47 to fire at the Americans, sparking the massacre. Broomfield shouts "cut" but the screams and the tears don't stop. Afterwards I [the reporter Catherine Philp] go to comfort Shukrieh. "It was like my son was killed all over again, right now," she sobs. Broomfield is asked why he uses such people. "Her performance is a thousand times more convincing than most actresses," Broomfield enthuses' (Philp 2008).

37 See www.outfoxed.org/Clips.php

38 By co-starring with black actress Rosalind Cash in *Omega Man* (1971), Heston was actively involved in breaking the Hollywood race barrier (Skovmand, n.d.).

39 Arguably, politicians and celebrities, who are powerful and therefore perfectly able to defend themselves, should not be offered control: if they are, the film runs the risk of descending into a public relations vehicle for their image or message, without any critical questioning.

40 Lesbian 'offences' are not mentioned in the Qur'an.

41 Sharma's blog documents both emails from film critics who praise the film's bravery and damning comments from Muslim clerics and hardliners. He also announces that he will screen his film worldwide. Available at: http://ajihadforlove.blogspot.com/search?updated-min=2007-01-01T00%3A00%3A00-05%3A00&updated-max=2008-01-01T00%3A00%3A00-05%3A00&max-results=43 (accessed 11 November 2008).

42 Before the trial, no right of privacy existed in the State, so the legislature quickly drafted a right of privacy statute and passed it (Taylor 1988: 101). Wiseman twice petitioned the US Supreme Court to get the restrictions lifted, losing both times by a vote of four to three. In a further law suit in 1971 for invasion of privacy damages, the presiding judge ruled that the film was protected by the First Amendment.

43 *New York Times*, 13 March 1984: A18.

44 Aaron Russo was interviewed by Alex Jones about his alleged conversation with Nicholas Rockefeller. The full undated interview is available at: http://video.google.com/google-player.swf?docid=5420753830426590918&hl=en&fs=true (accessed 12 November 2008).

45 Though the film's website has a 'sources' page the list is incomplete and of limited value for verification of facts.

46 The literature on Grierson is extensive. See in particular Winston (2008).

47 *Broadcast*, 13 April 2006.

Bibliography

Adam, David (2007), 'Move to Block Emissions "Swindle" DVD', *Guardian*, 25 April.

Adorno, Theodor (1967), *Prisms*, trans. Samuel and Shierry Weber (London: Neville Spearman).

Agee, James and Walker Evans (1960), *Let Us Now Praise Famous Men* (Boston: Houghton Mifflin).

Aitken, Ian (ed.) (2006), *Encyclopedia of the Documentary Film* (New York and London: Routledge).

Allen Greene, Richard (2006), 'Film Sees War Through Soldiers' Eyes', BBC News (online), 2 June: http://news.bbc.co.uk/1/hi/entertainment/5038172.stm (accessed 12 September 2007).

Allen, Jeanne (1977), 'Self-reflexivity in Documentary', *Cine-Tracts* 1 (2): 37–43.

Allen, Robert C. and Douglas Gomery (1985), *Film History: Theory and Practice* (New York: Knopf).

Ammu, Joseph (2002), 'India: Soft on Porn, Hard on Peace: Cinema Censorship by Mob Rule Threatens Free Expression', *Index on Censorship: For Free Expression* (online), 4 July: http://www.indexonline.org/en/news/articles/2002/3/soft-on-porn-hard-on-peace.shtml (accessed 12 April 2006).

Anderson, C. and T. Benson (1991), *Documentary Dilemmas: Frederick Wiseman's Titicut Follies* (Carbondale, IL: Southern Illinois University Press).

Ang, Ien (1991), *Desperately Seeking the Audience* (London: Routledge).

Arthur, Paul (1993), 'Jargons of Authenticity: Three American Moments', in M. Renov (ed)., *Theorizing Documentary* (New York and London: Routledge).

Arthur, Paul (1998), 'Media Spectacle and the Tabloid Documentary', *Film Comment* 34 (1): 74–80.

Arthur, Paul (2003), 'Essay Questions', *Film Comment* 39 (1): 58–63.

Austin, Thomas (2005), 'Seeing, Feeling, Knowing: A Case Study of Audience Perspectives on Screen Documentary', *Particip@tions* 2 (1): http://www.participations.org/volume%202/issue%201/2_01_austin.htm (accessed March 2009).

Austin, Thomas (2007), *Watching the World: Screen Documentary and Audiences* (Manchester: Manchester University Press).

Avery, Dylan (2005), *Loose Change*: http://www.YouTube.com/watch?v=7E3oIbO0AWE (accessed 3 Sept 2008).

Avery, Dylan (2008), *Loose Change*: http://loosechange911.com/get_involved.shtml (accessed 3 Sept 2008).

Babcock, Barbara (1975), *Mirrors, Masks and Metafiction* (Chicago: University of Chicago Press).

Babcock, Barbara (1984), 'Reflexivity: Definitions and Discriminations', *Semiotica* 30: 1–14.

Bakshian, Aram, Jr. (1985), 'PBS Tries Playing it Straight', *National Review* 37 (10): 49–50.

Barnouw, Erik (1992), *Documentary: A History of the Non-Fiction Film* (New York: Oxford University Press).

Barrett, Amy (2003), 'The Truth Hurts', *Screen International*, 21 November: 18.

Barthes, Roland (1977), 'The Rhetoric of the Image', in *Image, Music, Text* (London: Fontana).

Bell, Rose and William L. Webb (eds) (1998), *An Embarrassment of Tyrannies: 25 years of Index On Censorship* (London: Victor Gollancz).

Benjamin, Walter (2008), 'The Work of Art in the Age of Mechanical Reproduction', in M.

Jennings, B. Doherty and T.Y. Levin (eds), *The Work of Art in the Age of its Technological Reproducability, and Other Writings on Media* (Cambridge, MA: Belknapp).

Bhaskar, Roy (1993), *Dialectic: The Pulse of Freedom* (London: Verso).

Blue, James (1965), 'Thoughts on Cinema Verité and a Discussion with the Maysles', *Film Comment* 2 (4): 22.

Bourdon, Jerome (1998), 'Censorship and Television in France', *Historical Journal of Film, Radio and Television* 18 (2): 231–5.

Bowles, Brett (2006), 'Jean Renoir's *Salut à la France:* Documentary Film Production, Distribution, and Reception in France, 1944–1945', *Historical Journal of Film, Radio and Television* 26 (1): 57–88.

Bruzzi, Stella (2000), *New Documentary: A Critical Introduction* (London: Routledge).

Burton, Julianne (ed.) (1990), *The Social Documentary in Latin America* (Pittsburgh: University of Pittsburgh Press).

Butchart, Garnet C. (2006), 'On Ethics and Documentary: A Real and Actual Truth', *Communication Theory* 16: 427–52.

Butler, Margaret (2000), *Images of Community in British and French Cinema 1939–1951*. Phd Thesis. University of Essex.

BBC (1965), Written Archives Centre (WAC T56/263/1), Wheldon to Adam, 22 February.

BBC (1965), Written Archives Centre (WAC T56/261/2), Watkins to Geoff White, 15 July.

BBC (1965), Written Archives Centre (WAC Box 8), 'The Story of *The War Game*'.

BBC (n.d.), Written Archives Centre, 'The War Game', WAC internal circular R44/1334.

BBC (1985), Documents Released under the Freedom of Information Act, www.mediaguardian.co.uk.

Camy, Gérard (2002), *50 Films qui ont fait scandale*, 'Le Chagrin et la Pitie', Enrique Seknadje-Askenazi, *CinemAction*, 103 (2): 101–3.

Carroll, Noel (1983), 'From Real to Reel: Entangled in Nonfiction Film', in *Philosophic Exchange* (Brockport, NY: State University of New York).

Caughie, John (ed.) (1981), *Theories of Authorship: A Reader* (London and New York: Routledge).

Chanan, Michael (1997), 'The Changing Geography of Third Cinema', *Sight and Sound*, Reports and Debates, Special Report 38 (4): 372–88.

Chapman, James (2006), 'The BBC and the Censorship of the War Game (1965)', *Journal of Contemporary History* 41 (1): 75–94.

Chapman, Jane (2005), *Comparative Media History: 1789 to the Present* (Cambridge: Polity Press).

Chapman, Jane (2006), 'Reflections on 15 Years of Activist Media and India's Narmada Dams Controversy', *International Journal of Communication (IJC)*, India, September–December: 16 (2).

Chapman, Jane (2007), *Documentary in Practice* (Cambridge: Polity Press).

Chapman, Jane (2009), *Journalism Past and Present* (Oxford: Blackwell Wiley).

Chen, Pauline (1996), 'Screening History: New Documentaries on the Tiananmen Events in China', *Cineaste* 22 (1): 18–23.

Cheng, Scarlet (1996), 'China-born Filmmaker Casts Tiananmen in a New Spotlight', *Far Eastern Economic Review*, 16 May: 90.

Chiu, Kuen-feu (2005), 'Taiwan and its Spectacular Others: Aesthetic Reflexivity in Two Documentaries by Women Filmmakers from Taiwan', *Asian Cinema* (Spring/Summer): 98–107.

Christie, Ian (2006), 'Lights, Camera, Discord', *Sight and Sound*, Reviews, March: 88.

Clifford, James and George Marcus (eds) (1986), *Writing Culture: The Poetics and Politics of Ethnography* (Berkeley: University of California Press).

Cogswell, David (1996), *Chomsky for Beginners* (New York and London: Writers and Readers).

Coles, Robert (1968), 'Stripped Bare at the Follies', *The New Republic*, January 20: 18, 28–30.

Cook, John R. and Patrick Murphy (2000), 'After the Bomb Dropped: The Cinema Half-life of *The War Game*', *Journal of Popular British Cinema* 3, March: 129–32.

Cooper, Sarah (2006), *Selfless Cinema? Ethics and French Documentary* (Leeds: Legenda, Modern Humanities Research Association and Maney Publishing).

Corner, John (1996), *The Art of Record: A Critical Introduction to Documentary* (Manchester: Manchester University Press).

Corner, John (2000), 'What Can We Say about Documentary?', *Media, Culture and Society* 22 (5): 681–8.

Corner, John (2001), 'Documentary and Realism', in G. Creeber (ed.), *The Television Genre Book* (London: BFI).

Corner, John (2002), 'Performing the Real: Documentary Diversions', *Television & New Media* 3 (3): 255–69.

Corner, John (n.d.), 'Documentary in a Post-Documentary Culture? A Note on Forms and their Functions':   http://www.lboro.ac.uk/research/changing.media/John%20Corner%20paper.htm (accessed 15 March 2009).

Cottle, Simon (1997), *Television and Ethnic Minorities: Producers' Perspectives* (Aldershot: Avebury).

Crick, Benny (2004), 'Documentary Schooled in the Art of "Feel-Good"', *Screen International*, 4 October: 24

Crowdus, Gary and Richard Porton (1991), 'American Dream: An Interview with Barbara Kopple', *Cineaste* 18 (4): 38.

Currie, Gregory (1999), 'Visible Traces: Documentary and the Contents of Photographs', *The Journal of Aesthetics and Art Criticism* 57 (3): 285–97.

Curtain, Michael (1995), *Redeeming the Wasteland: Television Documentary and Cold War Politics* (New Brunswick, NJ: Rutgers University Press).

Dahlgren, Peter (1995), *Television and the Public Sphere* (London: Sage).

Darnton, Robert (1995), 'Censorship, a Comparative View: France 1789 – East Germany 1989', *Representation* 49 (Winter): 41–61.

de Beauvoir, Simone (1985), 'Preface' to Claude Lanzmann, *Shoah: An Oral History of the Holocaust* (New York: Pantheon Books).

Debord, Guy (1983), *Society of the Spectacle* (Detroit: Red and Black).

Denby, David (2006), 'An Inconvenient Truth', *The New Yorker*, 19 June.

Devereaux, Leslie and Roger Hillman (eds) (1995), *Fields of Vision: Essays in Film Studies, Visual Anthropology, and Philosophy* (Berkeley: University of California).

DiMaggio, Paul J. (1991), 'Decentralization of Arts Funding from the Federal Government to the States', in Stephen Benedict (ed.), *Public Money and the Muse: Essays on Government Funding for the Arts* (New York: W.W. Norton).

Doherty, Thomas (2001), '"The Sorrow and the Pity": Chronicle of a French City Under the Occupation', *Cineaste* 26 (3): 50–2.

Dorst, John D. (1999), 'Which Came First, the Chicken Device or the Textual Egg?: Documentary Film and the Limits of the Hybrid Metaphor', *Journal of American Folklore* 112 (Summer): 268–81.

Douglas, Susan J. (1992), 'Notes Toward a History of Media Audiences', *Radical History Review*, 54: 127–38.

Dovey, Jon (2000), *Freakshow: First Person Media and Factual Television* (London: Pluto Press).

Eco, Umberto (1976), *Theory of Semiotics* (Bloomington: Indiana University Press).

Eco, Umberto (1986), 'De Consolatione Philosophiae', in *Travels in Hyperreality: Essays* (San Diego: Harcourt Brace Jovanovich).

Eisenstein, Sergei (1949), 'Methods of Montage', in *Film Form*, ed. and trans. Jay Leyda (New York: Harcourt, Brace and World).

Ellis, Jack C. and Betsy A. Mclane (2005), *A New History of Documentary Film* (New York: Continuum).

Ellis, John (2002), *Seeing Things: Television in the Age of Uncertainty* (I.B. Taurus Publishers, London).

Fetveit, Arild (1999), 'Reality TV in the Digital Era: A Paradox in Visual Culture?', *Media, Culture and Society*, 21: (787–804).

Fischer, Michael and George Marcus (1986), *Anthropology as Cultural Critique: An Experimental Moment in the Human Sciences* (Chicago: University of Chicago Press).

Foucault, Michel (1989), 'Film and Popular Memory', in *Foucault Live*, ed. Sylvère Lotringer, trans. John Johnston (New York: Semiotext(e))

Fraser, Nick (2004), 'A Dangerous Occupation', *Financial Times*, Weekend Magazine, 10 July: 34–6.

Freedland, Jonathan (2006), 'An Inconvenient Truth: Beware the Politician in Fleece Clothing', *Guardian*, 13 September.

Friedman, Edward (1997), '*The Gates of Heavenly Peace*', Review, *The Journal of Asian Studies* 56 (2): 582.

Fritz, Ben and Michael Learmonth (2007), 'Showbiz's Site-fright', *Variety*, 10 March: http://www.variety.com/article/VR1117960880.html?categoryid=13&cs=1 (accessed 13 February 2008).

Furman, Nelly (2005), 'Viewing Memory Through *Night and Fog, The Sorrow and the Pity*, and *Shoah*', *Journal of European Studies* 35 (2): 169–85.

Fusco, Coco (1988), 'The Tango of Esthetics and Politics: An Interview with Fernando Solanas', *Cineaste* 16 (1–2): 57–9.

Gabriel, Teshome (1982), *Third Cinema in the Third World: The Aesthetics of Liberation* (Ann Arbor: UMI Research Press).

Gaines, Jane M. and Michael Renov (eds) (1999), *Collecting Visible Evidence*, Vol. 6, (Minneapolis: University of Minnesota Press).

Gaylor, Brett. (2007a), *A Remix Manifesto:* http://www.opensourcecinema.org (accessed 24 September 2007).

Gaylor, Brett (2007b), *The Basement Tapes (wikifilm)*: http://opensourcecinema.org/wikifilm (accessed 24 September 2007).

Getty, Matt (2006), 'Keeping it Reel: Ethics in Media', *American Magazine*: http://veracity.univpubs.american.edu/magazine/magazine/fall0 (accessed 16 January 2007).

Gillespie, Marie (ed.) (2005), *Media Audiences* (Maidenhead: The Open University).

Gilley, Bruce (1997), 'Gate Crashers: A Controversial Film Attracts Crowds From China', *Far Eastern Economic Review*, 6 March, Arts & Society: 44.

Goddard, Peter, John Corner and Kay Richardson (2001), 'The Formation of *World in Action*', *Journalism* 2 (1): 73–90.

Gourevitch, Philip (1992), 'Interviewing the Universe', *New York Times Magazine*, 9 August: 18, 44–6, 53.

Govaert, Charlotte (2007), 'How Reflexive Documentaries Engage Audiences in Issues of Representation: Apologia for a Reception Study', *Studies in Documentary Film* 1 (3): 245–63.

Green, Darren (n.d.), 'William Raban': http://www.luxonline.org.uk/artists/william_raban/essay(1).html (accessed 26 February 2009).

Greenwald, Robert (2005), 'ABC and *Outfoxed* Ad, and Air America', http://rg.bravenewfilms.org/blog/147-abc-and-outfoxed-ad-and-air-america (accessed 5 November 2008).

Greer, Darroch (2002), 'Fade to Black', *Digital Content Producer* (online): http://digitalcontent-producer.com/mag/video_fade_black_11 (accessed 15 July 2006).

Griskop, V. (2005), 'Do the Maths', *Daily Telegraph Magazine*, 28 May: 38–44.

Gross, Larry, John Stuart Katz and Jay Ruby (eds) (1988), *Image Ethics: The Moral Rights of Subjects in Photographs, Film and Television* (Oxford and New York: Oxford University Press).

Guggenheim, Davis and Al Gore (2006), *An Inconvenient Truth*. Paramount Classic: http://www.climatecrisis.net (accessed 29 January 2008).

Habermas, Jürgen (1989), *The Structural Transformation of the Public Sphere: An Inquiry into a Category of Bourgeois Society*, trans. Thomas Burger (Cambridge, MA: MIT Press).

Hall, Jeanne (1991), 'Realism as a Style in Cinema Verité: A Critical Analysis of *Primary*', *Cinema Journal*, 30 (4): 24–50.

Hall, Stuart (1987), 'Minimal Selves', in *Identity: The Real Me*, ICA Documents 6: 44–6.

Hall, Stuart (1988), 'New Ethnicities', in D. Morley and K. Chen (eds), *Stuart Hall: Critical Dialogues in Cultural Studies* (London: Routledge).

Hall, Stuart (1991), 'Old and New Identities, Old and New Ethnicities', in A. King (ed.), *Culture, Globalization and the World-system: Contemporary Conditions for the Representation of Identity* (Basingstoke: Macmillan).

Hall, Stuart (1996), 'Who Needs Identity?', in S. Hall and P. du Gay (eds), *Questions of Cultural Identity* (London: Sage).

Hall, Stuart (2000), 'The Multicultural Question': www.sheffield.ac.uk/uni/academic/N-Q/lectures/htm (restricted access)

Haltof, Marek (1995), *When Cultures Collide: The Cinema of Peter Weir* (London: Prentice Hall International).

Hamsher, Jane (2005), 'ABC Refuses Outfoxed Ad, Censors Boston Legal': http://firedoglake. blogspot.com/2005/03/abc-refuses-outfoxed-ad-censors-boston.html (accessed 5 November 2008).

Harnden, Toby (2008), 'White Supremacist "Plot" to Assassinate Barack Obama Foiled', *Daily Telegraph* (online), 28 October: http://www.telegraph.co.uk/news/newstopics/uselection2008/barackobama/3270479/White-supremacist-plot-to-assassinate-Barack-Obama-foiled.html (accessed 4 November 2008).

Herman, Edward S. and Noam Chomsky (1994), *Manufacturing Consent: The Political Economy of the Mass Media* (London: Vintage).

Hesford, Wendy (1999), 'Reading *Rape Stories*: Material Rhetoric and the Trauma of Representation', *College English* 62 (2): 192–221.

Hesford, Wendy (2004), 'Documenting Violations: Rhetorical Witnessing and the Spectacle of Distant Suffering', *Biography* 27 (1): 104–44.

Hill, Annette (2005), *Reality TV: Audiences and Popular Factual Television* (London: Routledge).

Horkheimer, Max (1941), 'Art and Mass Culture', *SPSS* IX, 2: 291.

Hoveyda, Fereydoun (1961), '*Cinema Verité*, or Fantastic Realism', in Jim Hillier, (ed.) (1986), *Cahiers du Cinema: 1960–1968: New Wave, New Cinema, Re-evaluating Hollywood*, Vol. 2 (London: Routledge).

Iglesias-Prieto, Norma (2001), 'Who is the Devil and How or Why Does He or She Sleep: Viewing a Chicana Film in Mexico', in Rosa Linda Fregoso (ed.), *Lourdes Portillo: 'The Devil Never Sleeps' and Other Films* (Austin, Texas: University of Texas Press).

Ignatieff, Michael (1997), *The Warrior's Honour: Ethnic War and the Modern Conscience* (New York: Henry Holt).

ITC/BSC (2003), *Television: The Public's View* (London: Independent Television Commission and Broadcasting Standards Commission).

Jackson, Martin (1974), 'True, People Do Prefer a Bit of Make Believe', *Daily Mail*, 20 June.

Jacobs, Lewis (ed.) (1979), *The Documentary Tradition*, 2nd edn (New York: W.W. Norton).

Jaigu, Yves (1990), 'Television et service public: quel contenu?' *Le Debat* 61 (September–October).

Jakobson, Roman (1960), *Style in Language*, ed. Thomas Seboek (New York: Wiley).

James, Nick (2004), 'Secrets and Lies', *Sight and Sound* 14 (6): 5.

Jay, Martin (1996), *The Dialectical Imagination: A History of the Frankfurt School* (Berkeley: University of California Press).

Jeffries, Anice and Gabrielle Idlet (1997), 'State of the Filmmaker/Subject Relationship', *National Forum* 77 (4): 21–5.

Jenkinson, Michael (1993), 'The CBC Decides Bias is OK', *Alberta Report/Newsmagazine*, 20 (47): 49–51.

Jensen, Klaus Bruhn and Karl Erik Rosengren (1990), 'Five Traditions in Search of the Audience', *European Journal of Communication* 5 (2): 207–38.

Johnson, Paul (2004), 'Intellectuals, Ski Instructors and Other Militant Riff-Raff', *The Spectator*, 6 March: 25.

Jones, Derek (2001), *Censorship: A World Encyclopedia*, Vol. 2, E–K (Chicago and London: Fitzroy Dearborn Publishers).

Kaplan, E. Ann (1982-3), 'Feminist Documentary', *Millennium Film Journal* 12, (Theories and Strategies of the Feminist Documentary): 44–67.

Kay, Jeremy (2007), 'Hearts and Minds', *Guardian* (online), 6 September: http://www.guardian.co.uk/film/2007/sep/06/gayrights.religion (accessed 11 November 2008).

Kendall, Paul (2008), 'The Anti-Big Brother', *Sunday Telegraph*, Seven Magazine, 31 August: 22.

Kilborn, Richard (1996), 'New Contexts for documentary production in Britain', *Media, Culture and Society* 18 (1): 141–50.

Klein, Julia M. (2004), 'Whose News? Whose Propaganda?', *Columbia Journalism Review*, documentary, 43 (2): 54–5.

Kornatowska, Maria (1993), 'Polish Cinema', *Cineaste* 19 (4): 47–50.

Langlois, Suzanne (2001), *La Résistance dans le cinéma français 1944–1994* (Paris: L'Harmattan).

Lanzmann, Claude (1985), *Shoah: An Oral History of the Holocaust* (New York: Pantheon Books).

Larsen, Josh (2006), 'Al Gore Saves the Universe', *The American Enterprise*, 1 July.

Lawson, Mark (2006), Guardian Comments and Debates, *Guardian*, 18 August: 33.

Lazarus, Margaret (2001), 'Producing Feminism', *Feminist Media Studies* 1 (2): 245–9.

Lesher, John and Jeff Skoll (2006), 'Paramount Classics To Donate An Unprecedented One Million Dollars To Fight Global Warming', interview 4 August, *Paramount Vantage*: http://www.paramountvantage.com/blog/?cat=1&paged=3 (accessed 10 November 2008).

Leuthold, Steven (1997), 'Historical Representation in Native American Documentary', *Ethnohistory*, Review Essay, 44 (4): 728–39.

Lewis, Marlo (2007), 'Some Convenient Distortions', *On Point*, 16 March: http://cei.org/pdf/5818.pdf (accessed 30 July 2007).

Lindeperg, Sylvie (1997), *Les écrans de l'ombre: la Seconde Guerre mondiale dans le cinéma francais (1944–1969)* (Paris: Centre National de la Recherche Scientifique).

Livingstone, Sonia (1998), 'Audience Research at the Crossroads: The "Implied Audience" in Media and Cultural Theory', *European Journal of Cultural Studies* 1 (2): 193–217.

Lloyd, Fran and Catherine O'Brian (2000), *Secret Spaces, Forbidden Places: Rethinking Culture* (New York and Oxford: Berghahn Books).

Lu, Xinyu (2003), *Documenting China: The New Documentary Movement in Contemporary China* (Beijing: Sanlian Shudian).

Lubelski, Tadeusz (2002), 'Polish Contemporary Documentary Film', *culture.pl*: http://www.culture.pl/en/culture/artykuly (accessed 16 June 2006).

McGarry, Eileen (1975), 'Documentary Realism and Women's Cinema', *Women in Film* 2 (7): 50, 51, 53.

MacLennan, Gary and John Hookham (2001), 'Documentary Theory and the Dialectic: A Dialectical Critical Realist Approach', paper presented to IACR Conference 'Debating Realisms', Roskilde University Denmark, 17–19 August: 1–15.

MacNab, Geoffrey (2008), 'Not Everything Is As It Seems In Documentary-Making', *Independent* (online), 11 January: http://www.independent.co.uk/arts-entertainment/films/features/not-everything-is-as-it-seems-in-documentarymaking-769516.html (accessed 11 January 2008).

McQuail, Dennis and Sven Windahl (1993), *Communication Models for the Study of Mass Communications* (London: Longman).

Maher, John C. and Judy Groves (1999), *Introducing Chomsky* (Cambridge: Icon).

Maingard, Jacqueline (1995), 'Trends in South African Documentary Film and Video: Questions of Identity and Subjectivity', *Journal of Southern African Studies* 21 (4): 657–67.

Marcellus, Jordyn (2008), 'Zeitgeist ist "time ghost" auf Deutsch, ja!', *Gauntlet* (online), 13 March: http://gauntlet.ucalgary.ca/story/12284 (accessed 23 June 2008).

Marcuse, Herbert (1991), *One Dimensional Man*, 2nd edn, introduction by Douglas Kellner (Boston, MA: Beacon Press).

Marks, Laura U. (2000), *The Skin of the Film: Intercultural Cinema, Embodiment, and the Senses* (Durham, NC: Duke University Press).

Maslin, Janet (1997), 'Iranian Film Makes it Past Censors to Cannes', *New York Times*, 17 May: 13.

Mayne, Judith (1977), 'Kino-Truth and Kino-Praxis: Vertov's Man with a Movie Camera', *Cine-Tracts* 1 (2): 81–91.

Media Guardian (2007), 'Does Britain Trust the Media Anymore?': http://www.mgeitf.co.uk/home/news.aspx/does_britain_tust_the_media_anymore (accessed 4 December 2008).

Mercer, Kobena (1994), *Welcome to the Jungle: New Positions in Black Cultural Studies* (London: Routledge).

Metz, Christian (1974), *Film Language: A Semiotics of the Cinema*, trans. Michael Taylor (New York: Oxford University Press).

Milestone Films (2000), *Woody Allen Presents Marcel Ophüls' "The Sorrow and the Pity"*, Press Screening Kit (Harrington Park, NJ: Milestone Films).

Mills, Lisa (2008), *A Tarnished Golden Age: Political Documentary on Television Networks in the 1960s*, paper submitted to the Documentary Division of the Broadcast Education Association, 53rd Annual Convention, Las Vegas, 16–19 April.

Monbiot, George (2007), 'A 9/11 Conspiracy Virus is Sweeping the World, But it Has No Basis in Fact', *Guardian* (online), 6 February: http://www.guardian.co.uk/commentisfree/2007/feb/06/comment.film (accessed 3 December 2008).

Morley, David (1980), *The 'Nationwide' Audience: Structure and Decoding* (London: BFI).

Morris, Errol (1989), 'Truth Not Guaranteed: An Interview with Errol Morris', *Cineaste* 17: 16–17.

M.T. (n.d.), Interview with Anne Crilly: http://www.tallgirlshorts.net/marymary/anne.html

Muir, Gregor (2003), 'The Documentary Style', *Flash Art*, International Edition, 36 (January): 78–81.

Mulvey, Laura (1975), 'Visual Pleasure and Narrative Cinema', *Screen* 16 (3): 6–18.

Murphy, Patrick (1997), 'The Film the BBC Tried to Bury', *New Statesman*, 22 August, Issue 4348: 22–4.

Naficy, Hamid (2001), *Accented Cinema: Exilic and Diasporic Filmmaking* (Princeton: Princeton University Press).

Nichols, Bill (ed.) (1985), *Movies and Methods*, Vol. 2 (Berkeley: University of California Press).

Nichols, Bill (1986), 'Questions of Magnitude', in John Corner (ed.), *Documentary and the Mass Media* (London: Edward Arnold).

Nichols, Bill (1991), *Representing Reality: Issues and Concepts in Documentary* (Bloomington: Indiana University Press).

Nichols, Bill (1994), *Blurred Boundaries: Questions of Meaning in Contemporary Culture* (Bloomington: Indiana University Press).

Nichols, Bill (2001), *Introduction to Documentary* (Bloomington: Indiana University Press).

Nolley, Ken (1997), 'Finding Alternatives to Gossip: Reflexivity and the Paradigm of Traditional Documentary', *Visual Anthropology* 9: 267–84.

O'Brien, Harvey (2004), *The Real Ireland: The Evolution of Ireland in Documentary Film* (Manchester: Manchester University Press).

O'Connor, Rory (2005), 'Free Speech Impediment', *Alternet*, 10 March: http://www.alternet.org/mediaculture/21463 (accessed 5 November 2008).

Ophuls, Marcel (1980), 'La zivilcourage et les diners en ville', *Positif* 20: 61–3.

Parry, Bruce (2008), 'What is *Tribe* to Me?': http://www.bbc.co.uk/tribe/bruce/index.shtml (accessed 27 October 2008).

Patwardhan, Anand (2004), Keynote address to the International Documentary Conference, Silverdocs Documentary Film Festival, 16 June, www.centerforsocialmedia.org.

Pauwels, Luc (2004), 'Filmed Science in Search of a Form: Contested Discourses in Anthropological and Sociological Film-making', *New Cinemas* 2 (1): 41–60.

Peary, Gerald and Maureen Turim (1973), 'An Interview with Marcel Ophüls', *Velvet Light Trap*, Issue 9 (July): 40–5.

Perrott, Lisa (2002), 'Rethinking the Documentary Audience: Re-imagining The New Zealand Wars', *Media International Australia*, 104: 67–79.

Philp, Catherine (2008), 'Will This be Iraq's Apocalypse Now?', *The Times* (online), 10 May: http://entertainment.timesonline.co.uk/tol/arts_and_entertainment/film/article1767527.ece (accessed 24 June 2008).

Pilger, John (1998), *Hidden Agendas* (New York: The New Press).

Plantinga, Carl. R. (1997), *Rhetoric and Representation in Nonfiction Film* (Cambridge: University of Cambridge Press).

Privett, Ray and James Kreul (2001), 'The Strange Case of Noel Carroll': http://www.sensesofcinema.com/contents/01/13/carroll.html (accessed 10 July 2006).

Procter, James (2004), *Stuart Hall* (London: Routledge).

Pryluck, Calvin (1976), 'Ultimately We Are All Outsiders: The Ethics of Documentary Filming', *Journal of the University Film Association* 26 (1): 21–30.

Pye, Douglas (2008), 'Reclaiming the Real', paper delivered at the Visible Evidence XV Conference, University of Lincoln, 7 August.

Rabinowitz, Paula (1993), 'Wreckage upon Wreckage: History, Documentary and the Ruins of Memory', *History and Theory* 32 (2): 119–37.

Rabinowitz, Paula (1994), *They Must Be Represented: The Politics of Documentary* (London and New York: Verso).

Rabinowitz, Paula (1999), 'Sentimental Contracts: Dreams and Documents of American Labor', in Diane Waldman and Janet Walker (eds), *Feminism and Documentary* (Minneapolis: University of Minnesota Press).

Raeburn, John (1996), 'Rendering Lives: Documentary and its Audience', *European Contributions to American Studies* 37: 195–201.

Rajagopal, Avind (2002), 'Reflections on a Controversy', *Critical Asian Studies* 42 (2): 279–83.

Rayns, Tony (1997), 'The Chinese Syndrome', *Sight and Sound*, July: 25.

Reedy, Margie (2003), 'A Documentary Examines Cable News Coverage', *Nieman Reports* 57 (4): 87–8.

Renov, Michael (ed.) (1993), *Theorizing Documentary* (New York and London: Routledge).

Renov, Michael (1999), 'New Subjectivities: Documentary and Self-representation in the Post-Verité Age', in Diane Waldman and Janet Walker (eds), *Feminism and Documentary* (Minneapolis: University of Minnesota Press).

Renov, Michael (2004), *The Subject of Documentary* (Minneapolis: University of Minnesota Press).

Richter, Erika (1993), 'Drehbuch: Die Zeiten', 23. *Internationales Forum des jungen Films Berlin*, Berlin: Internationales Forum des jungen Films (Freunde der deutschen Kinemathek).

Robertson, G. and A. Nicol (1992), *Media Law* (London: Penguin).

Rolston, Bill and David Miller (eds) (1996), *War and Words: The Northern Ireland Media Reader* (Belfast: Beyond the Pale Publications).

Rony, Fatimah (1996), *The Third Eye: Race, Cinema and the Ethnographic Spectacle* (Durham, NC: Duke University Press).

Roscoe, Jane (1999), *Documentary in New Zealand: An Immigrant Nation* (Palmerston North, NZ: Dunmore Press).

Roscoe, Jane (2000), 'Documenting the *Immigrant Nation*, Tensions and Contradictions in the Representation of Immigrant Communities in a New Zealand Television Documentary Series', *Media, Culture & Society* 22 (3): 243–61.

Roscoe, Jane and Craig Hight (2001), *Faking It: Mock-documentary and the Subversion of Factuality* (Manchester: Manchester University Press).

Roseman, Sharon R. (1991), 'A Documentary Fiction and Ethnographic Production: An Analysis of *Sherman's March*', *Cultural Anthropology* 6 (4): 505–24.

Rosenthal, Alan (ed.) (1988), *New Challenges for Documentary* (Berkeley: University of California Press).

Rosenthal, Alan (2002), *Writing, Directing and Producing Documentary Films*, 3rd edn (Carbondale and Edwardsville: South Illinois University Press).

Rosenthal, Alan and John Corner (eds) (2005), *New Challenges for Documentary*, 2nd edn (Manchester: Manchester University Press).

Rotha, Paul (1983), *Robert J. Flaherty: A Biography* (Philadelphia: University of Pennsylvania Press).

Rousso, Henry (1990), *Le syndrome de Vichy. De 1944 à nos jours*. Deuxième édition revue et mise à jour (Paris: Seuil).

Ruby, Jay (1977), 'The Image Mirrored: Reflexivity and the Documentary Film', *Journal of the University Film Association* 29 (4): 3–12.

Ruby, Jay (1980), 'Exposing Yourself: Reflexivity, Anthropology and Film (1)', *Semiotica* 30 (1/2): 153–79.

Sadasgige, Jacqui (1997), 'Film Reviews: Forgotten Silver', *American Historical Review*, 102 (3): 87–8.

Said, Edward (1978), *Orientalism* (New York: Pantheon).

Scannell, Paddy, Philip Scheslinger and Colin Sparks (eds) (1992), *Media and Culture: A Media, Culture and Society Reader* (London: Sage).

Scott, A.O. (2007), 'Now Playing: Inconvenient Truths', *New York Times*, 23 February: http://www.nytimes.com/2007/02/23/movies/awardsseason/23docs.html?_r=1&scp=15&sq=a%20o%20scott%20%20february%202007&st=cse (accessed 30 March 2007).

Scranton, Deborah (2006), Interview: http://www.pbs.org/kcet/tavissmiley/special/election06/2006/10/war_tapes.html (accessed 12 September 2007).

Scranton, Deborah (2007), 'Deborah Scranton: Scenes from "The War Tapes"', interview, *TEDtalksDirector*: http://uk.YouTube.com/watch?v=bGV5-DJ5_QU (accessed 30 October 2007).

Searls, Doc, et al. (2007), 'The Manifesto on Monday Morning', *Technorati*: http://technorati.com/about/resources/ManifestoOnMondayMorning.pdf (accessed 10 November 2008).

Sharma, Parvez (2007), 'About A Jihad For Love': http://www.ajihadforlove.com/about.html (accessed 23 September 2008).

Sharma, Parvez (2008), 'Love Jihadi': http://www.ajihadforlove.blogspot.com (accessed 11 November 2008).

Sheng, Michael (1996), '*The Gate of Heavenly Peace*', Film Review, *American Historical Review*, 101 (4): 1150–5.

Sherzer, Dina (ed.) (1996), *Cinema, Colonialism, Post Colonialism: Perspectives From the French and Francophone World* (Austin: University of Texas Press).

Silverstone, Roger (1990), 'Television and Everyday Life: Towards an Anthropology of the Television Audience', in M. Ferguson (ed.), *Public Communication: The New Imperatives* (London: Sage).

Singer, Jane B. (2006), 'The Socially Responsible Existentialist: A Normative Emphasis for Journalists in a New Media Environment', *Journalism Studies* 7 (1): 2–18).

Skaff, Sheila (2003), 'Marek Haltof, *Polish National Cinema*', Book Review, *Journal of Visual Culture*, 2 (1): 131–3.

Skovmand, Michael (n.d.), '*Bowling for Columbine:* "I Want Them to Leave Angry"': http://pov.imv.au.dk/Issue 16/section 1/arte3A.html (accessed 14 March 2008).

Smaill, Belinda (2006), 'Diasporic Subjectivity in Contemporary Australian Documentary: Travel, History and the Televisual Representation of Trauma', *Continuum: Journal of Media and Cultural Studies* 20 (2): 269–83.

Smith, Jonathan (2008), 'The Making of *The Family*': http://www.channel4.com/health/the-family/the-making-of/the-making-of-the-family-documentary-2008-08-08-28_p_1.html (accessed 1 September 2008).

Sobchack, Vivian (1984), 'Inscribing Ethical Space: Ten Propositions on Death, Representation and Documentary', *Quarterly Review of Film Studies* (4): 283–300.

Spiegelman, Arthur (2006), 'Bush Assassination Film Set for US Release': http://today.reuters.co./news/articlenews.aspx?type=entertainmentNews&StoryID=2006-09-12T050038Z_01_N11475432_RTRKOC-US-LEISURE-FILMFEST-PRESIDENT.xml (accessed 3 December 2008).

Stevens, Chris (2007), 'A Conspiracy Theorist's Paradise', *Daily Telegraph* (online), 14 April: www.telegraph.co.uk/scienceandtechnology/3352794/A-conspiracy-theorist's-paradise.html (accessed 11 March 2009).

Sutherland, Allan T. (1978), 'Wiseman on Polemic', *Sight and Sound*, Spring: 82.

Swinford, Steven (2007), 'Scientologists to BBC: What Planet Are You On?', *Sunday Times*, 13 May, News: 3.

Tagg, John (1988), *The Burden of Representation: Essays on Photographies and Histories* (Basingstoke and London: Macmillan Education).

Taylor, Charles (1988), 'Titicut Follies Freed?', *Sight and Sound*, Spring: 98–103.

Thompson, Clifford (2001), 'Showing Complexity in Documentary Portraits: An Interview with St. Clair Bourne, *Cineaste* 26 (3): 36–7.

Thompson, Graham (2003), 'Review of P.R. Klotman and J.K. Cutler (eds), *Struggles for Representation; African American Documentary Film and Video*', in *Journal of American Studies* 37 (3): 492–3.

Thompson, John B. (1990), *Ideology and Modern Culture: Critical Social Theory in the Era of Mass Communication* (Cambridge: Polity Press).

Thompson, John B. (1995), *The Media and Modernity* (Cambridge: Polity Press).

Tien, Yu-wen (1994), 'The Heteroglossia in *Voices of Orchid Island*: A Transcript', *Film Appreciation Journal* 12 (3): 23–35.

Trinh T. Minh-ha (1992), *Framer Framed* (London and New York: Routledge).

Trinh T. Minh-ha (1993), 'The Totalising Quest of Meaning, in Michael Renov (ed.), *Theorizing Documentary* (New York and London: Routledge).

Ungar, Steven (2003), 'In the Thick of Things: Rouch and Morin's *Chronique d'un été* Reconsidered', *French Cultural Studies* 14 (1): 5–22.

Usborne, David (2006), 'First Night: An Inconvenient Truth, New York', *Independent* (online), 26 May: http://www.independent.co.uk/arts-entertainment/films/reviews/first-night-an-inconvenient-truth-new-york-479774.html

Vighi, Fabio (2002), 'Beyond Objectivity: The Utopian in Pasolini's Documentaries', *Textual Practice* 16 (3): 491–510.

Waldman, Diane and Janet Walker (eds) (1999), *Feminism and Documentary* (Minneapolis: University of Minnesota Press).

Ward, Paul (2005), *Documentary: The Margins of Reality* (London and New York: Wallflower).

Weiner, Annette (1978), 'Epistemology and Ethnographic Reality: A Trobriand Island Case Study', *American Anthropologist* 80 (3): 752–7.

Williams, Linda (1993), 'Mirrors Without Memories: Truth, History and the New Documentary', *Film Quarterly* 46: 9–21.

Williams, Linda (1999), 'The Ethics of Intervention: Dennis O'Rourke's "The Good Woman of Bangkok"', in Jane Gaines and Michael Renov (eds), *Collecting Visible Evidence* (Minneapolis: University of Minnesota Press).

Winston, Brian (1993), 'The Documentary as Scientific Inscription', in Michael Renov (ed.), *Theorizing Documentary* (New York and London: Routledge).

Winston, Brian (1995), *Claiming the Real: The Documentary Film Revisited* (London: British Film Institute).

Winston, Brian (1999), 'Documentary: How the Myth Was Deconstructed', *Wide Angle* 21 (2): 71–86.

Winston, Brian (2000), *Lies, Damned Lies and Documentaries* (London: British Film Institute).

Winston, Brian (2008), *Claiming the Real: The Documentary Film Revisited*, 2nd edn (London: Palgrave Macmillan/British Film Institute).

Yergin, Daniel (1973), 'Politics and Autobiography: An Interview with Marcel Ophüls', *Sight and Sound* 43 (4): 20–2.

Zimmerman, Patricia R. (2000), *States of Emergency: Documentaries, Wars, Democracies* (Minneapolis: University of Minnesota Press).

Zhang, Yinglin (2004), 'Styles, Subjects and Special Points of View: A Study of Contemporary Chinese Independent Documentary', *New Cinemas* 2 (2): 119–35.

Zinn, Daniel (2000), 'By the End of the War We Were Our Own Censors', Review Essay, *Peace Review*, 12 (4): 627–33.

Filmography

(* = Case Study)

*9/11 Chronicles, The: Part 1: Truth Rising (2007). Alex Jones. 115 min. Available at http://video.google.com/videoplay?docid=-6558849874454763730 (accessed 15 August 2008).

20th Century, The (1957–70). 30 min. 120 episodes. CBS Television.

60 Minutes (1968–). Don Hewitt. 68 episodes. CBS Television.

Aileen Wuornos: The Selling of a Serial Killer (1993). Nick Broomfield. 87 min. DEJ Productions.

Airline (1998–). Independent Television (UK).

*Amazon (2008). Bruce Parry. 360 min. BBC Worldwide.

American Dream (1990). Barbara Kopple and Cathy Caplan. 98 min. Buena Vista Home Entertainment (US).

American Family, An (1973). Alan and Susan Raymond. 720 min. PBS.

Angola: Journey to a War (1961). Robert Young. NBC.

Appearance, The (1996). Harun Farocki. Facets Multimedia Distribution.

*Autism: The Musical (2007). Tricia Regan. 94 min. HBO Documentary.

Babewatch (1998). Nick Lord. 60 min. 6 episodes. Yorkshire Television.

Basement Tapes, The (wikifilm) (2007). Brett Gaylor. Available at: http://opensourcecinema.org/wikifilm (accessed: 24 September 2007).

*Battle for Haditha (2007). Nick Broomfield. 97 min. Channel 4 Films.

Battle of Chile, The (1979). Patricio Guzmán. 100 min. Unifilms.

Berkeley in the Sixties (1990). Mark Kitchell. 117 min. California Newsreel/PBS.

Beyond Killing Us Softly: The Strength To Resist (2000). Margaret Lazarus and Renner Wunderlich. 30 min. Cambridge Documentary Films.

Black Journal (1968–70). National Educational Television. PBS.

Blood of My Brother (2005). Andrew Berends. 90 min. Lifesize Entertainment

Boston Legal: Series 1 (2005). 'Let Sales Ring'. Episode 16. David E. Kelley. (Broadcast 13 March 2005). ABC.

Bowling for Columbine (2002). Michael Moore. 120 min. United Artists; Alliance Atlantis Communications.

Brief History of Time, A (1992). Errol Morris. 80 min. Triton Pictures.

Calling the Ghosts (1996). Mandy Jacobson and Karmen Jelincic. 160 min. Women Make Movies.

Capturing the Friedmans (2003). Andew Jarecki. 107 min. HBO.

Chinese Takeaway (2002). Mitzi Goldman. 52min. Ronin Films.

Chronicle of a Summer (1960). Edgar Morin and Jean Rouch. 85 min. Pathé Contemporary Films.

City, The (1939). Pare Lorentz, Ralph Steiner and Willard Van Dyke. 43 min. Civic Films.

*Complete History of My Sexual Failures, A (2008). Chris Waitt. 90 min. Optimum Releasing.

Control Room (2004). Jehane Noujaim. 84 min. Magnolia Pictures.

Crisis in Central America (Frontline) (1985). Neal B. Freeman. 240 min. PBS series.

Daughter Rite (1980). Michelle Citron. 49 min. Iris Films.

David Holtzman's Diary (1968). Jim McBride. 74 min. Direct Cinema Ltd.

*Death of A President (2006). Gabriel Range. 90 min. Newmarket Films.

Death on Camera (2004). 60 min. BBC.

Devil Never Sleeps, The (1994). Lourdes Portillo. 87 min. Independent Television Service.

Die Kinder von Golzow (1961–). Winfried Junge. VEB Progress Film-Vertrieb.

Don't Look Back (1967). D.A. Pennebaker. 96 min. Warner Home Video.

Drifters (1929). John Grierson. 49 min. British International Pictures America Inc.

Drowned Out/The Damned (2002). Franny Armstrong. 75 min. Journeyman Films Ltd.

Earth (2007). Alastair Fothergill and Mark Lindfield. 90 min. Lionsgate.

Edwardian Country House, The (2002). Nick Murphy and Caroline Ross-Pirie. 50 min. 6 episodes. PBS.

Enthusiasm (1920). Dziga Vertov. 67 min. Edition Filmmuseum.

*Être et Avoir (2002). Nicholas Philibert. 104 min. Les Films de Losange.

Eyes on the Prize (1987). Henry Hampton. 360 min. PBS.

Fahrenheit 9/11 (2004). Michael Moore. 122 min. IFC Films.

Fall of the Romanov Dynasty (1927). Esfir Schub. 90 min. Sovinko.

*Family, The (1974). Franc Roddam and Paul Watson. 12 (60 min) episodes. BBC.

*Family, The (2008). Jonathan Smith. 8 (60 min) episodes. Channel 4 Television Corporation.

Far From Poland (1984). Jill Godmilow. 106 min. Beach Street Films.

Forgotten Silver (1995). Costas Botes and Peter Jackson. 53 min. First Run Features.

Gate of Heavenly Peace, The (1995). Carma Hinton and Richard Gordon. 108 mins. Frontline PBS.

Great Global Warming Swindle, The (2007). Martin Durkin. 74 min. Channel 4 Television Corporation.

Grey Gardens (1975). Albert and David Maysles. 100 min. Portrait Films.

Good Woman of Bangkok, The (1991). Dennis O'Rourke. 82 min. Roxie Releasing.

Handsworth Songs (1987). John Akomfrah. 61 min. The Other Cinema.

Harlan County USA (1976). Barbara Kopple. 103 min. PBS.

Harvest of Shame (1960). Edward R Murrow. 60 min. CBS Television.

Hill Street Blues (1981–87). Steven Bochco and Michael Kozoll. 7 seasons. NBC.

Hollywood Women (1993). Carlton Television.

Hoop Dreams (1994). Steve James. 170 min. Fine Line Features.

Hour of the Furnaces (1968). Octavio Getino and Fernando Solanas. 260 min. Tricontinental.

How the Myth Was Made: A Study of Robert Flaherty's Man of Aran (1976). George Stoney and James Brown. 56 min (1978 DVD). Films Incorporated.

How to Live in the German Federal Republic (1989). Harun Farocki. 83 min. Facets Multimedia Distribution.

Housing Problems (1935). 16 min. British Commercial Gas Association.

Human Remains (1998). Jay Rosenblatt. 30 min. Yleisradio.

Immigrant Nation, An (1997). Monique Ooman, et al. 7 x 46 min. Top Shelf Productions.

In the Name of God (1992). Anand Patwardhan. 90 min. First Run/Icarus Films/Samvaad.

In the Year of the Pig (1968). Emile de Antonio. 103 min. Pathé Contemporary Films.

*Inconvenient Truth, An (2006). Davis Guggenheim. 100 min. Paramount.

*Jihad For Love, A (2007). Parvez Sharma. 81 min. First Run Films.

Killing Us Softly (1979). Margaret Lazarus and Renner Wunderlich. 30 min. Cambridge Documentary Films.

La Bataille d'Algiers (1966). Gillo Pontecorvo. 121 min. The Criterion Collection (US); Argent Films (UK).

La Rabbia (1963). Giovanni Guareschi and Pier Paolo Pasolini. 104 min. Warner Bros.

Land Without Bread (1933). Luis Buñuel. 30 min. Kino Video.

Le Joli Mai (1963). Chris Marker. 165 min. Pathé Contemporary Films.

Les Maitres fous (1955). Jean Rouch. 36 min. Les Films de la Pléiade.

*Les Plages d'Agnès (2008). Agnès Varda. 110 min. Ciné Tamaris.

Letter from Siberia (1957). Chris Marker. 62 min. New Yorker Films.

Life and Times of Rosie the Riveter, The (1980). Connie Field. 65 min. First Run Features.

Listen to Britain (1942). Humphrey Jennings and Stewart McAllister. 20 min. Image Entertainment Distributors (ABFD).

Living Desert, The (1953). James Algar. 69 min. Buena Vista Distribution Company.

Lonely Boy (1962). Wolf Koenig and Roman Kroitor. 27 min. NFB.

Loose Change (2005). Dylan Avery. 61 min. Louder Than Words.

Loose Change 2nd Edition (2006). Dylan Avery. 82 min. Louder Than Words

Loose Change: Final Cut (2007). Dylan Avery. 130 min. Louder Than Words.

Man Bites Dog (1992). Rémy Belvaux and André Bonzel. 95 min. The Criterion Collection.

Man of Aran (1934). Robert Flaherty. 76 min. PBS.

Man with a Movie Camera (1929). Dziga Vertov. 86 min. BFI.

Mandate Years, The (1978). 75 min. Thames Television.

March of the Penguins (2005). Luc Jacquet. 85 min. National Geographic Feature Films.

March of Time (1935). Jerry Kuehl. BFI.

Memory of the Camps (1985). Sidney Bernstein. 56 min. Frontline.

Men Who Killed Kennedy, The: The Guilty Men (2003). Nigel Turner. The History Channel.

Mighty Times: The Children's March (2004). Robert Houston. 40 min. Home Box Office.

Modern Times (1936). Charles Chaplin. 87 min. United Artists.

Moi, un noir (1957). Jean Rouch. 70 min. Les Films de Pléiade.

Mondo Cane (1962). Paolo Cavara and Gualtiero Jacopetti. 97 min. Times Film Corporation.

Mother Ireland (1998). Anne Crilly. 52 min. Channel 4 Television Corporation.

Muriel, ou le temps d'un retour (1963). Alain Resnais. 115 min. Roissy Films.

Naked Spaces: Living is Round (1985). Trinh T. Minh-ha. 135 min. Women Make Movies; MoMA.

Nannies From Hell (1998). Jessica Fowle. 60 min. Yorkshire Television.

Nanook of the North (1922). Robert Flaherty. 79 min. The Criterion Collection.

Narmada Diary, A (1997). Anand Patwardhan and Simantini Dhuru. 57 min. First Run/Icarus Films.

Neighbours From Hell (1998–2004). Central TV.

New Earth (1934). Joris Ivens. 36 min. Capi-Holland.

New Zealand Wars (1998). Tainui Stephenson. TVNZ.

Night and Fog (1955). Alain Resnais. 32 min. The Criterion Collection.

Night Mail (1936). Harry Watt and Basil Wright. 25 min. Associated British Film.

No End In Sight (2007). Charles Ferguson and Audrey Marrs. 102 min. Magnolia.

No Lies... (1974). Mitchell Block. 16 min. Direct Cinema Ltd.

Not a Love Story: A Film About Pornography (1981). Bonnie Sherr Klein. 69 min. National Film Board of Canada.

Olympischespielen (1938). Leni Riefenstahl. 111 min. PBS.

Omar Is My Friend (1995). Mounaf Shaker. 15 min.

On the Bowery (1957). Lionel Rogosin. 65 min. Film Representations.

Outfoxed: Rupert Murdoch's War on Journalism (2004). Robert Greenwald. 77 min. Disinformation Company.

Painful Reminder, A: Evidence for All Mankind (1985). Brian Blake. 69 min. Granada Television.

Persecution of the White Car, The (2001). Sebastian Diaz Morales. 25 min. Just Like That Productions.

Pillar of Fire (1979). Ya'akov Eisenman. 420 min. Israel Broadcasting Authority.

Primary (1960). Robert Drew. 60 min. Drew Associates.

Rape Culture (1975). Margaret Lazarus and Renner Wunderlich. 33 min. Cambridge Documentary Films.

Rape Stories (1989). Margie Strosser. Women Make Movies.

Real Lives: At the Edge of the Union (1985). Paul Hamann. 45 min. BBC.

Reassemblage (1983). Trinh T. Minh-ha. 40 min. Women Make Movies.

Return of the Tribe (2007). Donal MacIntyre. 180 min. Channel 5.

River, The (1937). Pare Lorentz. 31 min. Paramount.

Rivers of Sand (1974). Robert Gardner. 83 min. Phoenix Films.

Roger and Me (1989). Michael Moore. 91 min. Warner.

Screw Loose Change (2006). Mark Iradian. 177 min. Available at: http://www.lolloosechange.co.nr (accessed: 14 March 2007).

Schindler's List (1993). Steven Spielberg. 195 min. Universal Pictures.

See It Now (1951). Don Hewitt. 30 min. CBS Television.

Selling of the Pentagon, The (1971). Peter Davis. 60 min. CBS Television.

Sense of Loss, A (1972). Marcel Ophüls. 135 min. Cinema5 Distributing.

Sherman's March (1986). Ross McElwee. 157 min. First Run Features.

*She's a Boy I Knew (2007). Gwen Haworth. 70 min. Outcast Films.

Ship, The (2002). Christopher Terrill. 60 min. 6 episodes. BBC.

Shoah (1985). Claude Lanzmann. 503 min. New Yorker Films; Eureka.

*Sicko (2007). Michael Moore. 123 min. Lionsgate (US); Optimum Releasing (UK).

Sink or Swim (1990). Su Friedrich. 48 min. Outcast Films.

Soft Fiction (1979). Chick Strand. 60 min.

Song of Ceylon (1934). Basil Wright. 38 min. World Pictures Corporation.

Sorrow and the Pity, The (*Le Chagrin et la Pitié*) (1969). Marcel Ophüls. 251 min. Channel 5 Distributing.

Still Life (1997). Harun Farocki. 58 min. Facets Multimedia Distribution

Still Killing Us Softly (1987). Margaret Lazarus and Renner Wunderlich. 30 min. Cambridge Documentary Films.

Strike (1925). Sergei Eisenstein. 82 min. Alta Films.

Super Size Me (2004). Morgan Spurlock. 100 min. Roadside Attractions.

Surname Viet Given Name Nam (1989). Trinh T. Minh-ha. 108 min. MoMA (USA); Cinema Contact Ltd (UK).

Taking Our Bodies Back: The Women's Health Movement (1974), Margaret Lazarus and Renner Wunderlich. 33 min. Cambridge Documentary Films.

*Tarnation (2003), Jonathan Caouette. 88 min. Wellspring Media.

Taste of Cherries, The (1997). Abbas Kiarostami. 95 min. Zeitgeist Films.

*Taxi to the Dark Side (2007). Alex Gibney. 106 min. Revolver Entertainment.

Thames Film (1986). William Raban. DVD 2004. BFI.

Thin Blue Line, The (1988). Errol Morris. 103 min. PBS.

Things I Cannot Change (1966). Tanya Ballantyne. 55 min. NFB.

This is Spinal Tap (1983). Rob Reiner. 84 min. Embassy Pictures.

*Titicut Follies (1967). Frederick Wiseman. 84 min. Titicut Follies Distributing Company.

To Render a Life (1992). Ross Spears. 88 min. James Agee Film Project.

Touching the Void (2003). Kevin Macdonald. 106 min. Pathé (UK); PBS (US).

*Tribe – Series 3 (2007). Bruce Parry. 360 min. BBC Worldwide.

Triumph of the Will (1935). Leni Riefenstahl. 114 min. Connoisseur Video.

Uncovered: The Whole Truth about the Iraq War (2003). Robert Greenwald. 56 min. Disinformation Company.

Union Maids (1976). Jim Klein and Miles Mogulescu. 50 min. New Day Distribution Co-op.

Uprising of '34 (1995). George Stoney. POV.

Valour and the Horror, The (1992). Brian McKenna. In three parts (104 min each). Canadian Broadcasting Corporation.

Victory at Sea (1952–3). Henry Salomon and Isaac Kleinerman. 26 (30 min) episodes. NBC.

Video Nation (1993–). BBC Community Programmes Unit.

Voices of Orchid Island (1993). Hu Lai-Ti. 73 min.

War And Peace (2001). Anand Patwardhan. 148 min. First Run Features.

*War/Dance (2007). Andrea Nix Fine and Sean Fine. 105 min. THINKFilm.

War Game, The (1965), Peter Watkins. 48 min. BBC; Project X Distribution (US).

*War Tapes, The (2006). Deborah Scranton. 97 min. SenArt Films.

We Are Not Your Monkeys (1993). Anand Patwardhan. 5 min. First Run/Icarus Films/ Samvaad.

What You Take For Granted (1984). Michelle Citron. 75 min. Iris Feminist Collective.

When We Were Kings (1996). Leon Gast. 89 min. NBC.

Who Killed Vincent Chin? (1987). Christine Choy and Renee Tajima-Pena. 87 min. PBS.

Wife Swap (2003). Martin Fuller and Sam Maynard. 20 (60 min) episodes. Channel 4 Television Corporation.

Winston Churchill: The Valiant Years (1961). Anthony Bushell and John Schlesinger. 30 min. 26 episodes. ABC/BBC.

Wiping the Tears of Seven Generations (1992). Fidel Moreno and Gary Rhine. 57 min. Kifaru Productions.

Wolves (1999). Chris Palmer. 40 min. E-Realbiz.com.

Woman's Film, The (1971). Louise Alaimo and Judy Smith. 40 min. San Francisco Newsreel Collective.

Word is Out (1977). Rob Epstein. 124 min. Adair Films/PBS.

World at War, The (1974), 26 (52 min) episodes. BBC.

World in Action (1963–98). 26 seasons. Granada/ITV.

You Are on Indian Land (1969). Mort Rantsen. 37 min. NFB.

*Zeitgeist: The Movie (2007). Peter Joseph. 122 min. Zeitgeist.

Zoo (1993). Frederick Wiseman. 130 min. PBS.

Index